Go Bucks!

Chic

The extraordinary rise of **Ohio State football**
and the tragic schoolboy athlete who made it happen

by Bob Hunter with Marc Katz

ORANGE FRAZER PRESS
Wilmington, Ohio

ISBN 978-1933197-487

Additional copies of *Chic* may be ordered directly from:

Orange Frazer Press
P.O. Box 214
Wilmington, OH 45177

Telephone 1.800.852.9332 for price and shipping information.
Website: www.orangefrazer.com

Jacket design: Jeff Fulwiler

Library of Congress Cataloging-in-Publication Data

Hunter, Bob, 1951-
   Chic : the extraordinary rise of Ohio State football and the tragic schoolboy athlete who made it happen / by Bob Hunter with Marc Katz.
       p. cm.
   Includes index.
   ISBN 978-1-933197-48-7
   1. Harley, Chic. 2. Football players--Ohio--Biography. 3. Ohio State University--Football--History. 4. Ohio State Buckeyes (Football team)--History. I. Katz, Marc. II. Title.
   GV939.H314 H85 2008
   796.332092--dc22
   [B]
                                        2008030377

To Mom, my most loyal reader.

Acknowledgments

When *Dayton Daily News* sportswriter Marc Katz first proposed this project to me several years ago, neither one of us had any idea how difficult it would be to research the subject. Researching a book where all of the principal characters are dead isn't easy, especially when not much beyond the basics has been written about them.

Because Chic never married, he has no direct descendents. A debt of gratitude is owed to Bob Harley, grandson of Chic's older brother, Bill, for offering stories about the brothers that have been handed down in the Harley family. A special thanks is also offered posthumously to Richard C. Wessell, son of Chic's sister Ruth, who was doing research on his uncle for a possible book before his death in 2003. Wessell hoped to disprove the rumors of the cause of his uncle's illness, which, we hope, has been done here.

Thanks due also to Doug Harlor, Mike Paul, Whitney B. Dillon, John P. (Jack) Havens, Dorothy Wilce Krause, John Giesy, Skip Yassenoff, Russ Finneran, Tom Selby, Hugh Miller, and Reverend Richard H. Gingher. All offered invaluable insights into the Harley story through the eyes of their parents and grandparents. Without them, it would have been extremely difficult to bring Harley's story back to life.

A special thanks is due to Bertha Ihnat and Michelle Drobik at the Ohio State University Archives. Ihnat was especially helpful in locating and copying letters pertaining to Chic and his illness and Drobik offered valuable assistance with the archives' vast photo collection.

Linda Deitch, archive and collection manager of the *Columbus Dispatch* library, was generous with her assistance with the newspaper's photo archive, and deserves a special debt of gratitude. She was as excited about some of the photos of Chic that she located in the newspaper's collection as we were. As reporters at the newspaper know, she is an invaluable resource for the staff.

Neva-Hall Jacobs, deputy clerk of the Franklin County Probate Court, also provided help in locating and copying trial records, and the staff at the Columbus Public Library patiently tried to answer numerous questions that at times must have seemed bizarre to them. Ione Benedetto remembered Chic through his years of employment for Leo Yassenoff, Harley's close friend. Gary Metzenbacher helped with the East High School archives. D.C. Koehl offered assistance with records in the Ohio State athletic communications office.

Thanks also to Martha Garland, vice provost for enrollment services and dean of undergraduate education, and Brad Myers, university registrar, for their assistance in providing an academic portrait of Harley during his years at Ohio State. Dr. Michael Craig, formerly chief of staff of Miami Valley Hospital in Dayton, helped explain and interpret Harley's medical records and diagnoses.

Katz deserves a lot of credit, both for seeing Chic as a story that needed to be told and for his enthusiasm for the project. He spent countless hours in the library, in courthouses, at the archives and on the phone, interviewing some of the sources for this work.

Finally, a special thanks to my wife, Margie, sons Bryan and Rob and daughter Amy, and to many of my good friends and newspaper colleagues, both for their support and for their willingness to listen to my interminable stories about places and teams they've never heard of and people they don't know. In the months preceding the final drafts, the repeated question, "When is this going to be done anyway?" has finally been answered. Now.

Bob Hunter
Westerville, Ohio
June, 2008

PHOTO CREDITS—*From The Ohio State University archives: pages 12-13, 16-17, 47, 70-71, 74-75, 110-111, 130-131, 184-185, 206-207.*
From the author: pages 42-43. From the Orange Frazer Press library: page 39.
From the Dayton Daily News: pages 209, 217, 219.
All others are from the Columbus Dispatch, with research by archivist
Linda Deitch whose good eye and diligence is owed a special debt.

Special gratitide to Rosemary Thurber and the Barbara Hogenson Agency Inc. for permission to quote from James Thurber's story, "University Days."

Table of contents

Prologue

From the press box of Ohio Stadium, a small patch of trees is visible a half-mile to the east. It looks to be about where Ohio Field stood almost ninety years ago, back when overflow crowds of 12,000 seemed gigantic and players such as Harley, Stinchcomb, and Yerges were creating wonder for those raised in a slower, simpler time.

The mind drifts. Does Ohio Field still exist in some mysterious time warp? Could it be that those players are out there somewhere, running and tackling and rousing all those deafening cheers?

The eyes begin to contract in a reflexive squint, trying to see something that's not there, trying to peer through the decades at a relatively small patch of green.

For a few moments, they lose sight of the colorful mosaic of 105,000 people crammed into the huge horseshoe-shaped stadium in front of them. The foreground blurs and the trees in the distance sharpen. There were woods immediately to the west of Ohio Field in those days. Farms still abutted the city. The area looked nothing like this.

For a few seconds, the trance breaks. The eyes shift to the right, to a jumble of fat, massive buildings bunched in an area where the first Ohio State students long ago tried their hand at this new game of football, in what was then an empty field to the north of the long gone North Dormitory.

No, those students are definitely not there, not in that dense mass of brick and steel. Time has been paved over by concrete and the ghosts have long since fled. But over there by those trees, just to the west of High Street, it almost seems as if something's there.

The mind wafts gently away from the reality of the moment. The eyes squint again, the trees sharpen, and there is a small swarm of people on the sidewalks near High, men in suits and hats and women in long dresses, leaving cars an aficionado would recognize as Reos and Packards and Ford Model Ts. They have come to see Jack Wilce's boys play football, come to see Harley perform feats of magic.

They are there somewhere. You're sure of it. There's no way to explain it, no way to prove it certainly, but that time and place is as real as this immense sea of red bodies before you, as real as the band now stepping out *Script Ohio* and the giant scoreboard flashing a colorful cartoon on a screen almost as large as Ohio Field's old east stands.

What happened over there, what may still be happening over there, created this incredible sight in front of you now.

You are as sure of that as you have ever been of anything.

THE OHIO STADIUM

It is difficult to imagine that the site of Ohio Stadium was once distant from the city, and Neil Avenue nothing more than a private dirt lane that led to Billy Neil's farmhouse. And that the stadium's predecessor, Ohio Field, once rented seats from a circus so 2,000 fans could watch OSU play Kenyon on Thanksgiving Day.

coming of age

He was an ordinary boy in an ordinary town. There was nothing all that unusual about him, at least in appearance, and there was nothing all that special about the town. Young Chic Harley and middle-aged *Columbus* seemed made for each other. They were neither the best nor the worst, and there was no reason to expect they would ever be either. They almost fit the definition of average. They didn't stand out in a crowd. Though Chic was a good-looking boy with a square jaw and a crooked grin, he was just another face

He wasn't a tall, muscular young man, but he had something else: an amazing physical gift.

in a group picture. He wasn't much of a student and even when he applied himself, he found learning to be a chore. He was neither tall nor muscular, and half the kids in the east Columbus neighborhood where he lived bore the same slight build. If you walked from one end of town to the other, you would probably see at least fifty kids just like him.

Chic could always run faster than the neighbor kids, not that it mattered. In the days just this side of 1900, being fleet of foot didn't get you much. It earned the respect of school friends and neighborhood rivals but it was mostly a worthless skill. It couldn't land a good job at the local factory or provide the money to open a business. It wouldn't pay the rent or feed a family. There wasn't much a kid could do with that special talent other than brag about it. It was like being the best tree climber or the best rock thrower. By the time a fleet runner reached a certain age, no one cared.

The city where his family had moved when he was 12 seemed every bit as average as Chic did. It wasn't the biggest or the smallest and didn't have the best or worst of anything. Outside of the state's borders, it didn't project much of an identity; it was a flat, medium-sized city surrounded by miles of cornfields. It served as Ohio's state capital and was defined by politics. In most cases, it was merely a transitory stop for those on the road to greatness somewhere else.

FIVE U.S. PRESIDENTS HAD COLUMBUS on their resumes, beginning with the ill-fated William Henry Harrison, a general during the War of 1812. He was noteworthy largely for giving—hatless on an unpleasant March day—the presidency's longest inaugural address, catching pneumonia, and dying within the month. The president with the most to say, someone wrote afterward, also had the shortest time in which to say it. The august presidential lineage of one-time Columbusites continued through Rutherford Hayes, James Garfield, and William McKinley, concluding with Warren G. Harding, an upstate newspaper editor and small town glad-hander whose matinee idol good looks propelled him out of Columbus and into history, such as it was. (He was not regarded kindly by it, being described once as "a cheese-paring of a man," and often much worse.)

As for Columbus and art, there was William Dean Howells, who worked for the *Ohio State Journal*, his springboard to *The Atlantic Monthly* and a walloping career as the Dean of American Letters. There was, too, another Ohio State youth, a strapping fellow from Central High named George Bellows, who was perhaps the only man in America to forsake professional baseball for art. It was a risky career move either way, although Bellows made it work for him; he was the most acclaimed painter of his generation, demonstrating that hitting for average in the art game was a tougher act than baseball.

Possibly the most intriguing person who spent most of his life in Columbus was widely-known in both state and national political circles but largely unknown by the public. Newspaperman Samuel Medary wielded considerable power in the Democratic Party, and as the Civil War approached, he published a nationally-circulated Copperhead newspaper called *The Crisis* in which he opposed the war effort. Twice, his newspaper offices were ransacked and burned and he was eventually arrested for aiding the escape of Confederate prisoners in Ohio.

Medary died in 1864 before his trial, and by the time the Harleys moved to town, he had been forgotten even by most of those who knew him. So Columbus had been home to a handful of unremarkable presidents, an author and an artist whose fame was achieved elsewhere, and a radical Copperhead editor long since forgotten. As legacies go, it wasn't much.

To some, Columbus was still the Arch City, known for a series of lighted arches that had spanned the city's major north-south artery, High Street, for most of the past twenty years. But like those energetic boys who ran like the wind, the city had nearly outgrown its adolescent reputation. Wooden arches lit by gas lamps had gone up every half block or so on High Street for a parade during the Grand Army of the Republic encampment in 1888 and because of their popularity, the arches stayed long after the Civil War veterans were gone. The wooden canopies were eventually replaced by metal arches with electric lights, and offered a means of stringing wires to power the electric streetcars. A few years later, when Chic was in high school, the arches came down and Arch City was no more.

The city also served as home to the Columbus Buggy Company, the largest buggy maker in America, and another two dozen buggy companies that were scattered about the city. But this, too, was no longer an image the city needed or wanted. Buggies were being replaced by the automobile, and being the buggy capital was something like being famous as a hub for steamboat-building. It had once been a distinction; now it wasn't much of one.

Chic

The city's most famous current resident, a local surgeon named Dr. Samuel Hartman, received the respect of local citizens; on the national level, he may have been more reviled than revered. He gained world-wide fame because of his Peruna elixir, a cure-all whose formula he said had been given to him by a dead Indian chief of that name in a dream. But the year before the Harleys arrived, federal investigators discovered that the elixir consisted mostly of alcohol, food coloring, and flavoring, and they told Dr. Hartman to ditch the alcohol or quit making the stuff. Some of his customers still swore by the new formula, but it was clear Peruna would never be the city's ticket to lasting fame.

LIKE MOST BIG AMERICAN CITIES, Columbus had grown dramatically in the last twenty years. The industrial revolution ushered in sweeping changes that were still occurring. The sleepy little state capital that had only 18,000 residents in 1861 at the start of the Civil War had grown to 90,000 by the 1890s, and was nearing 180,000 when Harley's family arrived from Chicago in 1907. It had burst out of the two-mile radius that had encircled the city for the past fifty years, partly because of the invention of the electric streetcar in the 1890s. When streetcars replaced their horse-drawn counterparts, Columbus's days as a walking city ended. The increased mobility made it possible for local citizens to move to new distant suburbs such as Marble Cliff and Grandview, although most still lived in neighborhoods that ringed the central city.

Charles and Mattie Trunell Harley and their seven children—Walter, Marie, William, Irene, Charles (Chic), Ralph, and Ruth—were in the latter group. (Another girl, Helen, had died at age 4 before they moved to Columbus.) They moved into a large, two-and-a-half story brick duplex at the southwest corner of Mound and Kelton Streets, in a neighborhood of tightly-packed brick houses on the city's eastern fringe. For them, it was a move back home. Charles had been born in Chillicothe and Mattie had been born in Columbus, and they had apparently married in the city.

Charles worked as a printer in Columbus throughout the 1880s, left for Chicago in 1892 when he was offered a job with the *Chicago Tribune*, and now he was back, having been offered a job at the *Columbus Evening Dispatch*. Robert Frederick Wolfe, who had written a popular column of local happenings for the *Sunday Capital* in 1889 and 1890 when Charles worked there, had purchased the

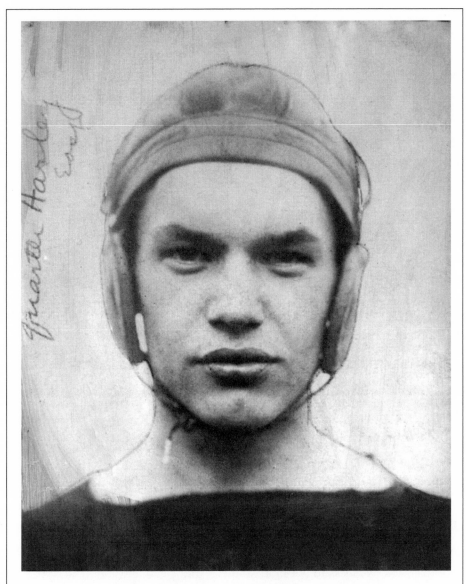

*As a skinny kid growing up on Columbus's East Side, Chic
Harley displayed only one trait that would set him apart
from his fellow schoolboys, and in an unimaginable way—
his speed. He was always faster than the others.*

Chic

Dispatch with his brother Harry P. Wolfe in 1905, knew Charles from those days, and seems to have been responsible for bringing him back.

They weren't in Columbus long before the neighborhood kids discovered that at least one of the new Harley boys could run.

"To add to family income," John C. Harlor said, "Chic had a paper route through our neighborhood which occasionally brought him under the rain of snowballs thrown by our neighborhood gang. Chic good-naturedly took the missiles without any signs of anger until one day he put down his sack of papers and started after us. Although we were able to retreat to safety, we then realized that the newcomer we had met, we were no match for the speed or the strength of his physique."

PAUL GINGHER'S FAMILY LIVED HALFWAY up the block and across the street from the Harley's—Gingher's father, Cassius, was a carpenter—and he said he remembered seeing the moving van unload the Harley family furniture. "He was several years older than I," wrote Gingher, later a successful attorney and chairman of the board and chief executive officer of State Automobile Mutual Insurance Company, "but still of elementary school age and we both attended East Main Street School. Chic quickly became the neighborhood leader in all things athletic, particularly in baseball and football, which we played on a group of vacant lots nearby and which this Chicago kid called a 'prairie.'"

Fewer than ten years before, the area had been farmland. Two blocks east of where the Ginghers and the Harleys lived, there was land that had been sold for development and subdivided into lots but was still empty. Four blocks to the east a hundred acres of open land stretched to the eastern limits of Bexley. Driving Park race track was six blocks to the south and everything east and southeast of that was farmland.

The Harleys didn't live a bucolic life, however. An interurban train ran up and down Mound Street, next to their home, and years later one of the Harley girls remembered how noisy it was. Sickness was also a frequent visitor. Chic's younger brother, Ralph, died a month before his 12th birthday of typhoid fever, a reminder that even in a city blessed with several fine hospitals—St. Francis, St. Anthony, Grant, and Children's all stood within a couple of miles of the Harley house—notions of immortality were foolish, even for the young. Chic was 13 years old at the time, and Ralph's death must have been both devastating and frightening.

In this Midwestern setting, it's hard to believe that a teenage boy from a working class family would someday change things in ways that could only be truly appreciated a hundred years later. If the gang in his neighborhood recognized his athletic skill—and this was an age when boys were always outside playing—those talents didn't mean much, even on the other side of town. Athletes didn't command much attention in those days and they weren't in much demand. An enormously talented baseball player could make a fair living, as long as he had a good job during the winter months when his team wasn't playing. A talented football player, if he were lucky, could only hope to make a little money on the side from one of the loosely organized pro teams that seemed to come and go with the wind. Basketball had recently moved out of YMCAs to school gymnasiums. Track athletes participated only for the thrill of competition. If a runner or field athlete were good enough, he might someday compete on an international level for the glory of his country. He had no hope of ever making any money.

THIS WAS A COLUMBUS FEW OF US WOULD RECOGNIZE. The riverfront was still an ugly mélange of old two- and three-story brick storefronts and warehouses, some of which had once housed small factories that had moved to other parts of the city. The ten-story Wyandotte building was the city's only "skyscraper" and the statehouse rivaled it for the title of tallest building in town. The grocery store, the drugstore, the jewelry store, the bookstore, and the restaurant had a face to go with the name on the sign out front. Ice wagons patrolled the streets, a necessity before the days of electric refrigeration. Fires were common—and deadly. Medicine was still primitive by modern standards. The average woman expected to live forty-seven years, the average man forty-six. The life expectancy of a black man was thirty-three.

With no television or radio to entertain them, family members gathered around the piano for sing-alongs in the evenings. Barbershop quartets harmonized on Saturday nights. Sears Roebuck and Montgomery Ward catalogs were read more widely than any book other than the Bible. Only one in seven homes had a bathtub. And one in thirteen had a telephone.

The world was changing, though, and Columbus was changing with it. The relatively small, quiet city of roomy, tree-lined streets in a state dominated by agriculture already seemed like a distant memory to its older residents.

Chic

Horse-drawn vehicles were still predominant on the streets, but cars were everywhere, particularly along elm-lined East Broad Street where some of the city's wealthiest families lived in homes that hinted at royalty.

Two bicycle shop owners named Wright in nearby Dayton had made their first flight in 1903 and ancient dreams of flying were made real; soon, even the heaviest-footed mortal would no longer be earthbound. Silent films spawned nickelodeons, where a customer could get twenty minutes of entertainment for five cents. In only a few years time, the impossible had become the possible had become the rage.

With a growing emphasis on leisure activities, athletics had begun to play a larger role in daily life and was beginning to take up more and more space in the only real source of news, the daily newspaper. Columbus Country Club opened in 1903 and forced the game of golf into the city's consciousness. An athletic-minded group of local Pennsylvania Railroad workers formed a professional football team, the Panhandles, that became the talk of people in other Ohio and Pennsylvania cities because it featured five talented brothers, the Nessers. At least one Ohio State professor, Thomas French, was already dreaming of the day when the school's football team would be popular enough to play in a horseshoe-shaped stadium.

A horseshoe-shaped stadium for a team that rarely drew more than 1,000 spectators? If a man ever fit the role of hopeless dreamer, French was surely it. Whether he was a quack or visionary, French couldn't possibly have known that a slightly built, average-looking 12-year-old on the city's east side possessed the physical tools to both make his dream a reality and alter the city's nondescript image forever.

Ordinary boy, indeed.

small time

OSU

When Chic Harley moved to town, Ohio State football was only a few years older than he was. Its birth in the spring of 1890 came after a difficult and prolonged pregnancy, with rough play on a rough field amidst relative *anonymity*. It wasn't king and it didn't have much hope of becoming one. It was a snot-nosed kid with ragged clothes and mussed hair, an ill-mannered creature that some didn't approve of and others passed on the street without seeing. Hugh Fullerton knew that scraggly

Football B.C.—Before Chic—had little in the way of equipment, rules, or fans. At right, Ohio Field in 1917.

brat intimately. When the well-known Chicago sportswriter came to Columbus in 1916 to help raise money for a new YMCA building, the Ohio State grad talked about what it was like to play on the team that first year. Even then, only twenty-six years later, most of those who heard the Hillsboro, Ohio, native describe those primitive days must have been appalled. The game sounded crude and barbaric, giving them a peek at a sordid past that almost didn't seem fit for respectable suitors such as they.

"A football game was just a slam-bang free-for-all in those days," Fullerton said. "We didn't have a coach and we didn't need one. The varsity got ready for the big games by beating up the scrubs. Everybody had sore knuckles and jaws. Kenyon was our mortal enemy. There were more knockdowns and dragouts in the Kenyon game than in any other."

Even this doesn't completely explain how different that Ohio State football was from the one that would become famous. But Fullerton's description of the second game in school history, a November 1, 1890, match with Wooster, does.

"Wooster took the field all togged out in new sweaters and wearing pretty stocking caps in place of headgears," Fullerton said. "I was playing halfback and we had a wonderful fullback in Dirty Mike Kennedy. He said, 'Let's get 'em.' And we got 'em. Before the first half was over, each Ohio State man was wearing his opponent's stocking cap tucked in his belt.

"Well, the rest of the game developed into a fight on our part to hold the caps and on the part of the Wooster fellows to get them back. Wooster won the game, but we won the fight."

IT SOUNDS LIKE A WASH AND MAYBE it truly seemed that way to Fullerton and his college pals. But the fact that Wooster won that game 64-0 says a lot about how little the students on the isolated, expansive seven-building campus north of the city knew about the game of football. The game was still a novelty in Columbus, and a relatively unknown one at that. Even though the college game was already flourishing in the East, football—for the longest time—didn't seem to have a place in this mostly-rural Midwestern world.

Students started playing football on the OSU campus in 1881, twelve years after Princeton and Rutgers met in the first official college football game. And while the world was shrinking, there was still a vast difference between the densely-populated eastern seaboard and agricultural-oriented Ohio, and the contrast was just as stark between Ohio and the untamed regions of the frontier West. The nation's population spread east to west like a coat of paint from a freshly-dipped brush, a thick coat of people gradually thinning through the Midwestern states until it was just a row of barely-discernible strokes on a vast expanse of western canvas.

ABOUT THE TIME A FEW BORED STUDENTS on the sleepy campus north of town decided to try this new game of football, the Earps and the Clantons were shooting it out at the tiny Arizona town of Tombstone in what became known as the Gunfight at the O.K. Corral. It was the same year Billy the Kid was killed by Sheriff Pat Garrett, a year before a reward-seeking pal shot and killed Jesse James. Even in places such as Columbus where civilization had sanded most of the rough edges, the crevices were still fresh in memory. Many Civil War veterans were still under fifty years old, and old Columbus residents still remembered when wagons dodged tree stumps in High Street.

Aside from the brutality, the games played on the dormitory grounds west of Neil Avenue in Columbus weren't a lot different than the ones you might see at a modern family picnic. There were few spectators. Uniforms were homemade. The players changed daily. The contests were played for fun, and the rules, if you can call them that, were vague.

The one thing the players had was room to play. While the city of Columbus was growing, it had just started to lap at the edge of the distant campus. The school had 340 students and its enrollment was exploding: only 235 had attended school the year before. Neil Avenue, a private dirt lane that had once led only to William "Billy" Neil's farmhouse, was gradually becoming lined with stately homes cast in a compelling mixture of styles: Italianate, Second Empire Mansard, Eastlake Victorian, and Richardsonian Romanesque. But Neil Avenue also led to the country, where land that had once been Neil's 300-acre farm had been purchased shortly after his death in 1870 for the establishment of a state land-grant college that eventually became Ohio State University. Though it was an impressive piece of property, one reason the Board of Trustees supposedly chose the Neil farm over a site near Worthington and the Nelson-Rees farms two and a half miles east of the city was the existence of a fine spring. Then in 1891, when the city ran a trunk

sewer line nearby, the spring suddenly receded and dried up, so that hardly made them visionaries.

Even in 1890, the area hadn't changed all that much from what Neil, owner of a hotel across High Street from the statehouse and a far-flung stagecoach business, knew twenty years before. Neil Avenue stopped at 11th. The huge, rambling farmhouse reputedly built in the southern style with a wide-covered porch encircling it had burned down in 1862; the open spot it had occupied would someday be the site of the William Oxley Thompson Memorial Library. The seven widely-separated buildings still looked a little out of place, as though they should be sharing the property with corn rows and dairy cows. The area screamed agriculture, not culture, which was probably as it should have been for a school that began as the Ohio Agricultural and Mechanical College. No one would ever mistake the place for Harvard, nor were they supposed to.

*Recreation Park, Thanksgiving Day, 1891. OSU tussles with Denison,
winning 8-4 in the penurious days when a touchdown was four points.*

The expansive area west of Neil to the tree-lined Olentangy River was open,
part of the Neil property that had stretched from First Avenue on the south to
what would someday be Lane Avenue on the north and from High Street on the
east to the river. The school's two dormitories—the aptly named North and South
dorms—were the only college buildings located west of Neil. The grassy land to the
west of them mostly bore the scruffy look of a man who had misplaced his razor
a week before and hadn't gone to the trouble of buying another. The South—the
little dorm—was a two-story brick structure that resembled a large house and stood
at the end of 10th. The much-larger North—the big dorm—was at the end of 11th,
and both were, in effect, located in a big field a block apart.

This field, on the opposite side of the street from where Oxley Hall stands
now, provided the students with the perfect spot to engage in games of every sort.
The only buildings to the north were a farmhouse and a barn, overlooking the

proceedings from the other side of a small creek called Neil Run. Across the river, there was farmland, as far as the eye could see. Even twenty years later, the school born with "agriculture" in its name was true to its roots.

If the football played there bore only a faint resemblance to the sport so popular in New York, Boston, and Philadelphia, the ball itself probably shared that same flaw. Real footballs were a scarce commodity. When students gave the new game a whirl, they almost surely used homemade balls. In 1886, the freshmen challenged the seniors to a game and the following year students at Marietta College challenged OSU students. If such a game occurred, it is lost to history, although there does seem to have been a game in October, 1887, between OSU students and a team from the Columbus Buggy Company. This drew some notice on campus, but it was at best an informal affair. Eight years before Chic Harley was born in Chicago, Ohio State didn't even have a football team.

IN THE SPRING OF 1889, a student named George Cole took up a collection to buy a real football. When it arrived in the mail, its elliptical shape so befuddled Cole and his buddies that they repacked the ball and prepared to send it back, thinking a mistake had been made. But before it could be returned, another student slipped into Cole's dorm room and took the ball, and a gang of boys started playing with it. Cole recovered it but because it had been used he had to keep it, as he later said, "much to our disgust."

Cole also wrote to the Spalding sporting goods company for a football rulebook, and upon its arrival, discovered that the unusual ball was exactly as it should have been. This is what passed for progress. Doubtless, the game would have developed more slowly at OSU had Cole not learned that one of his old Columbus schoolmates was back in town. Al Lilley had attended Princeton and played football there. Cole asked him if he would coach an Ohio State team, and when Lilley agreed, the makeshift team finally had a chance to become a good one.

Lest we forget that this was still that snot-nosed kid of game and that the times were simple enough to embrace it, Lilley provided another reminder. He lived at least three miles away, on Main Street, and rode to practice on an Indian pony. Presumably this was cheaper and more efficient than the horse-drawn streetcars of the Columbus Street Railroad Company, which ran lines to the campus up both High Street and Neil Avenue. Reasonable as the price of a ride seems—five cents a fare or twenty-four for $1—a football coach might need to call a meeting with his players when the cars weren't running. Under those circumstances, a good Indian pony was hard to beat.

The modern fan wouldn't have had to see the Ohio State coach riding a pony to know that this was a different era. The team Lilley coached wore uniforms that wouldn't be associated with football by any 21st century fan. Some of them didn't even look good to the players who were wearing them.

"They all had suits of heavy muslin," Cole said in the February, 1920, issue of *The Ohio State Alumni Monthly*. "My place on the second team did not assure me with a suit, so I got a suit of painter's white overalls and jumper, and after proper cutting down, puckering strings, and an old blanket cut up for padding it was quite a comfortable outfit to be thrown across the lot in. But I would note right here that the suit was always engaged weeks ahead by someone on the first team."

THE NEW SQUAD'S FIRST OFFICIAL GAME, against Ohio Wesleyan in Delaware, on May 3, 1890, is remembered as an historic occasion today; at the time, the city yawned and looked the other way. Football was a new sport and most Ohioans hadn't had much exposure to it. Baseball, horse racing, and boxing held sway in America, and baseball was the dominant sport in Columbus. Three major leagues existed in 1890: the National League, the American Association, and the Players League—the latter created by players who were unhappy with the salaries and working conditions imposed upon them by the owners of the other two leagues—and Columbus had a team good enough to finish second in the American Association. Its games were played at Recreation Park on the current site of a Giant Eagle grocery store on Whittier Street in German Village, a field that would be used for OSU's first home football game and many others for the next eight years.

What did the city of Columbus think of the first Ohio State football game? It didn't. Neither the afternoon *Columbus Dispatch* nor the morning *Ohio State Journal* made any direct mention of the game. A few weeks earlier, the *Journal* reported that OSU's new football team had ordered suits and would go to Delaware in style, and that was the extent of the pre-game news coverage. The only post-game coverage appeared in *The Lantern*, Ohio State's student newspaper, and given what the game was, that probably isn't surprising. There was none of the beauty and grace of the modern sport, nothing to inspire songs, cheers, mascots, or poetry.

A modern viewer would probably regard the school's first game as little more than an organized brawl.

"Anything went but brass knuckles," Cole said in 1938. "And there was none of this fancy forward passing or razzle-dazzle. It was all power-stuff and wedge work—the flying wedge, a sheer power play, was then in vogue. It was all right to step on a man's face, but you had to be careful how you did it."

THEY CALLED IT FOOTBALL, but that was pure semantics. The sport that drew thousands of fans on the east coast was a brutal if not downright malicious affair. A player on the line did everything—*everything*—to beat the man across from him. That might include punching, pinching, gouging, gnawing, or clawing at him. Only the year before, the *New York Herald* had reported that Harvard used a player who had advertised himself as a football slugger, available to the highest bidder. Then in the Harvard-Yale game, the newspaper indicated that the player had distinguished himself only by kicking a Yale player in the face. Throughout the 1880s, the game had developed a reputation for uncontrolled violence. In its report on the Yale-Princeton game in 1892, *The New York Times* offered the most popular ways to disable an opposing player: step on his feet, kick his shins, give him a dainty upper cut, or gouge his face while making a tackle.

The rules were also different. Forward passes were forbidden; only backward "passes" were permitted. Teams were required to make five yards in three downs rather than ten yards in four. Guards and tackles could line up anywhere, so they didn't have to stay at the line. Touchdowns counted for four points, not six, and the conversion kick was worth two points, not one. The field was 110 yards long and end zones didn't exist. Once a player left the game, he wasn't permitted to return, so eleven ironmen usually tried to play the entire game on both offense and defense. The operative word was "try." Serious injuries were as much a part of the game as the tackling.

In these early days, Midwestern football offered the mayhem and violence without the skill or the profit. In 1893, Harvard spent $18,754 on its football team. That included $3,226 for transportation, $1,887 on summer practice, and $3,469 for the training table. The players wore custom-tailored leather uniforms that cost $125 each. The school's receipts for the Yale game alone that season totaled $15,409.

Contrast that with a Midwestern game where Cole had to take up a collection to buy a real football, where players often played in their own clothing, and even devised their own ingenious forms of footwear by nailing cleats to the soles of old shoes, and it's easy to see how far removed this slap-dash sport was from the football affairs being staged before huge crowds back east.

INTEREST BEYOND THE CAMPUS GREW SLOWLY. Part of the problem was that Ohio State's teams weren't much different from the teams forming on other Ohio campuses. When OSU lost to Otterbein in nearby Westerville 42-6 in 1891, *The Lantern* asked, "Can not our institution of 600 students furnish as good men as smaller colleges of 200 to 500?" The answer seemed to be a resounding "no." OSU was merely one of several Ohio colleges fielding a football team, and that same year it joined with Denison, Kenyon, Buchtel (Akron), and Adelbert (Western Reserve) in forming a loose confederation of teams for scheduling purposes, a league that was a forerunner of the Ohio Athletic Conference.

There may have been other reasons Ohio State didn't stand out in that crowd. "Tramp" players who didn't even attend the college they played for had been a problem in the east. Now experienced players who had graduated from the eastern powers often came west, joined a college team in Ohio or Indiana under an assumed name, then moved on with the opponents none the wiser. At the University of Michigan in 1894, seven of the eleven regulars neither enrolled in school nor attended classes.

The practice was so widespread—and found so despicable by some of the school presidents—that it helped lead to the formation of the Western Conference, later known as the Big Ten. When the presidents of seven universities met in Chicago on January 11, 1895, their purpose was "to establish and maintain common standards of eligibility and common rules to curb practices which are detrimental to amateur sport or fair and friendly competition." This was a nice way of saying that vagabond athletes would be outlawed. The teams would be composed not only of students, but students who maintained a certain academic standard that determined eligibility.

The Western Conference's rules were the exception, however, and Ohio State's admission was far in the future. Eligibility rules among Ohio schools were loose and enforcement was left up to individual colleges. In 1896, OSU captain

Ed French was barred from play before a game against Oberlin because a faculty committee said that he "had been industriously working up the football team and as industriously cutting classes."

When the school lost the game 16-0, *The Lantern* demanded, "Who defeated the OSU team? The Oberlin team or the OSU faculty?" A few weeks later, in the wake of a 24-6 Wittenberg win over Ohio State, the winners were charged with using "ringers." Specifically, *The Lantern* quoted the Notre Dame *Scholastic* as saying that Nicholas Dinkle, who had graduated from the South Bend school the previous year, "is spending his spare moments playing right tackle on the football team at his home in Springfield, Ohio." The lineup that day had Dinkle at quarterback. *The Lantern* also noted that the Wittenberg left end had graduated from the Springfield school in 1895 and the left guard was a student at Springfield Business College.

DESPITE THE PROBLEMS, football gained in stature and popularity locally, and it happened even though Ohio State's teams were not particularly successful. For most of its program's first dozen years, a Thanksgiving Day game with Kenyon was one of the highlights of the sports year in Columbus. Kenyon held its own in this mini-rivalry, which was as much a social affair as an athletic event. The first lengthy top-of-the-page account of an OSU game in a Columbus newspaper—the *Dispatch*—concerned the 1892 Kenyon game, won by Ohio State 26-10. It was refereed by a master mechanic of the local Panhandle shops of the Pennsylvania Railroad named Samuel Prescott Bush, who became the grandfather and great-grandfather of two American presidents.

Though interest in the school's football team gradually continued to increase, not much happened in the years between the program's birth in 1890 and Harley's arrival in Columbus in 1907. Some of the games drew large crowds, but some of the newspaper estimates were probably exaggerated. It is doubtful that 8,000 attended the 1896 Thanksgiving Day game with Kenyon as the *Dispatch* reported, especially since many of the games at the time drew less than 1,000.

Twenty-one years later, 1894-95 team member George H. Calkins said as much when he told the *OSU Monthly* that the crowds of 11,000 and 12,000 the team was drawing then seemed almost unfathomable to him.

"It seems like a dream when I think of the crowds of today and the slim attendance of twenty years ago," Calkins said. "Then we had a grandstand which seated about sixty people—the rest stood around the edge of the field. And we didn't play in quarters and halves. We played until one side or the other was licked. I remember one game we played in the moonlight."

The grandstand was actually a 300-seat structure built in 1892 when the school set aside the area north of the North Dorm as University Field. The structure remained that way until 1898, when the faculty recommended that a new football field be constructed on High Street, north of the new armory and gymnasium.

The new University Field, where Chic Harley would roam as a college freshman a mere seventeen years later, was constructed with only 700 permanent seats. Two years later, when the Buckeyes had a "huge" Thanksgiving Day game with Kenyon at the end of a second consecutive championship season, the school's Athletic Board rented seats from the Columbus-based Sells Brothers Circus to increase seating capacity to 2,000. New bleachers seating 1,500 were finally added to the east side of the facility now called Ohio Field in 1904, three years before Harley moved to Columbus and eleven years before he first walked campus as a freshman.

With the seating capacity of Ohio Field just over 2,000, local people thought Ohio State football had finally hit the big time. Not until Harley arrived, however, did they discover what "big time" really meant.

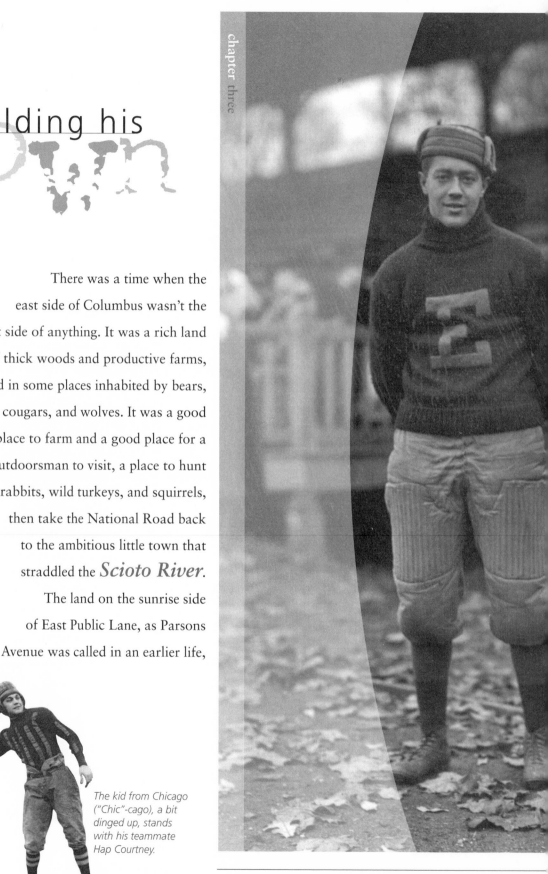

holding his
own

There was a time when the
east side of Columbus wasn't the
east side of anything. It was a rich land
of thick woods and productive farms,
land in some places inhabited by bears,
cougars, and wolves. It was a good
place to farm and a good place for a
outdoorsman to visit, a place to hunt
rabbits, wild turkeys, and squirrels,
then take the National Road back
to the ambitious little town that
straddled the *Scioto River*.
The land on the sunrise side
of East Public Lane, as Parsons
Avenue was called in an earlier life,

The kid from Chicago
("Chic"-cago), a bit
dinged up, stands
with his teammate
Hap Courtney.

was what the inveterate city dweller would derisively term "the country." It took the little town two miles to the west a while to get around to settling there, but once it did, it did so furiously. The wealthy came first, building brick mansions farther and farther out East Broad Street, and then some of the less-wealthy, seeing what the wealthy had done, began heading in that direction themselves. It wasn't long before it seemed like a stampede. Columbus's growth was slow at first and then extraordinary—a serene little burg of 18,554 in 1860 swelled to 125,560 by 1900—and those less wealthy than the less-wealthy wanted to live out there, too.

SO THE BIRTH OF EAST HIGH SCHOOL in the late 19th century sounds much like a story told repeatedly in exploding suburbs of the early 21st century. Columbus was oozing to the east, swallowing up farmland and planting houses on what had been empty land. The high school that served these new homes, Central, had more students than it was built to handle and its downtown location at the southeast corner of Sixth and Broad wasn't convenient for far east side families whose houses were sprouting like weeds.

A few visionaries proposed a new east side high school to take care of what they knew would eventually be an unacceptable problem and budget-conscious citizens all but laughed them out of the room. Building a new school way out there seemed like a colossal waste of money. Columbus was growing, yes, but it wouldn't need a new building out there for years, if at all.

In all of one year that notion began to crumble. Central grew so overcrowded that the school board decided to a establish a high school branch in eight rooms at one of its newer elementary schools on the south fringe of the new east side, the Ohio Avenue School, located at the southwest corner of Fulton and Ohio. First, they called it "South," then they changed the name to "East" in what seemed more of a hopeful image of a school than the real thing.

When expanding enrollment took two of those rooms back in 1897, more rooms were appropriated at the Felton Avenue School, fifteen blocks north. "East," the largest school geographically if not in enrollment, was now spread practically from the north end of town to the south. Sixteen teachers made the two-mile trip back-and-forth between the two buildings, and one of them, John D. Harlor, would be principal when Chic Harley went to school there.

Modern administrators deal with overcrowding by dropping portable buildings onto school parking lots like pieces on a chess board. Such options didn't exist, so construction of a new high school building on Franklin Street, a block east of Wilson Avenue, began the following year. The three-story building, Columbus brick and terra cotta trimmed with sandstone, was dedicated in April of 1899 and called "one of the most complete high school buildings in the state." Students no longer had to feel like renters. The shape-shifting East High School had become the real thing.

There was still open land within a few blocks of the new high school, but not for long. By the time Charles W. Harley and his family moved from Chicago to Columbus in 1907, East was surrounded by two- and three-story houses, mostly brick, and the city was still gobbling up land to the east and south. When Chic Harley enrolled in 1912, East's student population had doubled to over 800 students and the growth didn't stop. (In 1922, a more spacious East High School would open on East Broad Street for the expanding east side population and the "old" East became Franklin Junior High and welcomed students in the lower grades.)

THE NEIGHBORHOOD SERVED BY THE FIRST East High School wasn't much different than some of the upscale suburban developments on the city's outer fringes today. Most of the houses had been built in the previous twenty years. The area was clean. The schools were good. It was not only a good place to raise a family, it was good place to be a kid.

The Harleys moved a couple of times in the next six years, first to 1251 Mooberry, about five blocks to the southeast, and then to 689 South Champion, about five blocks southeast of the Mooberry address. The Mooberry house was surrounded by woods and was the most pastoral setting of the three; today the empty lot where the house once stood sits just across the street and above I-70, where thousands of cars whiz by daily.

The boys whom Harley played with in the vacant lots the big city kid called "prairie" recognized his athletic skill immediately. He was a quiet kid, so some of his grade-school playmates nicknamed him "Noisy," but his hand-eye coordination was amazing. He was good not only in sandlot football games, but excelled in baseball and boxing. This reticent, ordinary-looking kid could more than hold his own in a scrap.

Chic

"The greatest boxing match I ever saw was in our old barn," fellow east-sider Whit Dillon said in 1974. "Chic boxed John Vorys, who outweighed Harley by twenty or twenty-five pounds. Chic could box, but he could also slug if the other guy wanted to slug."

The Dillons lived in a huge brick house at 83 Wilson Avenue, half a block from the mansions on Broad Street—Whit's father, Edmond, was a well-known common pleas judge whom the Republican Party once tried to get to run for governor—and the barn in back was a remnant of horse-and-buggy days.

"My understanding from Dad was that there was no winner," Dillon's son, Whitney B. Dillon, said, "and Vorys was a lot bigger."

Being a little guy could be a problem in games like football where brawn seemed paramount, however. The boy who reputedly received the nickname he would carry forever from the Illinois city where he was born—Chic-ago—stood about 5-foot-6 and weighed only 125 pounds when he got to East High School as a sophomore in 1912. In sharing a field with the brawny upperclassmen on the school's football team, he still wasn't sure of his athletic skills.

"His modesty was evident when he entered East High School and had to be pressured to try out for the football team," Paul Gingher wrote. "He is quoted as having said to his young friends, 'You fellows think I'm good, but look at the size of those guys.'"

The transition from important ninth grader to lowly first-year high school student seems to have been a little daunting for Chic, as it is for many teenagers. And it is understandable. Vorys, the junior center whom Harley once boxed in Dillon's barn, would play football at Yale. Brothers Howard and Harold "Hap" Courtney, a senior and junior who played the two tackle spots, were talented enough that both would start at Ohio State in a few years, and at a respective 170 and 160 pounds they were two of the biggest players on the team. Senior captain Husky Thurman weighed 170 and senior Howard "Bugs" Schory weighed 168. They must have looked like men to the pint-sized sophomore.

East coach Frank Gullum knew this was no ordinary boy when he called his first practice at the east end of nearby Franklin Park. Gullum was 26, not much older than many of his players, but he knew football. A handsome, square-jawed man with dark hair, the school chemistry teacher possessed a sturdy build that hinted at an Ohio University athletic career still fresh in memory. Four years on the college gridiron had taught Gullum a little about talent, and this smallish sophomore could run like no one he had seen. Chic might be a little unsettled by the bigger, more mature bodies he saw all around him; to Gullum, it quickly became apparent that the older players' size would be more of a detriment than an advantage when dealing with Chic. The little sophomore was hard to miss. He flitted around like a firefly, changing speeds and directions so quickly that the others were left lunging and grasping for a body that was no longer there.

After only four days of practice sessions that he had to be "pressured" into attending, Harley was the first-team quarterback in East's intra-squad scrimmage. For some reason, Joe Murphy, East's starting quarterback the previous year, hadn't yet reported to the team, and it was a costly mistake. Whether Murphy realized he had jeopardized his job, he would know it soon. The *Dispatch* called Harley "a youngster who seems to be the most promising quarterback Mr. Gullum has had on the field since the passing of Ike Carroll."

That hardly meant Harley was on his way to national renown as a football player. The newspapers reported on the schools' practice sessions because the city had only four high school football teams at that point—East, North, South, and Aquinas. West was open, but had yet to start a football program and the High School of Commerce, which is what Central was now called, was in the process of trying to scare up enough players to field a team. The city's high schools didn't have a history of producing outstanding football players and East didn't have a track record of football success. Chic's practice exploits wouldn't mean anything unless it carried over into the games.

His first chance came on an unseasonably warm Saturday morning, October 5, 1912, in Recreation Park, the south end structure at Schiller (Whittier) and Jaeger streets that had once served as home to the city's professional baseball teams. With houses peering over the wooden fence that surrounded much of the field and a small crowd of people inside, Harley started the team's opener against Mt. Vernon. East won 16-0 in an ugly game where both teams fumbled repeatedly. Harley threw a "splendid" pass to Ed Gochenbach for a touchdown, then was "badly bumped" in the fourth quarter and Murphy replaced him. He was back in the lineup the following week, and East played a sloppy game in losing to Delaware

13-7. In two games, Harley's impact on the mediocre East program had been minimal. His play had been decent but not extraordinary, and his team was 1-1.

It may have been the last time in Chic's life he could still be described as ordinary. He was a high school sophomore like other high school sophomores, new to his school, new to many of his classmates and new to the increased workload from his high school teachers. While he knew the boys from his neighborhood and was getting to know those on the football team, he was still an uncertain first-year high school student, a baby-faced kid in a school where the older students strutted through the school's hallways with pride and confidence. It must have helped that he was from a large family, that he had older brothers and sisters to counsel him when school and practice was over, but for a while, he had to live with the anxiety that new high school students face everywhere.

His MISGIVINGS MELTED in the after-school practice sessions in Franklin Park. After the loss to Delaware, Gullum tried Harley at halfback during a scrimmage, then quickly moved him back to quarterback, which in the single-wing offense of the day was often called the "pivot." The single-wing quarterback often received the snap in a shotgun formation and usually pivoted either right or left to hand off to one of the halfbacks. But sometimes one of the halfbacks took the hike from center. The emphasis was on deception and the running game dominated. Early football games often turned into field position battles, and good kickers and punters were vital. Passing was an afterthought. When they did throw, some teams had their quarterback do it and others preferred to have a halfback pass. The quarterback sometimes punted or drop-kicked, and Chic's strong leg had already caught Gullum's eye. But Husky Thurman would do most of the kicking on this team, and to kick ahead of Harley, he must have been pretty good at it. Before the season had even started, the *Columbus Citizen* had marveled at the way little Chic could punt the football 50 yards.

Despite the slow start, it soon became obvious that East was better than usual and Harley was a big reason. He dazzled opponents with remarkable runs and crisp passing just about every game. His reputation grew quickly. In a game in Athens, Harley scored touchdowns on runs of 60, 40, and 60 yards in a 40-6 win over a team quarterbacked by future Ohio University star Ross Finsterwald, whose son Dow would become a famous professional golfer. But East also tied Springfield 7-7

(Harley's 30-yard run the only East touchdown) and lost in a light snow at Newark, and it wasn't until the game against North, East's rival, that it became clear how much things had been changed in local football circles.

East played the role of little brother in the annual scrap. The schools had played every year since 1899, and North held the lead, 10 wins to two with a 0-0 tie on a muddy field in 1911. East had won only one of the last seven games, and the sudden parity was one reason the city had been anticipating the game since early in the season. Although neither team was undefeated, both had good players. North guard Charley Seddon, quarterback Gordy Rhodes, and halfback Ray Pennell would play football at Ohio State.

Headlines promoted the game all week until the *Dispatch*, now riding shotgun on the Harley bandwagon, bannered, *Harley and Thurman Expected To Do Sensational Stuff For East On Morrow*. Underneath, the headline identified him as "East High's midget quarterback, who is said to be some speed merchant."

A big, enthusiastic crowd at Ohio Field discovered his speed wasn't just hearsay. Harley scored two touchdowns, one on a fumble recovery and the other on an interception, in a 20-3 victory that sent a wave of excitement through the east side. The fans saw a miniature version of the Harley that would star on this same field later, an elusive runner who would sometimes deliberately slow his gait long enough to deceive a defender into thinking he intended to maintain that speed. Chic patiently waited for blockers to clear his path and then suddenly shifted gears, often catching the poor saps trying to tackle him flat-footed.

"As a player he was not only lightning fast, but he had an instinctive change of pace and direction that demoralized his pursuers," Gingher wrote, "and all the while, he was as graceful as a ballet dancer."

HARLEY'S RUNNING STYLE COULD BE AS HYPNOTIC as it was breath-taking. He changed directions and speeds like a wind before a storm. He almost daintily pranced his way toward a defender, then exploded past him in a furious burst. He made sharp cuts that were sudden and erratic, and just as a turbulent wind might dislodge a hat and send it flying, a turbulent, shifting Harley cast off his defenders.

Harley shed his "ordinary" label the way a boy removes his coat on the playground on a warm day; he wasn't even aware of it. East closed out the season with an 82-6 win over outmanned South and the *Dispatch* named Harley second-team All-City, behind South quarterback Hal Gaulke. If this seems like one of those senior vs. sophomore all-star decisions that confound football purists, the newspaper justified it by explaining that Gaulke received the nod "because of his weight and experience. He is about as good as the East quarterback in open field running and is better at boring through the line."

Gaulke was no slouch. Even though he didn't go to college, the former South star ended up playing for the Columbus Panhandles professional football team for five seasons, a stint that started a forty-two-year career as a clerk, inspector and bookkeeper for the Panhandle division of the Pennsylvania Railroad. The newspaper had no way of knowing what the future held for either player. In the narrow focus of 1912 high school football, Gaulke's selection may have been perfectly reasonable.

IT DIDN'T MATTER TO CHIC, ANYWAY. He didn't have the ego to be bothered by the snub; this was a boy who had to be urged to go out for the team. And he was too busy. He played basketball and baseball and ran track, and excelled at all three. He also frequently found his way to a short retail district on Oak Street, two blocks north and west of the school. Today that section of Oak is devoid of life, a pock-marked row of vacant lots and rundown buildings, with no sign of the bustle known by Chic and his East classmates.

They hung out in Hahn's Confectionary, a popular ice cream shop and bakery wedged between a dry cleaning company and the Oak Theater at 1256 Oak. Owners Joe and Grace Hahn offered an assortment of fine delicacies, though the delicacies Chic likely focused on were just as interested in him. His popularity was growing and his humility emphasized his good looks and athletic ability all the more.

Deep, substantial changes were coming to Chic's life, though. Sometime in 1913, his father was offered a job by his old employer, the *Chicago Tribune*, and he decided to take his family back to Chicago. Chic was comfortable at East, had a lot of friends, and wanted to continue his football career there. His pals and classmates didn't want him to go, either, and they were determined to find a way for him to stay. To solve the problem, the family of John Vorys, who had been voted captain of the football team, offered to take Chic in. Charles and Mattie Harley didn't like the idea. Chic lobbied. His parents still didn't like it. Chic lobbied some more and, finally, his parents reluctantly agreed. The Harley family moved to Chicago, and Chic moved into attorney Arthur Vorys's home at 441 East Town Street for the first part of his junior year.

Although great things were expected of him by his friends, Chic didn't begin his second year of high school as the prep football icon he would soon become. Outside of his east side circle, others were waiting to see just how good he was. Harley was not mentioned in the *Dispatch* report of East's first practice, with the team's opener against West at Indianola Park only a week away. Five days later, another story about East was accompanied with a head shot of John Vorys titled "Leader of East High Squad." Again, Harley didn't get a mention.

ONCE THE GAMES STARTED, HOWEVER, he couldn't be ignored. In East's 32-6 win over West at Indianola Park, Harley scored two touchdowns and was called a "marvel (who) shone above the other men on the field as a blue diamond would if surrounded by so much coal." In his second game, Chic took the opening kickoff 90 yards for a touchdown in what would be a 59-0 victory and a *Dispatch* headline writer dubbed East "Harley Hi." In week three, Harley scored the only touchdown in a 6-0 win over Springfield that was the only close game East would play all year. Chic was getting noticed now, both in the newspapers and back in his east side neighborhood.

"When I was in grade school we used to get on our bikes and race to Franklin Park to get a place to play what we called 'rough and tumble,' which was a game of football, the number on a side depending upon how many kids were around," *Dispatch* sports editor Russ Needham wrote in 1948. "It wasn't long until there weren't enough to play because the kids would rather watch East High School practice. The reason was a little kid about 130 pounds making monkeys out of 200-pound bruisers like Joe Mulbarger, Husky Thurman, the Courtneys, John Vorys, and the like.

"Talk about your will o' the wisp, a phantom or a ghost, this little Harley squirt could outrun them all and he would out-punt them and he threw a pass like he was pegging a baseball. Kids by the hundreds used to stand around watching East practice just to watch this marvel of football."

East practiced at the east end of Franklin Park and a north-south railroad track occupying a hill east of the field offered the perfect vantage point. And the show only got better. East beat South 82-6. It beat Mt. Vernon 62-0, in a game where the *Ohio State Journal* noted that Harley's "open field runs were most sensational." It was leading Newark 40-0 in the final minute of a game certain to generate another round of superlatives for the little quarterback when the story took a turn as abrupt as one of his pinpoint cuts.

Newark drove the ball to the East 20 and was desperately trying to avoid the shutout. A pass was thrown to Newark captain Merle Orr, running with his head down toward the goal line. Harley, playing defensive back, saw the play develop and dove for the ball at the same time Orr did. The two players rammed heads and both dropped to the ground. Orr suffered a "horrible gash" to his forehead, which was bleeding profusely. Harley suffered several severe cuts over the eye.

The two players were hurt badly enough that it didn't make sense to finish a game that had already been decided, and the officials stopped it with thirty seconds left. It may have been just another injury; Harley played the following week against North. But it's hard not to wonder if that collision didn't result in a serious concussion and he returned from the injury too soon. The flimsy leather helmets the players wore in those days offered scant protection from serious head injuries; when a player got hit in the head the way Harley did, the leather didn't absorb much of the blow. A serious shot to the skull hurt almost as much as if a player were helmetless, and Chic apparently knew how that felt: as a small boy he had been hit in the head by a baseball bat.

IF HARLEY SUFFERED A SIGNIFICANT head injury from the impact of his collision with the Newark quarterback, no one at the time knew the dangers of playing with it. The timing also couldn't have been worse. The North game was up next and Harley wasn't about to miss it because of a bad headache.

Gullum held him out of an intra-squad scrimmage the following week. Missing the game was something else. There were huge school rallies and secret practice sessions and ticket sales were brisk even outside of the school; Ohio State was out of town and the game would be played at Ohio Field. A tragedy added further intrigue. Former East captain Jay Thomas was killed in an accident, and his brother, George, who started at right halfback opposite Chic, would miss the game.

For all the anticipation, the game was a total mismatch. North coach Harry Swain had geared his defense to stop Harley's explosive runs and the ploy worked—

sort of. The East dynamo scored only one touchdown himself on a 20-yard run, but he was 10 for 23 passing—this in the day when teams seldom passed—including one of 25 yards.

Harley was so good that East students began to worry they were going to lose him. There were perhaps three games left, if East were able to schedule a game on Thanksgiving. Would that be the last time they would see him play football? For several weeks, rumors had been swirling that he planned to move to Chicago at the end of the semester and the rumors had some basis in fact. When John Vorys's older brother, Webb, came home from college for Christmas, there would be no more room in the family home for Chic. It was nice that he had been able to stay through the football season, but in the absence of other arrangements, it seemed logical to assume that Chic would finish the term and move to Chicago.

Gullum grew tired of all the speculation and tried to put an end to it before his team played in Marietta the following Saturday. He told the *Dispatch* that his young star planned to stay at East through his senior year.

"Harley has told me he intends to finish his high school course at East, which means he will be available for another football season," Gullum said.

As if to celebrate his decision, Harley intercepted a Marietta pass and sprinted 95 yards for a touchdown in a 13-0 East win. He scored three touchdowns in a 27-0 win over Delaware the following week—one on a 40-yard run and two on punt returns of 30 and 55 yards. He returned a punt 50 yards for a touchdown against Norwood, the Cincinnati champion, on a rain-soaked field on Thanksgiving Day, a 52-0 East victory.

"It was an absolutely miserable hard rain and it rained for some time," Whitney B. Dillon said. "Chic did everything. He punted, he drop-kicked, he ran and passed, and John Vorys told the story that he almost swam into the end zone."

Near the end of that game, Chic faked a punt and streaked 30 yards to near the goal line, where he was decked by three players. The extent of his injuries weren't revealed but he was forced to sit out the last few minutes. It was East's last game, so the blow he suffered didn't have an impact on the game or the season, but it again emphasized some of the dangers that all early players faced.

With the inferior equipment of the day—the leather shoulder pads were strapped to a player's shoulders and they also lacked the cushion of modern equipment—it's possible that the blows had a cumulative effect.

His growing legion of local fans weren't worried about his health as much as his destination. Gullum's contention that Harley would stay at East hadn't quelled the rumors. "'Chic' Harley will not go to Notre Dame University before he finishes his high school education, if Mr. (John) Harlor, principal of East High, has anything to say about the matter," the *Dispatch* reported in December of 1913. "Harley will confer with Mr. Harlor Thursday afternoon and at that time it is thought that 'Chic' will be persuaded to finish his academic course before taking up university work, for which he would be far from fitted should he leave at the present time."

As CURIOUS AS THIS SEEMS TODAY, some colleges, including Notre Dame, had their own prep schools. The lines were sometimes blurred regarding who went to the prep school and who was enrolled at Notre Dame. Harley wasn't a good student, but that didn't seem to matter. Notre Dame had difficulty scheduling Western Conference opponents because its eligibility requirements were regarded as much less stringent. The Western Conference snub caused Notre Dame football coach Jess Harper to accept a game against Army at West Point in 1913, and the victory gave the program a significant boost toward the national stature it would soon enjoy. So Notre Dame had a growing football reputation, it had a place where it could put Chic even before he was out of high school, and South Bend was a lot closer to Chic's family in Chicago than Columbus was.

The East principal, however, did more than persuade Chic to stay in Columbus; he invited him to move into the Harlors' big frame house across Franklin Street from the high school. The Harlors had three boys—Donald, Allen and John C.—and Allen was on the football team. Donald was four years older, Allen was in Harley's class, and John was a few years younger, but only a year behind him in school. Donald and Allen would share one room and Chic and John C. would share another.

"The association with Chic throughout this period was one of the happiest experiences of my youth, enhanced, I must admit, by a certain amount of hero worship on my part," John C. said. "It was then that I got to know him intimately, to marvel as his physical feats to be sure, but also to admire his composure, his politeness, his readiness to help about the house and the yard and, above all, his innate modesty. He never became rancorous to others, but joined in the idle pleasures of his youth with his winning smile."

Years later, John fondly recalled going fishing with friend Willie Williams in Alum Creek. He said he was sitting back, quietly watching his bobber when he heard a rifle crack behind him,

"My bobber jumped out of the water and I rather irately looked back to see Chic with one of his friends, standing well back of the creek, his face wreathed in smiles," Harlor said. "He was obviously elated that from sixty feet he had made such a fine shot, not only to hit the bobber, but to cut the line."

POOL WAS ANOTHER ONE OF CHIC'S pleasures and Nel Mason's pool room stood near the corner of Oak and Wilson, in that small retail district. Young John wasn't allowed to go there, but he entered into a "conspiracy" with Chic. He sometimes gave his roomie his key so he could slip away to meet his friends for a few games of pool and still get back into the house after the doors were locked. One night, Chic had gone to Mason's and had forgotten to ask for a key, and when he returned, the house was locked and everyone was asleep. Chic sized up the situation. If he climbed the trellis by the front porch and made it to the roof, he might be able to climb into the second story window without awakening anyone. He was halfway up when James Sims, the local beat cop, happened along, saw a figure halfway up the trellis and figured he had caught a burglar. Fortunately, John was the only one who heard the voices in front of the house, and he was able to explain that the human spider actually lived in the house he was climbing. Chic and John were able to sneak off to bed without anyone else finding out about it.

That spring, Chic apparently suffered another serious blow to the head in a baseball game with Mount Sterling.

"Hap Courtney, who played third base for East, got into a fight with one of the Mount Sterling players," John C. said. "Chic went to Hap's assistance and in the fracas, the umpire hit Chic on the top of his head with a ball bat. He was badly hurt and I spent part of the night trying to dress the cut on his head."

Chic's roommate didn't mind. To the younger boy, it was exhilarating to be so close to the school's biggest hero, especially one whose athletic prowess never seemed to be out of season. Later that spring, Chic was a member of East's state championship track team, finishing third in Ohio in both the 100 and 220.

Chic

The "ordinary" Chic no longer existed. One copy of East's school newspaper, *The X-Rays*, from his senior year included a full-page drawing of him, arms crossed and wearing football gear, standing atop a pedestal. The illustration had only one line of explanation: "This is our jewel." But the other parts of the paper showed that in some ways he could be just another high school kid:

"Miss Ferrell (in third period English): 'Harley, how many lines are there in a sonnet?'

"Harley: 'Five feet.'"

PAUL GINGHER'S SON, the Rev. Richard H. Gingher, said that his father always talked about how Chic spoke with a "a strange accent, a tough guy accent" and how his father used to do imitations of it. An example of that also showed up under Harley's name in *The X-Rays*, under the title Heard at Franklin Park: "If yez can't get de sijinels, git out o' de game." And there was also this line, under Guess Who Said This: "Gimme de ball."

These may have come from Karl Finn, *The X-Rays*'s athletic editor and one of Chic's friends. Finn's aunt, Anna Finn—"Miss Finn" to the students—had taught German at East since the day it opened, and she must have been a good influence on him; Karl was a good student and a good writer. He would attend Ohio State and write about Harley's exploits there both for the student newspaper, *The Lantern*, and as the campus correspondent for the *Dispatch*, and later help convince the *Dispatch* editors to hire James Thurber, another former East High alumnus.

The world around Harley was changing. John D. Harlor was no longer principal at East; he was just a teacher. When Chic returned from Chicago in the fall, he moved in with real estate man William W. Walker, a bachelor who lived with his widowed mother at 1418 Oak Street, directly behind the high school. Gullum was on his way back to coach at Ohio University. Palmer Cordray took over an East team that had Harley, Mulbarger, Dillon, and a lot of inexperience.

Chic now weighed 160 pounds, and the additional size helped him absorb the pounding. As good as he had been, he was even better now, but the team as a whole wasn't as good. It was the first time Chic hadn't played with at least one of the Courtney brothers. Howard had graduated in 1913, Harold in 1914, and they were both at Ohio State now, and Vorys had gone to Yale.

None of this diminished the enthusiasm for the East team. Watching it play

The near-idolatry of Chic Harley began at East High, as witnessed
by this drawing from East's school newspaper, run full page.

and practice was still the thing for neighborhood kids to do. They sometimes followed players as they walked from the high school to its Franklin Park practice field and watched the practices from that nearby hill. The younger kids sometimes waited around the school for the team to return.

"I was only 3½ years old at the time and all I can remember was filling up the tackling dummy with leaves," the *Dispatch's* Paul Walker wrote in 1948. Walker was nephew to the man Chic boarded with during his senior year. "The neighborhood kids out there on Franklin Avenue kept the thing filled and then we'd wait around the school yard till the squad came back from practice in Franklin Park. It was fun watching them work on the dummy, which had a rope and pulley and was yanked back into place by a sandbag running down one side."

For a while, this team seemed just as powerful as the previous one. East spanked Doane Academy 59-0 in the opener, with Harley either passing or running for every touchdown but one. Chic injured his foot the following week in practice and missed a 21-0 win over Aquinas. When he returned, Cordray experimented with moving him to left halfback; that didn't seem to matter much in a 33-0 win over Delaware. After the game with South was called off because of heavy rain, Cordray moved him back.

Chic's senior season passed in a colorful whirr. He scored on a 35-yard run and a 55-yard punt return in a 42-0 win over West, then starred again—briefly—in a 55-0 win over South where the regulars were on the bench in the third quarter. He threw three touchdown passes in a 75-0 win over Springfield, the last mismatch that stood between East and a rematch with North.

Despite all of East's easy wins, local reporters seemed to sense what was coming. North had also been winning, and its players had been stung by successive losses in this game the past two years. It had better players than East and more of them. Harley was trumpeted as the most gifted player ever in the city, but newspaper reports hinted that even he might not be enough.

George Selby said his father, E.M. Selby, a teacher at North, talked about how Swain received encouragement on stopping Harley in that game from Ohio State coach Jack Wilce, who was worried that Chic might go to Michigan.

"He said you guys are going to play East and there's gonna be a whole lot of scouts there," Selby said in a 2000 interview. "He told him to put three guys on him if he has to, so nobody else will recruit him. If Chic had known that, he probably would have been pretty ticked."

Wilce wasn't telling Swain anything he didn't already didn't know. His strategy—everybody's strategy—was to send waves of defenders at Chic. This time, Swain's smaller but more experienced defenders beat the East linemen off the ball and got to Harley in the backfield several times before he had a chance to perform his magic. With North leading 14-0, Chic made one last desperate effort, mostly on his own, "dodging and squirming" his way for 35 yards to the North 15 late in the fourth quarter. But East got no closer and the 14-point margin stood. For the first time since he was a sophomore, Chic Harley had lost.

EAST PLAYED ONE MORE GAME. In light of the loss, Cordray decided against the usual Thanksgiving Day affair in Columbus and instead chose to go to Bellaire for a game that ended in a 6-6 tie. A crowd of 1,500 came out to see Harley, who scored East's only touchdown and missed the conversion kick. A news account in the *Dispatch* said Chic "played the most spectacular game ever witnessed in this city," and it may have been. But a loss and a tie in his last two games gave Chic a disappointing finish to what had been an outstanding high school football career.

Chic made it back to the Ohio Field one more time as a high schooler that May for the state high school track meet. Young John C. Harlor was assistant athletic editor of the school paper at that point and it must have thrilled him to be so close to the school's biggest sports story.

"We were at lunch one Saturday in the afternoon and Chic was entered in several events at the Ohio high school track meet on old Ohio Field," Harlor recalled. "Mother asked, 'Chic, do you think you will win today?' Chic, who had trouble with his h's, replied, 'I don't know whether I'll win, but I 'sink I'll be pretty good.'"

Harley was indeed pretty good, finishing second in the 220, just ahead of a Fostoria junior named Pete Stinchcomb, and third in the 100. Given their radiant athletic futures, it was a prophetic snapshot: Harley and Stinchcomb would meet again in this same place, eventually sharing the same backfield at Ohio State. "Pretty good" wouldn't begin to describe their success.

aligning the
stars

God had a plan. He must have. The arrival of John W. (Jack) Wilce in Columbus in 1913, about the same time Chic Harley burst on the scene as a wildly-talented high school junior, seems almost too propitious to have occurred without the intervention of some powerful force. *Wilce* was 25. He was only one year removed from a job as athletic director and football coach at LaCrosse (Wisconsin) High School. The year before, he had been an assistant football coach and assistant professor of physical education

When John Wilce got the OSU coaching job, he wasn't much older than his players. At right, Chic's high school team in 1913, the year Wilce arrived.

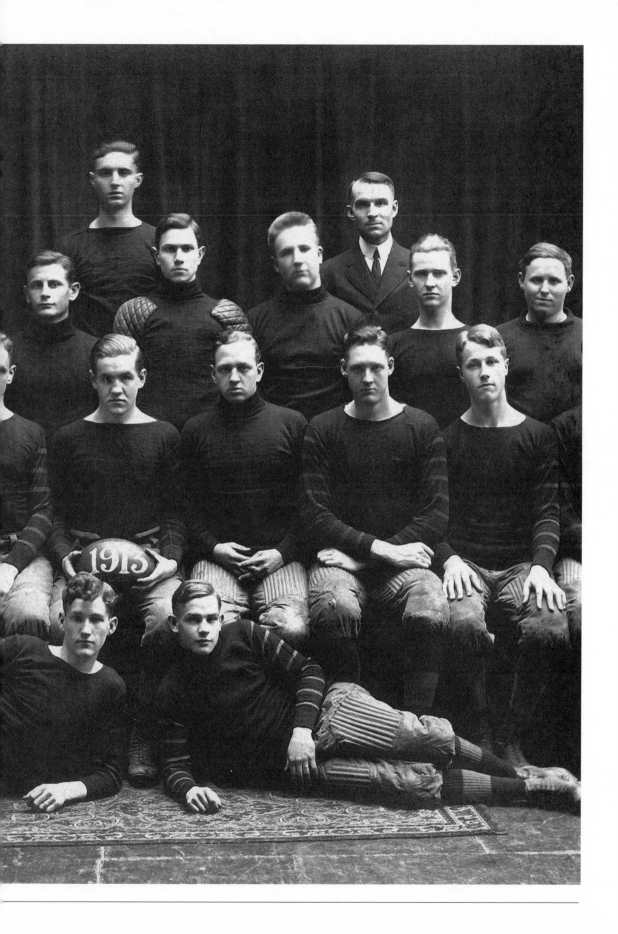

at Wisconsin, where he had once starred on the football, basketball, and crew teams. He was good but he was green.

A young man with Wilce's relative inexperience could never be hired as the head football coach at a major school today, regardless of his reputation as athlete or human being. Even a prospective job seeker with Wilce's glowing references would be both too young and too inexperienced to be considered a serious candidate. He would be told to return in a few years when he had built his resume. While dramatic promotions of this kind occurred more frequently in 1913, they weren't common. For Jack Wilce to become Ohio State's head football coach at a time when the school prepared to embark on its first season in the prestigious Western Conference, the pieces to a divine puzzle had to fall—almost mystically— into place.

It all started with John R. Richards, who had been the Buckeyes' head coach for only a year. Richards had been head football coach at Wisconsin when Ohio State hired him as football coach, track coach, and athletic director for the then-princely sum of $3,500 a year. He had coached at Colorado College and Shurtleff College before going to Wisconsin and was viewed as a knowledgeable coach and savvy administrator who could shepherd the program onto a higher plane. In short, he had the qualifications Wilce lacked. He figured to be the smart, steady hand needed by an ambitious program as it prepared to step up in class.

Others saw it, too. In November of 1912, word leaked out that Richards had been offered a position as head of the department of public recreation in Chicago, a post he had turned down once before. This time, it came with a $1,000 raise over his Ohio State salary, and while Richards said he wouldn't leave his post during the season, he said he might consider the appointment if he could start work after the first of the year. It quickly became obvious that he was as good as gone.

AT OHIO STATE, THIS STUNNING DEVELOPMENT qualified as business as usual. Since the program officially started in 1890, there had been eleven coaches, none staying longer than four years. Until recently, it hadn't even been viewed as a full-time job. Richards was supposed to change that. Now the responsibility fell to Lynn St. John, promoted from athletic business manager to athletic director.

St. John had come from Ohio Wesleyan only the year before as head coach of the baseball and basketball teams and assistant football coach, in part to pursue a medical degree. Now he was not only in charge of OSU's athletic program but was the man consigned to find a new football coach. With Ohio State preparing for its first season in the Western Conference, this would be an important hire.

All of this argued against Wilce. His only head coaching experience had come in high school. He had been one of Richards's Wisconsin assistants in 1911 and, on his way out the door, Richards strongly recommended Wilce for the Ohio State job. Although St. John respected Richards's opinion, Wilce wouldn't have been hired if fate hadn't intervened—not once but twice.

St. John and the OSU athletic board wanted Colorado College coach Carl Rothgeb, an Illinois alumnus. Rothgeb was interested but negotiations bogged down. So St. John and the board turned to their second choice, former University of Chicago multi-sport star John Schommer. Schommer had been a three-time All-American in basketball, and had also played end on Chicago football teams that won Western Conference titles in 1905, 1907, and 1908. He had served as head basketball coach and assistant football coach for the Maroons for two years, and left in 1911 to become athletic director, coach, and professor at the Illinois Institute of Technology. His association with famous Chicago football coach Amos Alonzo Stagg made him an attractive candidate. Again, Ohio State officials couldn't close the deal.

WITH THE BETTER KNOWN CANDIDATES out of the picture, St. John finally turned to Wilce, whose knowledge and integrity had impressed St. John in the interview. St. John understood the risk involved, but after two turndowns Wilce also had an upside: the young Wisconsin assistant would be happy to take the job.

The process demonstrated Ohio State's place as a football program. Schools of athletic renown—Michigan, Chicago, Princeton, Yale, and Harvard—would never have settled for a 25-year-old Wisconsin assistant whose only head coaching had been done in high school. They could have compiled a list of the best coaches and hired almost any one of them. Ohio State's program wasn't held in the same high regard. The move to the Western Conference would help, but the program's 23-year track record didn't scream success or potential. As a job, truth be told, it just wasn't that good.

This, too, seems part of the divine plan. Wilce's youth made it easy for him to embrace new ideas. He recognized that Ohio State's program didn't have players with the size and strength of many of the teams it would now have to compete with, so he became a proponent of the "open game" and embraced the then-radical concept of the forward pass. His system was made to order for a player such as the slightly-built Harley. He may not have had as many opportunities to blossom into the star he became if he had played under a coach married to the then-predominant power game. Wilce took an undersized team and won with it, in ways that at the time must have seemed a little shocking.

HE CAME TO COLUMBUS WITHOUT MUCH FANFARE. If Wilce's hiring or Ohio State's admittance to the Western Conference generated any excitement, it didn't show up in newspaper accounts or pre-season ticket sales. The newspapers accepted the Wilce hire with a figurative yawn. The students and alumni were indifferent. In 1912, 1,256 season tickets were sold. School officials were hoping to increase that total to 1,500 in 1913.

That small snapshot reveals the immaturity of Ohio State football, both as a program and as an entertainment option. Local newspapers reported that a special effort was being made to have co-eds purchase tickets. The program needed fans and St. John viewed women as an untapped market. "Last year, only a limited number of the girls availed themselves of the offer," the *Dispatch* reported, "but now it is arranged that if a sufficient number of the girls buy the tickets, a special section will be reserved for them. Plans have also been made to have suitable chaperons for the girls."

This football program was an entirely different animal from the one familiar to modern fans. An ornate two-and-a-half story frame house on the west side of High Street at 16th, which had been Professor B.F. Thomas's residence, had been converted into the school's "Athletic House" the year before and it was being hailed as a place where football players and coaches could "live on football from morning to night."

The house was equipped with offices, shower rooms, rubbing rooms, locker rooms, and "three large rooms downstairs with big chairs and tables for the comfort of the athletes before and after practice." As impressive as all this sounded, the home of Ohio State athletics was still just what everyone called it: a house.

Off-season conditioning was called by a different name: A job. A story in the *Dispatch* explained why Wilce would be pleased with the fitness of the squad he

John Wilce was the perfect hire for the less-than-plum Ohio State job—even if his head coaching had been only at the high school level.

inherited from Richards: "The old men of the squad have been for the most part putting in their time to good advantage during the summer and are coming back in fine physical condition. Red Trautman was a forest ranger out in California. (Ralph) Shafor, (W. Irving) Geissman and (Lou) Pickerel heaved iron all summer, and (Earl) Maxwell was on a farm. (Boyd) Cherry pounded iron for the Jeffrey Company, keeping in condition by playing plenty of tennis and getting out on the track occasionally. Eddie Morrissey was another cultivator of soil."

IT WOULD BE INTERESTING TO KNOW what the OSU players thought of Wilce on Monday, September 15, 1913, when he called them together at the Athletic House and explained what was expected of them. He was tall and lean, willowy, with short, closely-cropped hair and a stern expression that made it clear he was a serious man. Early practice photos show a virile Wilce wearing his Wisconsin letter sweater while coaching the Buckeyes' practices. That seems a little bizarre now, but no one complained about it publicly. It may have been his way of showing that beneath his youthful visage there was an experienced hand. If the older players thought their callow import was a step-down from vigorous, sometimes-brusque Richards, there is no record of any one of them saying so. They seem to have been impressed with him from the beginning.

"He was only a little older than some of the players," Charley Seddon recalled later. "But nobody ever called him Jack. . . ."

Wilce's first day offered no hints of future glories. The day didn't seem particularly momentous, even to those who monitored the program closely. While Wilce was introducing himself to his players, *Dispatch* sports editor Harvey Miller was in Milwaukee covering the Columbus baseball team in the American Association pennant race.

The first Ohio State game Wilce coached drew 3,950 fans. This included the 1,500 season tickets that school officials had hoped to sell, so the support pleased just about everyone. If the Buckeyes' 58-0 win over Ohio Wesleyan were cause for runaway optimism, the new coach's blunt assessment indicated that he didn't intend to feed it. He also showed that honesty was more important to him than making friends.

"The men played fairly good ball at times during the early part of the game, but the weakness of Wesleyan was responsible for the apparently good showing,"

Wilce said. "There must be vast improvement if Western Reserve and Oberlin are to be handled. The game was not a fair test of football ability."

HIS CANDOR OFFERED THE FIRST HINT of the aloof manner that many—particularly those who didn't know him well—regarded as a sense of superiority. His players and friends never saw him that way. To those who met him for the first time, his apparent lack of warmth was an understandable misinterpretation of who he was: a serious guy with serious goals and a steadfast determination to do the right thing, even if it meant losing a football game. It was clear he possessed the intense devotion to make the Ohio State football program successful.

What Wilce didn't have in experience, he made up for in energy. What he didn't have in qualifications, he made up for in creativity. The third choice for the job was undoubtedly the best choice—even if it wasn't readily apparent at the time.

The timing of his hiring didn't hurt, either. On the same day of Wilce's first game as Ohio State football coach, an undersized East High School junior named Chic Harley returned the opening kickoff 90 yards for a touchdown in East's 59-0 win over London at Indianola Park.

The stars were beginning to align.

freshman
chic

Mysteries always seemed
to follow Chic Harley, whether they
were his own mysteries
or *mysteries* that existed
in somebody else's mind.
The Phi Gamma Delta fraternity
recruited him to Ohio State
in the spring of his senior year, and
just about everybody in Columbus who
knew him joined in.
This was before the days of serious
recruiting by the coaches. Feelers
were sent out by coaches and school
representatives to let players know
they were interested and

*There was no dramatic
transition from East
to OSU, and in his first
scrimmage, Chic ripped
off a 75-yard TD run.*

sometimes there might even be a conversation or two between the coach and the player, but there was none of this sit-in-the-living-room-with-mama-and-tell-her-you-will-take-good-care-of-her-little-boy stuff. Coaches often didn't know who was going to be on the team until the players registered for classes in the fall. Even upperclassmen who had been on the team last year sometimes didn't return in the fall, much to the coach's chagrin.

Notre Dame wasn't the only school that had made a quiet run at Harley. Michigan had, too. Rumors during the summer after his high school graduation had Chic ending up in Ann Arbor, and there are signs he seriously considered going there. It's not hard to understand why. Michigan was the Midwest's reigning football power— it had been for almost twenty years—and Fielding Yost was one of the nation's most famous coaches. Ohio State ranked nowhere near Michigan in terms of football prestige, and its youthful coach lived in a different universe. On the Western Conference block, it was the baby.

NONETHELESS, THE PHI GAMS had made an impression on Chic, he had school friends on the Ohio State team already, and as far as Jack Wilce knew, the East star was all set to enroll in school in the fall. Then Chic went home to Chicago that summer and for the last month prior to fall registration, nothing much was heard from him. When students registered for classes and school started, Harley wasn't there, and even his friends began to suspect the worst.

Sixty-five football players, including thirty-five freshmen, reported for the first practice on September 20 and Chic wasn't among them. Was he at Michigan? No one knew. One practice was held, then another. On the seventh day of practice, the varsity scrimmaged the freshmen and didn't impress; the student newspaper, *The Lantern*, noted that "six touchdowns in ninety minutes of fierce scrimmaging was the best the varsity could do."

Finally, a week after school started, Chic showed up and enrolled in what university registrar Brad A. Myers described in 2007 as "general education courses—what we would refer to as a basic liberal arts core of classes." Two days later, a story about it appeared in *The Lantern*, an indication that the rumors had become a source of concern both in town and on campus.

"Contrary to reports that have been circulating rather freely about this campus and downtown, 'Chic' Harley, one of the best all-around athletes ever turned out by a Columbus high school, is enrolled in the University," *The Lantern* reported. "Harley has been away from Columbus for almost a month and returned last Monday. He did not register the first week, and this led a number of people to float the rumor that he had decided to enter the University of Michigan."

In some ways, this may have been easier for Chic than his first day of high school. The transition from high school to Ohio State wasn't quite as dramatic as it is today. There were 4,897 students on the OSU campus and more than 800 at East, which made OSU about six times larger than the school across town Harley had attended the past three years. Today, Ohio State is about fifty times larger than a high school with an enrollment of 1,000. Harley's Ohio State was still big; the school was comprised of forty-two buildings on 582 acres. But Chic had played several games on Ohio Field and had competed in the state track meet there. The area was comfortably familiar.

Chic also knew he could play with the other players on the team. He had been a teammate of Howard and Hap Courtney at East and senior Bill Havens had played at East the year before Harley arrived. Upperclassman Charley Seddon and Howard Yerges had played at North, and Gordy Rhodes was on the freshman team. His success in the past with and against all of these players gave him confidence.

IT WAS BY NO MEANS CERTAIN CHIC would become a star. But in a scrimmage against the varsity in his first day in uniform, Chic scored a touchdown on a 75-yard run. Even against the stepped-up competition, he had amazing skills. He could execute sharp turns like an expensive sports car, and together with his speed—he ran a 10.2 100-yard dash in high school—and change of pace, he was difficult to tackle in the open field.

"My dad (Whit Dillon) always said he never saw anybody, either in high school or in college, ever tackle Chic Harley one-on-one once he got into the secondary," Whitney B. Dillon said.

But as with many freshmen, his first year of college presented him with some major adjustments. It was anything but easy. Harley injured a shoulder and missed more than a week of practice and the injury seemed to slow him down when he got back. He had never been a good student and he struggled with his school work, partly because of its difficulty, partly because of his football responsibilities, and partly because college opened up a new world of possibilities for a young fraternity pledge.

He started to frequent Hennick's, a popular college hangout at the northeast corner of High and 15th Street, a restaurant advertised as "the only place around the campus where you can get a fudge sundae." Herb Hennick's restaurant occupied the bottom floor of an expansive two-story brick building with a skinny, one-and-a-half story rectangular sign that screamed *HENNICK'S* at cars and pedestrians, across 15th from the College Book Store. It was also located directly across High from President William Oxley Thompson's house, a sprawling two-story brick farm house that had been constructed in 1855, sixteen years before Ohio State opened. More important to Harley and the other football players, Hennick's was only half a block south of the Athletic House. The restaurant was a handy place to meet before or after practice, a mere block from Ohio Field.

THE FRESHMAN TEAM WAS COACHED by Campbell (Honus) Graf, who had been captain of the team the year before. Max Friedman was the quarterback when Chic arrived and Graf put Chic at one of the halfback positions and kept him there, effectively ending his career at the pivot. Once the season started, the freshmen were charged with mimicking each opposing team's offenses and defenses against the varsity. They did their job well, even if they played under a cloak of anonymity.

The 1915 varsity team was a good one but there was still only lukewarm interest in it from the general public. Ohio State football was still an afterthought to most Columbus residents. Most of the Buckeyes' games didn't draw crowds as big as the ones for the East-North games Harley had played at Ohio Field. Even good freshmen didn't generate a lot of interest. There was no way to be sure their success would translate to the varsity, or if they would even be in school the next season.

One game did hint at Harley's future success however. On November 13, Graf's freshman team scrimmaged a team of sophomores coached by Frank Castleman, the school's track coach and one of Wilce's assistants. While it was only a scrimmage, the freshmen ripped the sophomores 49-0. Harley scored three touchdowns and had 40- and 55-yard runs. He wasn't the only freshman star; Rhodes, the other halfback, had a spectacular 70-yard punt return and Friedman contributed several long runs and at least one long touchdown pass.

The freshmen were obviously good and *The Lantern* said as much in a story on November 30. The varsity had completed a fine 5-1-1 season the week before.

"With a lineup composed of "Chic" Harley, "Gordy" Richardson, Captain Friedman, (James) Flowers and (Fritz) Holtkamp, along with thirty other men of exceptional ability, the 1915 freshman football team was considered one of the best that has ever faced a Varsity organization on Ohio Field," *The Lantern* reported.

"'Chic' Harley, the East High star, was all that was promised of him. His end running was a serious worry for the Varsity and his line plunging kept the Wilce linemen busy.

"'Gordy' Rhodes, who hails from North High, made a good running mate for Harley. Critics looking forward toward next year's football prospects are giving these two Columbus men the once over. Dorer the fullback hit the line like a thunderbolt and was a hard tackler. Captain Friedman at quarter ran the team in snappy fashion and exhibited a sterling brand of quarterback play. On the line, Flowers stood out as a stellar performer. . . ."

It all sounded good but over the course of their Ohio State careers, the last four players *The Lantern* mentioned won a total of three letters between them. Freshman success was no guarantee of varsity success.

If Chic Harley was really that good, he was going to have to prove it.

chapter six

OSU's biggest
win

The summer of 1916 was the calm before Chic Harley. It was the last time *Ohio State* football was ever out of season, the last time it wasn't given a place at nearly every Columbus dinner table and accorded the affection bestowed upon a member of the family.

Ohio State football wasn't treated as religion that summer. It wasn't a passion, or even much of a hobby. The football goliath modern fans know and obsess over didn't exist. It was on the birthing table, but no one knew it, not Jack Wilce nor Lynn St.

Chic brought an excitement to Ohio Field that had never been there before.

John, not even the seer-of-all-things-John, nor even the seer-of-all-things-grand-and-great-for-Ohio State-football, Thomas French. The OSU football that existed that summer didn't demand racks of scarlet and gray clothing in the local department stores. It didn't require an outdoor palace with enough room to accommodate every beating heart in a city the size of Canton or Youngstown. It had trouble filling all the seats in its own unimpressive anthill of a stadium. It couldn't have raised one good tailgate party or inspired even a small flurry of letters to the local newspapers. The newspapers didn't run pages of stories about it to satisfy the insatiable thirst of their customers because the customers weren't thirsty.

The football team wasn't a common topic on every Columbus street corner. Attending a game might find its way onto a local citizen's autumn to-do list, but it could still lose out to raking leaves or taking a stroll in Goodale Park. Ohio State football wasn't so much an obsession as a curiosity, and most Columbus residents still hadn't discovered it.

Chic Harley, standout high school player though he was, was lost somewhere in all this apathy. He was merely a local kid who might have a chance to play as a sophomore, one of the promising young players on a roster with so many new players that it was shrouded in mystery. It wasn't even certain if he would be eligible, and there was no real reason to worry if he weren't.

The *Chicago Tribune's* preview of the 1916 Western Conference race summed up what the world outside of Columbus thought of Chic: "Ohio coach Wilce is happy to welcome local boy Chas. Harley, who might find the going too much when he starts playing with the big boys."

A sports-minded Ohioan had more pressing things to focus on during the summer. Mostly, he read and talked about baseball, which most Americans followed closely for eight months a year. The Boston Red Sox were trying to win their second straight American League pennant after selling star outfielder Tris Speaker to Cleveland a few days before the season opened. (It was over a salary dispute; Speaker wanted a minimum of $12,000, the Red Sox offered $9,000.) It didn't look good for Boston for a while, but the Red Sox charged back and took the American League lead, partly because of a fantastic 21-year-old left-handed pitcher named Babe Ruth.

Ruth and Harley were the same age, but the similarity stopped there. Ruth had already won 18 games the previous year as a rookie and had played in the big leagues briefly in 1914 when Harley was still in high school. Ruth had been a troubled youth; "incorrigible" was the word used to describe him when he entered St. Mary's Industrial School for Boys in his hometown of Baltimore, and he had spent most of his childhood there. Now he was the best pitcher in the American League, a voracious, unrestrained kid in a man's body who was even better than Washington's Walter Johnson. He beat the Big Train four times with one no-decision that season, and in one memorable game on August 15, Ruth was a 1-0 winner over the Senators' star in 13 innings. Ruth was on his way to a 23-win season with a league-leading 1.75 ERA and a record nine shutouts. If he kept this up, he would someday be one of the greatest pitchers in major league history.

THE AMERICAN PUBLIC FACED MORE SERIOUS concerns but mostly tried to ignore them. Europe had been at war for two years, and Americans had been angered by the sinking of the British passenger liner *Lusitania* by a German U-boat the previous year, mostly because there were 128 Americans onboard. The act drew a condemnation from President Wilson but nothing more. He adhered to a strict policy of neutrality and the nation nodded its approval and returned to its daily routine. If war news appeared on the front pages of local newspapers daily, it didn't dominate them. For the moment, at least, it was somebody else's war.

Life in Columbus was so good that its mayor, George Karb, constantly referred to the city as "Good old Columbus town." Karb was the quintessential politician, an exuberant, friendly figure who had served as mayor, sheriff, city councilman, and was now mayor again. He was often seen strutting around the city in a long black coat, wing collar, bushy moustache, and pince nez glasses, both the picture of the past and the messenger of a bright future. His characterization of Columbus as a "town" was repeated by local residents years after Karb was out of office because that's the way most of its citizens saw it—a friendly, neighborly place with a small town feel, like cities a third or a quarter of its size.

In reality, the "town" designation fit like a jacket that was two sizes too small. The east side neighborhood where Harley had lived as a youth was by no means the only example of the geographic expansion the city was experiencing. It had, in fact, become old news to local residents looking to move farther away from the growing poverty in older inner city sections like Franklinton, Middletown, Hickory Alley, the Badlands, and Flytown. The papers carried full-page ads with attractive pictures of the new homes that were being built in "Grand View Terrace," a place "safe from the noise, dirt and smoke of the city." It was a sign of change, a new suburban world Columbus residents were just discovering.

IT WAS AN EXCITING, CONFUSING TIME, a time when countless issues seemed more important than football games—the war, progressivism, women's suffrage, the temperance movement—and there were more compelling places to go for entertainment. At Keith's Theatre on Gay Street between High and Third, Gentleman Jim Corbett, former world heavyweight boxing champ, had a leading role in a vaudeville skit, and boxing towered over football in those days.

September wasn't much of a month to talk football, anyway. Wilce and St. John didn't return from their summer vacations until after Labor Day. School didn't open until September 19, and the first player to report, Dick Boesel, showed up on September 13. A few players trickled in the following days, but the Buckeyes' first game wouldn't be played until October 7, the same day as the first game of the World Series.

The word Wilce used for his team's prospects was "fair." Coming off a good 5-1-1 season the year before—albeit one that included a 21-0 loss to Wisconsin—his assessment offered no hint that a historic season might lie ahead. He probably didn't even know it himself.

"It was a pleasant surprise to have Mr. Wilce say. . . that the outlook at present is fair," the *Dispatch* reported, "and that it was excellent at the end of last season before losses by ineligibility and defections for other reasons turned the prospect from excellent into a milder form of efficiency."

The reporter listed six players who had graduated—including one who dropped out, got married, and became a farmer—and several freshmen who were ineligible. He also listed "quite a number of men who still have ineligibility delinquencies which may possibly be written off or removed by further classroom work," and Harley was one of fourteen listed. That was it for press coverage. The sophomore who had quietly shown flashes of brilliance amidst the relative obscurity of the freshman team was now just one of the guys.

Then came the first practice and Harley leaped to the lead of the newspaper's brief report: "To 'Chick' Harley went the first kicked ball on Ohio Field Wednesday afternoon in the initial official practice session of the year. Harley eluded his interference and his would-be tacklers who had come charging down the field to intercept him and the real season was on. . . . "

Three days later, Wilce put his team through "stiff scrimmage work," and Harley broke loose for a 70-yard touchdown run, one of only two scores during the session. His play raised eyebrows at the field on High Street, but this was still just practice and the dark cloud of ineligibility still hovered over him. Not until two days before the opener against Ohio Wesleyan was the sophomore halfback cleared to play, and the next day Wilce announced that Chic would start.

THERE WAS NO BUZZ. Prospects for the team were still murky. Only three players who started the season opener for the Buckeyes a year ago—tackle Howard Courtney, quarterback Fred "Fritz" Norton, and fullback Shifty Bolen—were back, and Norton was now a halfback and Bolen an end. Ohio Wesleyan was the first opponent and no longer one that generated much enthusiasm. Even though the Buckeyes won 12-0 and Harley was one of five new performers the *Dispatch* said had "won their spurs creditably"—he was the Buckeyes' leading grounder gainer with 87 yards—the lead headline in the sports section was Boston's 6-5 win over the Brooklyn Dodgers in the first game of the World Series.

The attendance at the football game was 4,889, not even half Ohio Field's capacity, but the newspaper was still impressed. It was called one of the biggest crowds ever for an OSU season opener, and the *Dispatch* implied that it had been beefed up by local people who were curious about the former East High School phenom.

"I have not seen an Ohio State game in two years," a 70-year-old man told the paper. "But I saw Harley play in high school games and I want to see what he will do."

His uncertainty about Harley's success was just as notable as his presence there. Those who had seen Chic perform some of those marvelous feats at East still weren't sure he could do it at the college level. Impressive as he had been in high school, he wasn't very big, and people, then as now, were obsessed with size and strength. Even an inspiring duel between the sophomore Harley and freshman

Chic

Pete Stinchcomb in a varsity vs. freshman scrimmage the following week didn't generate much enthusiasm for the upcoming game with Oberlin and once the game started, it was apparent why. The Buckeyes beat the visitors by a 128-0 score that still stands as a school record. Harley was impressive again, although none of the starters played much, including him. The announced attendance of 3,300 is as good a sign as any that Harley was not yet a drawing card, and the hysteria that would come to be associated with Ohio State football didn't yet exist.

THAT WOULD SOON CHANGE. The Buckeyes' next game would be played at Illinois, which was becoming a conference power under Bob Zuppke. The Illini had won the league championship with a perfect record in 1914 and finished second with two ties and no losses in 1915. The Illini weren't viewed as unbeatable—one of those two ties in 1915 was a 3-3 affair with the Buckeyes—but in 1912, the last time OSU visited Illinois Field, the Illini won 37-0. Illinois hadn't lost a conference game since 1913. Wilce drove his team hard in practice, and on Wednesday three players, including Harley, were hurt. Chic badly split a finger while fielding a punt, but was still expected to play.

Local fans, the few of them there were, expected the worst. There was no pre-game hype, no torrent of eager anticipation. The Buckeyes were given a nice sendoff by students when they boarded the train at Union Station on Thursday night and arrived in Champaign in time for lunch Friday. Zuppke gave the Ohio State players a tour of the Illinois trophy room, more of a psychological ploy than a genuine display of hospitality. As it turned out, the weather would play a larger role in the game than psychology.

A cold rain fell in Champaign on game day, and only 4,388 fans came out. The field turned to mud, the ball turned into a lump of lead, and the game became a sluggish, defensive affair. Illinois led 6-0 at halftime on a pair of field goals by Bart Macomber, and it began to look as though it would end that way.

The clock was winding down. The Ohio State offense had been all but non-existent, partly because Harley—due to the poor footing—couldn't use his speed to get around the ends. Wilce sent in tall end Clarence McDonald, who had been out with injuries, and Harley completed a pass to him around midfield. Chic followed that with a few good smashes up the middle, and then he threw another pass, this one to Norton, who carried it to the 20.

62

Now the Illinois defensive stiffened. One minute, ten seconds remained, and it was fourth and three for the Buckeyes from about the 16. Most press reports put it there, but some have it as close as the 13 and far away as the 20 because the sloppy field had erased the markings. Ohio State came out in Wilce's version of the T-formation, with Harley about eight yards back. Wilce called for what he termed a "spot zone" pass play, flooding one area of the defense with five receivers, leaving the other side open for Harley to perform his magic.

Abracadabra.

The OSU line shifted to the right, Harley went left, faked a pass, then angled toward the northwest corner of the end zone. One tackler hit him and Chic straight-armed him away. He eluded another, then another, and about three yards from the end zone, lunged forward in a desperate dive. . . and scored. The spectral, impossible-to-grab Harley—the one his East High School classmates knew—had almost magically appeared and the game was tied.

Extra point kicks were harder and more complicated in those days. The scoring team had to kick the ball from behind the goal line at the point from which the ball carrier entered the end zone. A member of his team had to field the ball cleanly on the field of play, and from that spot, the kicker was given a chance to make the conversion with either a place kick or drop kick. If the receiver of the "kick-out" dropped the ball or missed it entirely, no try for the extra point was permitted.

Harley produced the kick-out to halfback teammate Fred Norton, who caught the ball on the 22 near the sideline. The spot was less than ideal, particularly because of the muddy conditions, but the Buckeyes had another problem. Most of Wilce's regulars had been substituted off the field. The rules of the day said they couldn't return, and no one in the lineup had ever held the ball for a place kick. Up stepped Kelly Van Dyne to offer his services.

"Hell, throw the damned thing to me," Van Dyne said. "I've never held one before, but I'll hold this one."

The volunteer had taken a role in a dramatic scene that would be replayed by OSU fans for years. As Harley readied for the placement that could be the game-winner, he looked at the mushy field, looked down at his wet and mud-caked shoe, called time out and walked over to Trainer Doc Gurney.

"Gimme a shoe," he said.

Gurney complied and Harley took his time changing it. While all of the fans and players watched him and the tension grew, Chic carefully laced up the shoe and hitched up his pants. Then, in just his third college game, he stepped up and calmly booted the ball through the uprights, breaking the tie. The desperate Illini tried a few trick plays to go the length of the field, but Bolen intercepted a final pass as the game-ending whistle blew. Ohio State had a 7-6 victory and a story to tell for the next fifty years. A small band of 175 OSU rooters—they had come over on the train from Columbus—celebrated as if this were the biggest win in school history, which to that point, it probably was.

As the players headed to the locker rooms, an exuberant Bolen yelled over to Zuppke, "Hey, Zup, how would you like to have Harley's shoe for your trophy room?"

The remark didn't set well with the Illini players or their fans and a small skirmish on the field was quickly broken up by the campus police.

Back in the locker room, the star of the game may have been the least excited member of the team. While his rambunctious teammates enjoyed a milestone victory, Harley simply sat there and smiled "in his modest way." Then, while the other players went to the station and caught a train back to Columbus, Chic hopped on one for Chicago.

"Saturday night, he rode alone to Chicago to visit his parents, whom he had not seen since last Christmas," Harvey A. Miller reported in the *Dispatch*, "and perhaps there in the bosom of his family he will expose the concealed joy that he no doubt feels over his wonderful share in the victory."

IN ONE COLD, RAINY AFTERNOON IN ILLINOIS, Harley and his teammates had given birth to the Ohio State football behemoth that lives nearly a century later. This was the Big Bang of Buckeye football. On the Columbus campus, the sport would never again be the same. By Monday, plans were already being made for the Wisconsin game, even though it was two weeks away. The Buckeyes had a week off, which gave even the football-deficient time to get onboard, and by Wednesday, the newspapers were already reporting that the game would draw a record crowd. St. John announced that he would be able to take care of 12,000 spectators—an unheard of number in Columbus at the time—thanks in part to the erection of bleachers at the south end of Ohio Field and permanent boxes in front of the east

bleachers. Construction on both projects had already begun and mail orders
for tickets were streaming in.

A noticeable crescendo of interest gripped Columbus in the week that
followed. Two days before the game, the headline in the *Dispatch* added to the
hysteria: *Ohio State Football Eleven and Its Supporters Primed for Biggest Game in
History of Scarlet and Gray Athletics.* It wasn't hyperbole, even if James E. Pollard's
story indicated that the Badgers may not have had quite the same appreciation
of the occasion as the Buckeyes did.

"It is more than possible that the Madison contingent may return home with
much more respect for the Scarlet and Gray squad than they are bringing with
them," Pollard wrote. "After reading reports from Madison, one is inclined to
believe that the visiting eleven does not appreciate the true worth of Ohio State,
even after the Illinois win. Throughout the conference, the opinion generally
expressed is that Illinois is weaker than usual this fall, all of which detracts in some
degree from the Buckeyes' splendid win two weeks ago."

THE NEXT DAY, WISCONSIN COACH PAUL WITHINGTON physically confirmed as
much when the Badgers arrived and checked into the Southern Hotel without
their head coach. Withington had put assistant Ed Soucy in charge for the Ohio
State game, and instead went to Minneapolis to scout Minnesota's game with
Chicago, two strong teams he probably thought his Badgers would have to beat
in November to win the Western Conference title.

There is no record of Wilce giving his players a pre-game speech about the lack
of respect that Withington had shown them, but it surely must have happened.
This was the Buckeyes' big day. It was the city's big day. At Friday night's
homecoming rally, Wilce confessed that "I want to win this game tomorrow worse
than any other game in my life."

That the opposing coach was so sure of victory he had gone off to scout
another game made the outcome much sweeter. There were 12,268 people in
the stands, more than the school home record of 8,200 who attended the 1902
OSU-Michigan game. While the Badgers took a 7-0 lead in the second quarter,
they were about to be given a rude introduction to the little sophomore halfback
who had burst on the scene like a meteor two weeks before.

First, Harley threw a 33-yard pass to end Dwight Peabody that he carried to the Wisconsin 27-yard line. On the next play, Chic took the ball and swept around the right end, then squirted back through a small hole just beyond the line of scrimmage. He veered sharply to the left and streaked toward the end zone. He still had one man to beat, but made a quick cut to the right, froze the helpless defender, and shot across the goal line. His extra-point kick tied the score, and that's the way it stood at halftime.

After a scoreless third quarter, Harley added to his growing legend with eight minutes left in the game. He fielded a Glenn Taylor punt at the 20-yard line and cut a speedy, diagonal swath across the field, streaking past the befuddled Badger defenders and using a key block by Bolen to go 80 yards for the go-ahead score.

THE RUN WAS A PRIME EXAMPLE of Harley's unique running style, one that not only flummoxed his opponents but sometimes drove some of his own fans a little crazy. Russ Needham's description of it in the *Dispatch* in 1938 explains why.

"Maybe he would catch a punt on his own goal line," Needham wrote. "But he wouldn't start up the field pell-mell, as practically every running back you ever saw. Not Harley. He advanced at a dog trot, usually a slow one at that.

"He would drive you mad with his deliberation. 'Why, oh why,' you'd scream at yourself, 'doesn't he hurry?' But that wasn't the Harley technique. He'd loaf along hoping to string out his field of tacklers so he could meet them one by one. If he could, he was gone. Because no single tackler ever brought Harley down in the open field.

"When the first man to reach him would make his dive, Harley would quicken his pace for a step or two and the defender would keep diving right on past—frequently on his face. You'd chuckle. Possibly the next man would change his tactics, would wait for Harley to come to him. Here Harley would go into a Pavlowa sidestep, shoot out his straight-arm and go skidding by to the next man.

"He had made runs more than half the length of the gridiron which took long enough for every single man on the opposing team to have a chance to tackle him—and miss. The number of times one man has missed a tackle, got up and missed him again, never will be known, but there must at least have been several."

This may have been one of those runs. The scene Needham described off the field was almost as amazing as the one that was occurring on it.

"I've seen grown men with tears in their eyes as they watched him run through

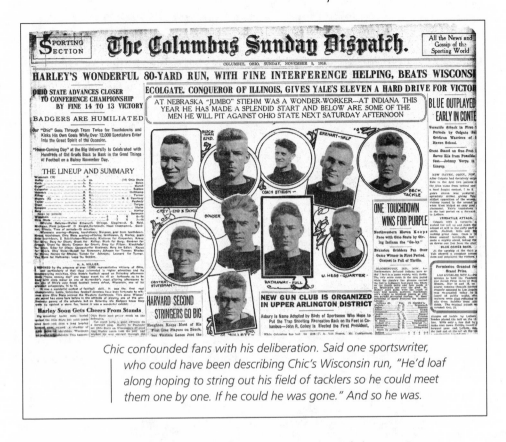

Chic confounded fans with his deliberation. Said one sportswriter, who could have been describing Chic's Wisconsin run, "He'd loaf along hoping to string out his field of tacklers so he could meet them one by one. If he could he was gone." And so he was.

a helpless opponent," Needham wrote. "There is on record the time Joe Mulbarger, a husky, 220-pound professional tackle who was a high school teammate of Harley's, fell out of his field box seat in tears when Harley cut loose with an 80-yard touchdowns run in. . . a Wisconsin game."

Mulbarger surely wasn't the only one. Chic's extra-point kick made it 14-7 and a surge of electricity ran through the overflow crowd in Ohio Field. The excited fans sensed history in the making, although it wouldn't be so easy.

The stunned Badgers woke up and made a determined march to move back down the field, helped in part by a pass interference call on Norton. With about two minutes remaining in the game, Lou Kreutz ended up going in for a touchdown on a fourth and one. Wisconsin might have tied it, but Taylor missed catching the kick-out, in part because of a good play by a hard-charging Fritz Holtkamp. The Buckeyes used two plays to run out the clock and broke into a wild celebration over the momentous 14-13 victory. While the happy Columbus fans stormed onto the field in a chaotic mob scene, jubilant students hoisted a smiling but reluctant Harley onto their shoulders and carried him off the field.

The victory brought the Buckeyes—and Harley—more national acclaim than they had received after the Illinois game. Wisconsin was one of the seven charter members of the Western Conference and had won four league titles before the Buckeyes were even granted membership. It was Wilce's alma mater and a school Ohio State had lost to three successive years. As if anyone needed to be reminded of how immature the OSU program was, Harley was presented with "a big silver loving cup," a suit of clothes, and a life insurance policy from the Midland Mutual Life Insurance Company for scoring the first touchdown at Ohio Field against a Western Conference opponent.

In a span of just three weeks, Ohio State had moved into an astonishing new world. Like the lovesick boy who falls for a pretty girl the first time he sees her, the city had fallen for the team and especially for Harley, whose play had proved every bit as electrifying as it had at East High School. In the crowded produce district near the Central Market, in the smoke-filled manufacturing ward near the Scioto River, in the old frame houses in Franklinton, and in the magnificent mansions along East Broad Street, an enchanting stranger called football had abruptly become a prime topic of conversation. The presidential election was only three days away, and in a place where politics was a way of life, as many people were talking about Harley and his Ohio State football team as they were about Woodrow Wilson's chances of being reelected over Supreme Court justice Charles Evans Hughes. Even when viewed through a ninety-year prism, the infatuation hit so fast and hard it is difficult to fathom.

THREE GAMES REMAINED IN THE SEASON, and the surprising Buckeyes had the inside track on their first league championship. Indiana was next, and while the newspapers tried to portray the Hoosiers as a dangerous team, it was no easier to sell in those days than it is now. Indiana wasn't in the same football class as Illinois or Wisconsin and even the local rooters knew it. "Only" 8,000 showed up to watch the Buckeyes beat the Hoosiers 46-7. Harley played on the first two scoring drives, contributing runs of 30 and 18 yards to the effort, and then was pulled from the lineup, supposedly to show that the Buckeyes weren't a one-man team.

The size of the crowd seemed the more salient point. The attendance had nearly duplicated the old record set in 1902 despite an opponent known to be among the weakest of the Western Conference schedule.

Harley was the toast of Hennick's, the favorite son in the Phi Gamma Delta fraternity house on East 17th where he lived, the hero to all the kids in his old east Columbus neighborhood, and a student who couldn't walk from one campus building to another without getting a handshake from one or more of his peers. He had always been popular because he didn't act like a football star, and his success only accentuated his modesty.

Football was now in style, mostly because of Chic, and it seemed as if nothing could stop the runaway enthusiasm for it. The Buckeyes' next game against Case in Cleveland was a case in point; it almost begged to be ignored. In over 20 games against Ohio State, Case had won 10 and tied two but those were ancient history; it had lost four straight to OSU by an aggregate score of 68-12. The match-up seemed grotesquely out of place, a vestige of the days when the Buckeyes couldn't line up games with teams such as Illinois and Wisconsin. It didn't matter, however, for a week without football was becoming unfathomable for many who had paid no attention to it before. Some students actually planned to take the train to Cleveland to see the Buckeyes play this mid-season scrimmage of a game.

Cleveland newspapers reported intense excitement over the Buckeyes' visit. As Ohio State ticked win after win over reputable opponents, state pride had swept through northeastern Ohio. Clevelanders tried to get Case officials to move the game to League Park, home of the Cleveland Indians, so that more fans could be accommodated. School officials resisted, hoping that their smallish stadium would aid their team. It was an expensive dream. After Ohio State cruised to a 28-0 win with Harley again the star, Case administrators must have realized they could have sold all 10,000 seats in the east side ballpark and had blown a chance to make a financial killing. It proved to be their last chance at a windfall. Ohio State hammered Case in Columbus the next two years, 49-0 and 56-0, and the schools never met on the football field again.

Back in Columbus, the Case contest proved more of an exercise in patience than a football game. With a Western Conference championship at stake—one that didn't seem even remotely possible prior to the season—fans had been buying up tickets for the Northwestern game at a frenetic pace. It was the Wisconsin buildup all over again. The Wildcats didn't have the prestige of the Illinois and Wisconsin

teams the Buckeyes had already beaten, but they were also unbeaten and harbored the same dreamy thoughts of a league title.

Northwestern coach Fred Murphy wouldn't repeat the mistake made by his Wisconsin counterpart. He would not underestimate the Buckeyes and their frenzied fans. The town's football hysteria concerned him almost as much as the opposing players, and upon arrival at Union Station, he loaded his twenty-nine players into twelve touring cars. Rather than stay at one of the usual downtown hotels, they were driven eleven miles south to the little country town of Groveport and lodged at the Elmont Hotel.

Harley's end run against Northwestern in 1916 is most often referred to as "the perfect play."

It was an admirable move and a futile one. Before a crowd of 11,979 that the newspapers called "disappointing"—despite frigid temperatures that doubtless kept some fans away—the Wildcats were outclassed 23-3 in another game where Harley made the big plays.

This time, the sophomore halfback kicked a field goal in the first period and then broke free for two touchdown runs in the fourth quarter, one for 63 and another for 16 yards. He also had a fourth quarter interception.

The crowd at Ohio Field celebrated as if it had won the World Series, which wasn't far from the truth. The Sunday *Dispatch* ran a giant *Ohio, Champs of the West* headline that took up nearly a third of the first sports page, and Harvey A. Miller wrote, "November, 25, 1916 will go down in athletic history as marking a new epoch in Ohio State football."

It had been a day of firsts. Chic's oldest brother, Walter, made the trip from Chicago to watch him play for the first time. Even though he sat with his mother and sister, he ducked and hid his face every time Chic came his way. He didn't want his kid brother to see him because he was afraid it would put too much pressure on him. Walter Harley was ten years older than Chic and had been living in Chicago for the past ten years. Not until Chic scored his second touchdown did he give any of those seated around him even the slightest hint of who he was.

"Chic's my brother," he finally said to the man next him. "I've never seen him play before. I didn't know he could play so well. The Chicago papers have said little about him, and the kid never would send us local clippings or tell us about his games."

After seeing Chic's effort against Northwestern, the *Chicago Tribune's* Walter Eckersall, respected as a former Chicago star and one of the nation's leading college football authorities, announced that "Chic Harley will be placed on my All-American team. He's one of the greatest players I've ever seen. Harley is as great as Willie Heston."

Heston was the 5-foot-8, 185-pound dynamo who starred on Fielding Yost's famous point-a-minute Michigan teams, teams that compiled a remarkable 43-0-1 record from 1901 to 1904 and were considered the standard by which all Midwestern football teams were judged. Heston was both fast and powerful, a 10-flat, 100-yard sprinter who could not only break tackles but often leaped over players who were trying to tackle him.

At the time, Heston was the most famous player in Western Conference history. And the kid to whom Eckersall compared him was only a sophomore.

life off the turf

The pretty female student found it fascinating to watch the awkward, rumpled male who sat next to her in Chief Myers's Ohio State journalism class. Peering through thick, steel-rimmed glasses, he would rapidly knock out his assignments on the *typewriter* in front of him and then continue to madly tap away. After a while, he would jerk the page out, wad it, and file it in a nearby wastebasket. In the fall of 1916, Minnette Fritts got to know the shy young man well enough to walk

The 1916 team sits for a field portrait. Chic is in the second row, third from right.

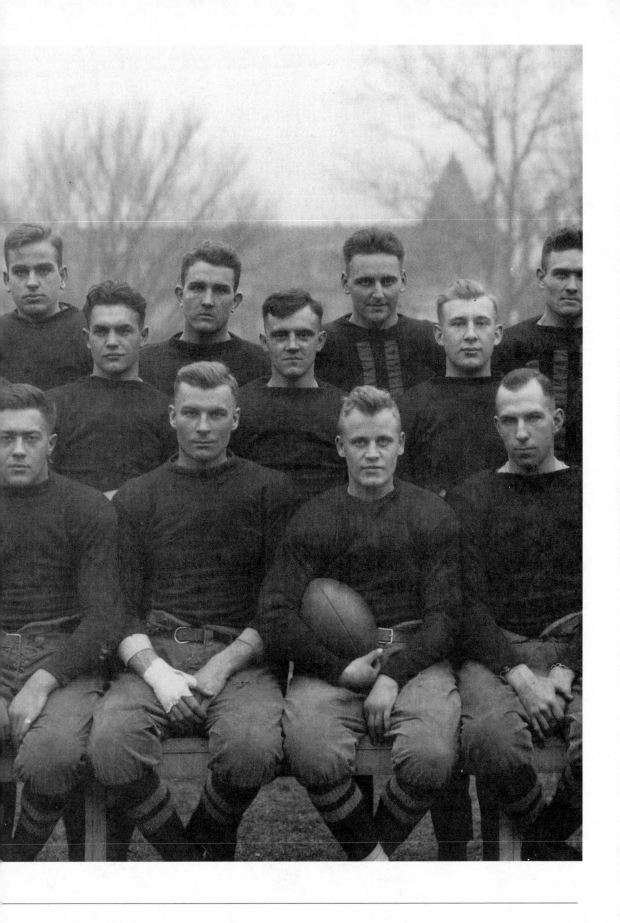

with him to the English department when class was over. One day she made an excuse, hung back, and fished one of his discarded papers out of the waste bin. When she saw how good the writing was, she showed the clever prose to her professor. Both, on a regular basis, fell into the habit of reading the young man's trash.

If James Thurber didn't cut a dashing figure, his writing did. Fritts and her professor thoroughly enjoyed the little comedic dramas he created, even if they were done only for his own pleasure. They began to see this thin, gawky figure as no one else in class saw him. Beneath that unimposing, townie exterior lay a rare creative talent. He was a literary genius in disguise.

THURBER WAS A JUNIOR IN 1916, one year ahead of Chic Harley. He was almost a year older than Harley and graduated from East High School in 1913, two years before Harley did. Harley played shortstop on the East baseball team captained by Thurber's younger brother, Robert. Because young Jim was two grades ahead of Harley and because he didn't participate in athletics due to his poor eyesight—he lost an eye in an accident when he was a boy—they weren't close friends. If they didn't have a lot in common, they did share many of the same east side memories.

Frank Gullum, Harley's first high school football coach, was Thurber's chemistry teacher and one of his favorites. Though Thurber was unable to compete athletically, he was as consumed by the rivalry between East and North as any east side youth. The pep rallies, nightshirt parades, and devilish pranks that preceded the games helped define the high school experience for all East students, Thurber and Harley included.

Thurber was a bit of a bookworm; his schoolmates later remembered that he was always reading. Harley was a student only in the narrowest sense of the word. Thurber wasn't popular in a Harley sense—few were—but he was well-liked by those who got to know him. Thurber could be funny and entertaining, and most of his classmates got to know him well enough that he was elected class president during his senior year. By his senior year, Harley probably could have been elected mayor. The dynamic young star's athletic exploits thrilled Thurber, even though he was already out of school by the time Harley became a local legend. Harley's decision to attend Ohio State and play football there delighted the young writer, even if by that time he had become more consumed by his own social inadequacies.

Chic's bookish classmate, Thurber, showed little evidence of what would one day be an enormous fame of his own. In time, Thurber's fame eclipsed that of Chic, and he would write the enduring description of Chic's running style.

Harley was as much a hero to Thurber as he was to any of his East High classmates. In later years, Thurber's description of Harley's running style would be the one that was most quoted in newspaper and magazine articles about Chic and even appears on a plaque about him that hangs in the Woody Hayes Athletic Center today. But there, as in most places, it is attributed to *Ohio State Journal* sports editor Robert E. Hooey, who unabashedly printed the line under his byline eight years after Thurber wrote it for the short-lived New York newpaper *PM* in 1940.

"If you never saw him run with a football, we can't describe it to you," Thurber wrote. "It wasn't like (Red) Grange or (Tom) Harmon or anybody else. It was a kind of a cross between music and cannon fire, and it brought your heart up under your ears."

As exquisite as that description is, it would be intriguing to see how a high-school age Thurber would have written of Harley's mystical running skills.

Chic

Unfortunately, Thurber didn't write anything for the school newspaper, *The X-Rays*, until May, 1913, a month before his graduation. The only piece he appears to have written for the paper was a Western potboiler called "The Third Bullet," and there was little in it to suggest Thurber would go on to international fame as a writer or that he planned to take up writing as a career. It's doubtful Thurber would even have gone to Ohio State if enrollment hadn't been tuition-free to every Ohio resident with a high school diploma. His father, Charles, was hardly a failure—he had been press agent for the mayor and had held similar respected positions in government—but he had three boys and not enough money to send them away to college. And, too, Thurber didn't have the vaguest notion of what he wanted to do with his life. OSU worked for him mostly because he could commute from across town for the cost of a ten-cent trolley ride.

HARLEY HAD MORE CHOICES and he made the same one as Thurber, albeit for different reasons. While Chic was actively recruited by Phi Gamma Delta, one of the most popular fraternities on campus, it seemed for a time that Thurber would not get into one at all. Fraternities and sororities dominated campus social life, so recruitment was a bigger event than it seems now.

Thurber was a "townie," so he didn't have the benefit of dormitory friendships. He wore cheap, ill-fitting clothing and a sheath of insecurity, a combination that didn't put him in high demand. His best friend from high school, the well-to-do Ed Morris, also attended OSU and he was quickly pledged by the Chi Phi house. Morris' father owned Buckeye Steel Castings, a large steel and iron company on the south side that had once been headed by Samuel Prescott Bush. Morris was bright and well-connected. The seedy-looking Thurber was not. The same fraternity rejected Thurber after briefly rushing him, and he was soon left behind. With his frat activities and friendships increasing, Morris no longer had much time to spend with his high school pal. Thurber's humbling experience as a college freshman eventually led him to drop out of school for a year in 1914, which is why he was now only a year ahead of Harley.

Thurber had other problems that Harley didn't. The university required students to take a gymnasium course and swimming was a requirement for graduation. Given that his great-grandfather had drowned in the Hocking River and Thurber had inherited his mother's fear of water, this didn't set well with him.

But it was the other requirement that caused him the most trouble. The university forced all male freshmen and sophomores to attend military science and tactics classes in the afternoon, which meant learning to march in close-order drill. The courses were taught by Captain George L. Converse Jr., a West Point grad who had been a classmate of General John J. Pershing, soon to be commander of the American Expeditionary Force in Europe. "Commy," as he was called by OSU students who weren't in his presence, had lost an eye Indian fighting shortly after graduation and wore a black patch. He had a reputation for being fair, but a bit of a martinet, rigid and strict. Some called him the third most powerful figure at the university, behind the president and athletic director.

There is no record of Harley having any more trouble with Commy or his military drills than the average student, but the instructor and his class were the banes of Thurber's existence. Converse seemed to delight in making life miserable for the clumsy one-eyed student. Thurber biographer Harrison Kinney later speculated that "he seemed to feel the ungainly young man was a disgrace to the ranks of one-eyed persons," and Thurber so hated the class that he wrote about it almost twenty years later. In "University Days," he gave Converse the name "General Littlefield" and wrote of how he once "popped in front of me during a regimental drill and snapped, 'You are the main trouble with this university!'"

"I think he meant. . . my type. . . ," Thurber wrote, "but he may have meant me individually."

When Thurber was finally invited to pledge Phi Kappa Psi because of the lobbying of another friend in Chief Myers's journalism class, he would slap a patch on his eye and regale his Greek brothers with hilarious imitations of Commy Converse. It was a stage Thurber would never have had if popular journalism classmate Elliott Nugent hadn't come to recognize his wit and talent. Nugent was also in Myers' class with Fritts and Thurber, and he insisted that his frat brothers take Thurber or risk losing both of them. Most of the other Phi Psis were never able to appreciate Thurber the way Nugent did, but after a while they began to recognize what he could bring to the membership. Nugent, who went on to a prominent career as an actor, writer, and film director, saw more than that. Years later, he and Thurber collaborated on the comic play, *The Male Animal*.

On what was then a relatively small campus, relationships could be unusually intertwined. Thurber went to work for both *The Lantern* and the school's monthly humor magazine, *The Sun-Dial*. He worked nights on *The Lantern*, and one of his friends there, Karl Finn, also attended East High School. Finn wrote stories about Harley and the Buckeyes as student sports correspondent for the *Dispatch*, and he also became a rival for the affection of Minnette Fritts, the girl Thurber met in journalism class. Finn eventually landed a full-time job at the *Dispatch* and helped Thurber get his own job there. Thurber more or less won out over Finn for Fritts's affections, although Fritts eventually married a former classmate from her prep school days in Illinois.

THURBER AND HARLEY MOVED IN DIFFERENT CIRCLES, but then Ohio State and Columbus were smaller circles that sometimes intersected. High Street was even more of a center of activity. While Chic spent a lot of his free time at Hennick's, Thurber was a regular at Marzetti's restaurant, another popular student hangout at the northeast corner of High and 10th, and it was open late. Thurber and his *Lantern* pals often stopped there around 11 p.m., after putting the paper to bed.

Hennick's and Marzetti's were but two of a range of options for Harley and Thurber. Just a mile north of campus on High Street, at the end of the streetcar line, was the thriving Olentangy Park, which occupied a 100-acre site west of High at Arcadia and featured several roller coasters, a dance pavilion, and a huge swimming pool with a waterfall at one end and beach sand shipped in from the shores of Lake Erie.

In those days, Ohio State students spent much of their free time in downtown Columbus, for the heart of town was both the shopping and entertainment district. There were eight downtown theaters and so many nickelodeons they were too numerous—and transitory—to count. The Exhibit at 155 North High was the most notable; it seated 200 and had a marbled lobby and a numbered shelf where male customers could park their expensive cigars until after the show. Botts Brothers offered forty fine billiards tables and a buffet at its location on North High, and at the high end of the leisure time spectrum, Lazarus installed a tea room where ladies could meet in the afternoon, a tradition that carried on for generations. Harley worked at Lazarus at various times throughout his college years and even appeared, anonymously, in a few of the store's clothing ads. Over 140 trains daily passed through either Union Station or the Toledo & Ohio

Central depot, and intown transportation was served by rickety orange and yellow streetcars. The early century world of Columbus held an enviable symmetry.

WHILE THURBER WAS JUST BEGINNING to earn the notice of a few classmates in Chief Myers's journalism class, Harley already had the city's attention and would soon demand it from football fans everywhere. Even as a sophomore, Harley was a familiar face to many students who knew him from his athletic exploits in high school. By the time he was a senior, it would have been next to impossible to find a student or faculty member who didn't know who he was. Thurber also grew in stature during his days at OSU; he just did it much more slowly and started from a much lower rung than Harley did. He never made it close—even to the pre-college Harley level—while he was in school there and wouldn't for years afterwards.

At that point, it never occurred to Thurber it would ever be any other way. A few years after they were both out of college, Thurber saw the dedication of the new Ohio Stadium as an opportunity to write and publish a poem glorifying Harley in the *Dispatch*. Thurber was a reporter for the newspaper at the time he wrote *When Chic Harley Got Away*:

> *The years of football reach back a long, long way,*
> *And the heroes are a hundred who have worn red and gray;*
> *You can name the brilliant players from the year the game began,*
> *You can rave how this one punted and praise how that one ran;*
> *You can say that someone's playing was the best you ever saw—*
> *You can claim the boys now playing stage a game without a flaw—*
> *But admit there was no splendor in all the bright array*
> *Like the glory of the going when Chic Harley got away. . . .*

COMPARED TO HARLEY, Thurber was a nobody. While he never approached the success of his fellow East alum during their college days, the growth in confidence and bearing that Thurber gained during his time on campus nonetheless helped him achieve his later renown. And while Thurber admired Harley all his life, his admiration didn't stop him from writing about Harley's academic struggles. Thurber never let his personal relationships with his subjects stand in the way of a good story. Just as he often relied on the foibles of family members to provide the basis for some of his best humor, in "University Days," he disguised Harley as a dim-witted tackle named Bolenciecwcz:

Most of his professors were lenient and helped him along. None gave him more hints, in answering questions, or asked him simpler ones than the economics professor, a thin, timid man named Bassum. One day when we were on the subject of transportation and distribution, it came Bolenciecwcz's turn to answer a question. "Name one means of transportation," the professor said to him. No light came into the big tackle's eyes. "Just any means of transportation," said the professor. Bolenciecwcz sat staring at him. "That is," pursued the professor, "any medium, agency or method of going from one place to another." Bolenciecwcz had the look of a man who is being led into a trap. "You may choose among steam, horse-drawn or electrically-propelled vehicles," said the instructor. "I might suggest the one which we commonly take in making long journeys across land." There was a profound silence in which everybody stirred uneasily, including Bolenciecwcz and Mr. Bassum. Mr. Bassum abruptly broke this silence in an amazing manner. "Choo-choo-choo," he said, in a low voice, and turned instantly scarlet. He glanced appealingly around the room. All of us, of course, shared Mr. Bassum's desire that Bolenciecwcz should stay abreast of the class in economics, for the Illinois game, one of the hardest and most important of the season, was only a week off. "Toot, toot, too-toooooot!" some student with a deep voice moaned, and we all looked encouragingly at Bolenciecwcz. Somebody else gave a fine imitation of a locomotive letting off steam. Mr. Bassum himself rounded off the little show. "Ding, dong, ding, dong," he said, hopefully. Bolenciecwcz was staring at the floor now, trying to think, his great brow furrowed, his huge hands rubbing together, his face red.

"How did you come to college this year, Mr. Bolenciecwcz?" asked the professor. "Chuffa, chuffa, chuffa, chuffa."

"M'father sent me," said the football player.

"What on?" asked Bassum.

"I git an 'lowance," said the tackle, in a low, husky voice, obviously embarrassed.

"No, no," said Bassum. "Name a means of transportation. What did you ride here on?"

"Train," said Bolenciecwcz.

"Quite right," said the professor. "Now, Mr. Nugent, will you tell us—"

Harley was a hero to Thurber, but he was also a good story topic. As a writer interested in producing an entertaining yarn, there seems little doubt which characteristic Thurber viewed as the most important.

the Panhandle
pros

On the other side of town,
in a noisy cluster of buildings
that seemed like the other side of the
world, sweaty men pounded bolts and
rivets, rebuilt and repaired locomotive
engines, forged iron and steel,
and engaged in other feats
of hard labor in the workshops
of the *Panhandle* Division
of the Pennsylvania Railroad.
Many of the workers were
immigrants or sons of immigrants,
men willing to accept positions
that required long hours
of back-breaking work

The Panhandle pros
simply carried their work
ethic over onto the
football field. Pounding
iron or their opponents,
it was all much the same.

in order to feed their families and pay their bills. The work wasn't easy, but most of them did their jobs—boilermaker, blacksmith, machinist, welder, carpenter, and countless others—without complaint.

They were men who could hoist a load of heavy pipe using muscle the average attorney, clerk, or college professor didn't know he had, and they performed those tasks wearing thick work clothes in steamy conditions Satan would have found uncomfortable. Some of them possessed characteristics shared by the best athletes of the day. What they lacked in grace, they made up in muscle. What they lacked in poetry, they made up in power. There were no mama's boys in the Panhandle Division of the Pennsylvania Railroad.

When local railroad officials formed the Panhandle Athletic Club to give employees an outlet for their athletic talents, baseball was the most popular pursuit. But there were also boxers and track and field men, eager to test their skills against men from other Pennsy shops in nearby states. Football seemed like a natural pursuit, but it was still mysterious, particularly to the older workers. Its time was at hand, but it had not yet arrived.

THE RAILROAD'S WORKSHOPS—machine shop, boiler shop, tank shop, foundry, storage yards, and the rest—were located in an expansive complex at 20th Street, in the recently annexed Milo-Grogan community on the near northeast side of the city. Today, the mostly empty patch of land where the shops once stood is easy to locate: a tarp-covered mountain of salt standing in the lot just north of I-670 and west of Leonard Avenue. Except for a couple of neglected railroad sidings, it offers few clues as to what once transpired there.

The field to the north of the shop complex wasn't much more than that. The ground was hard, rocky, uneven in spots. On some of it, dry clods of dirt occupied space that would have been better served by grass. A baseball field was carved out of part of this space, and this was where the Panhandle football team practiced during the workers' forty-five-minute lunch hour.

This place, these men, these conditions all contributed to the humble beginnings of the sport that grew into today's NFL. No fastidious groundskeeper had care of this weed patch. The less-than-perfect conditions didn't bother the coach; he had played real games on fields worse than this. He didn't spend much time thinking about grass.

He was 34 going on 44, his face a flesh and blood roadmap of cuts and bruises that traced his tortuous journey across similar lots over the past fifteen years. His

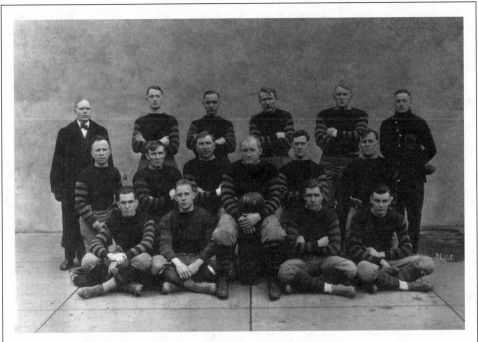

*They were Columbus's professional footballers—the Panhandles,
a team whose nucleus was the famed Nesser brothers, six siblings
known for their rugged play. Their business manager joked that
there weren't three good ribs among the lot of them.*

nose had been broken eight times and he had broken twice that many on faces across from him. He didn't preach "intestinal fortitude" the way the Wilce fellow on the other side of town did, and he gave no long speeches about character-building.

This wasn't college. This wasn't a place to dabble in psychology or to seek the deeper meaning of poetry. The Panhandle shops of the railroad affectionately called "the Pennsy" were a branch campus of the School of Hard Blocks. And one glance at that lumpy grapefruit on Ted Nesser's shoulders said if that imaginary institution granted degrees, he would have held a doctorate.

Nesser knew of Chic Harley, of course. Everybody in town did. But as long as Harley was at Ohio State, he lived in a different world. It was three miles from the Panhandle shops' practice field to Ohio Field and light years to a different universe.

Chic

The Panhandles were professionals; they were paid for the games they played on Sunday. Compared to many pro teams of their day, they did okay. The Panhandles' name meant something to many outside of Columbus, mostly because Ted Nesser's five brothers also played on the team. When the Nesser boys came to town, attendance usually surged. If the local Pennsy outfit didn't field the best pro team around, it ranked among the most famous. Six brothers on the same team—a small army of talented siblings known for their toughness—was a novelty even in those days. Whether they visited Toledo or Canton, Cleveland or Detroit, Akron or Pittsburgh, people were almost always willing to pay to see them play.

THERE WAS THE TIME TED NESSER stayed in a game with two broken bones protruding from an arm because he thought his brothers needed him. "I ain't gonna desert the boys; they like to know I'm here," he said. And Joe Carr, the team's business manager, told a reporter that there weren't three good ribs among all the Nessers. (Years later, we know the truth; there might not have been any). There was also the time Ted Nesser visited Dr. Charles Turner in his office on Mount Vernon Avenue after breaking his nose for the eighth time and was told, "We're not going to set that nose any more; you'll just break it again."

A crooked nose, though, was less a defect than a badge of honor. Mary Katherine (Babe) Sherman remembered how her father Ted used to talk about how his nose was like Knute Rockne's. "Dad used to say, 'We both have our nose all over our face.'"

The pay the Panhandles received was a pittance by modern standards, but a good wage for pro football players of their day. "When I first started playing, the players split $500 or $600 at the season's end," Al Nesser remembered later. "But in 1915, one of our most successful years, the first-stringers collected $1,500 apiece. I felt like a millionaire."

The key word is *felt*. Millionaires don't do back-breaking work for the railroad. Millionaires don't practice football during their lunch hour. Millionaires don't sleep in barns on the road as the Panhandles sometimes did, just to make sure there were profits to divvy up at the end of a trip. (Their snoring teammates in the haylofts didn't bother them; after all those years in the noisy boiler factory, many of them were almost deaf.) The Panhandles were just a bunch of regular working stiffs, both athletic and tough enough to excel at football and they had discovered a way to supplement their incomes by mixing it up on fall weekends with other players like themselves.

A few of them had played in college. Over the course of twenty years, the Panhandles welcomed a small handful of players from Ohio State and other Ohio colleges. Those were the exceptions. A gulf existed between the two that most of them didn't cross. Most of the Panhandles were railroad workers first and football players second, or at least they were supposed to be.

BY THE TIME OF HARLEY'S JUNIOR YEAR in high school, it was obvious the East High star was destined for a college campus, although that wasn't the case even for some of the better high school football players. One of Harley's teammates and best friends at East, Joe Mulbarger, decided to get a job when he got out of high school in 1915. He went to work for Schlotman's Clothing Store and then moved to Walker's Clothing, where he sold men's suits. In the fall of 1916, he joined the local Mendel Pirates pro football team to earn a little extra money, and in 1917, he was recruited by Joe Carr to play for the Panhandles.

Mulbarger never worked for the Pennsy but he played with the railroaders for six seasons. After they folded in 1923, he played four more seasons for the Columbus Tigers, one with the Portsmouth Spartans (who eventually became the Detroit Lions), and two with the Ironton Tanks before finally giving up football. He continued to work at Walker's all this time—football was never a living for any of the early stars—and was still working there in 1951 when he died of a heart attack.

When Mulbarger joined the Panhandles, pro football was even more of an option for young players than ten years earlier when 12-year-old Chic Harley moved to town. The Panhandle footballers had just returned to the field after an absence of two years and 1907 was the first year that they competed with the better teams from other Ohio towns. The early railroad teams, from 1900 to 1904, played mostly local teams, and in those days, the Panhandle baseball team—away from the railyards—got as much, if not more, notice than the football team.

In Columbus, the evolution of amateur, college, and professional football into distinct categories was just beginning. The early Panhandles were merely teams of railroad workers who played other teams of railroad workers, the local military team, a good amateur team or two, and even the Buckeyes. The Panhandles and Buckeyes are known to have scrimmaged a few times, and in 1904 the two teams drew a crowd of 1,200 for a game at University (later Ohio) Field three days before the Buckeyes officially opened their season against Otterbein. Viewed from another century, the meeting itself seems much more important than the final score, a 21-0

Ohio State win. Just the fact there was a game shows how little separation existed between what in time would be two distinctively different forms. In central Ohio, at least, amateur, college, and professional football all stood closely under the same umbrella. The distinctions among them weren't noticeable.

By the time the Panhandles reappeared in 1907, differences were evident. The Buckeyes' stature as a college program had gradually increased and the Panhandles were now as much a professional team as a railroad team. Few college players saw pro football as an option, even after their playing days were over. It wasn't lucrative enough to be a full-time job, particularly for a man who had a college degree. Professional football was a rougher game with rougher characters, and many college football coaches frowned upon it. Few could see any kind of marriage between the two, let alone one in which major college programs functioned as a training ground for young men interested in pursuing professional football careers.

WHEN CHIC HARLEY PURSUED A PRO football career in the early 1920s, he was at the forefront of this change; only a few Ohio State players had gone from college to professional teams, and none stayed long enough to make an impact. Harley's family arrived in Columbus the same year as the Panhandles' re-birth as a professional team, and their first game, a 38-0 win over a local team called the Columbias, was played at Driving Park, six blocks south of Chic's house. Whether any of the Harleys were among the 400 who attended, they were almost certainly aware of it. The Pennsy team surely became a topic in their household as the Panhandles' schedule unfolded.

One of the games drew so much attention around town that the *Ohio State Journal* gushed, "No athletic event that Columbus has produced in a long time is the subject of so much comment as the big Panhandle-Massillon game at Neil Park next Sunday afternoon." That game, on November 17, 1907, drew 4,000 spectators; Ohio Field, the Buckeyes' home field, seated only 2,000.

It is clear that Ohio State football did not yet own the city. The race for fans and attention was just beginning, and in Columbus, both the college and pro games had run the first few laps at a slow jog. The Buckeyes were in the midst of their third consecutive successful season, but one of their two losses was a 22-0 drubbing by Michigan. There was still room for other teams; until Ohio Medical College stopped playing football in 1904 (and later became part of OSU), its football team got almost as much space in the local press as the Buckeyes did.

There was another reason the Panhandles suddenly began to receive more

coverage in the Columbus newpapers: the local team was now being managed
by Joe Carr, the former assistant sports editor of the *Ohio State Journal*. Carr was a
saavy businessman and a tireless worker, and he knew promotion. His friendship
with reporters on all three of the city's newspapers was a bonus. Thanks to Carr, it
wasn't long before everybody in town knew who the Panhandles were.

THERE IS NO WAY TO KNOW IF CHIC attended any of the Panhandles' games, but
every sports-minded boy in Columbus was aware of them. Pro football wasn't yet
a game for the masses, but it had earned a respectable standing in the region. The
sport had been centered primarily in Ohio and western Pennsylvania since its first
appearance in the 1890s, and it had developed a small but devoted following of
fans, who seemed to increase in number every year.

The Buckeyes and Panhandles coexisted in the years following young Harley's
arrival, but the pro team increasingly played more of its games on the road. As
employees of the railroad, the players were permitted to ride the trains for free,
and Carr recognized that if his team didn't have to rent a facility to play in and
travel expenses were minimal, the football team could turn a decent profit. The
arrangement put money in the players' pockets but diminished their standing
in their hometown. In the days before television and radio, it didn't take long
for local fans to lose interest in a team they seldom saw, particularly when the
Buckeyes were on the rise.

Still, Ohio was the center of the pro football universe and Columbus sat in the
middle of that. While northern Ohio produced most of the sport's most successful
teams—the Massillon Tigers, Canton Bulldogs, Cleveland Indians, Akron Indians,
Cleveland Tigers, and Akron Pros—Dayton (the Triangles and the Oakwoods),
Cincinnati (the Celts), Toledo (the Maroons), and Shelby (the Blues) all had
relatively successful pro teams. Columbus had several independent local teams
(the Northerns, Muldoons, Wagner Pirates, Nationals, and Columbus Barracks,
from the army base that was later called Fort Hayes), which were good enough to
play some of the better pro teams, even if they couldn't beat them. A fan couldn't
spend his Sundays watching pro football on television—those days were more than
fifty years away—but chances were good that he could watch a game in person at a
park only blocks from his home. Every fall Sunday, Ohio witnessed countless pro
football games of varying degrees of skill.

When Chic was in high school, the Panhandles played local opponents at
Indianola Park, the field that adjoined the amusement park of the same name.

But by 1916, when he was sophomore at Ohio State, the Panhandles had outgrown it and played most of their rare home games at Neil Park, a sign of their elevated status.

The Panhandles reached the height of their fame during Harley's years at OSU. If they had been able to enjoy the kind of football success that the Buckeyes did during that period, local competition between the two types of football— college vs. pro—might have been more interesting. But 1915, the year before Harley hit the OSU varsity, marked the height of the Panhandles' on-the-field success. They beat Massillon 16-0 at Driving Park, beat the Detroit Maroons 7-0, and lost 7-0 to the powerful Canton Bulldogs in League Park, home of the Cleveland Indians, en route to an 8-3 season.

While they were still respectable in 1916, the Buckeyes upstaged them. The Panhandles played four games in League Park that year, losing three. They won a pair of games against the Detroit Heralds at Navin Field, later known as Tiger Stadium, but alas, they played only two games in Columbus, a loss to Massillon in Driving Park and a 6-0 win over the Columbus All-Stars in Neil Park on December 6. With the Buckeyes on an attention-grabbing roll, the Panhandles' greatest glories had passed.

WHEN MULBARGER AND CHIC'S former South High rival Hal Gaulke joined the Panhandles in September, 1917, the railroaders were starting a downward spiral that made competing with Harley and the suddenly-popular Buckeyes all the more difficult. Ted Nesser was past his prime, and so were most of his brothers. The Panhandles were still a source of pride for the community, but without the six Nessers and brother-in-law John Schneider to form the backbone of the roster, the Pennsy couldn't continue to supply enough football talent to make the team viable. They never had another winning season.

It wasn't the end of pro football in Columbus and it surely wasn't the end of Carr. With the Panhandles gone, a new team called the Tigers joined the NFL, and they competed for four years with modest success. Carr became the league president, running the NFL out of an office at Broad and High until his death in 1939.

As much as pro football's popularity had grown, Carr had no way of knowing that the flimsy marriage of convenience between college and pro games would develop into an everlasting union, or that many high school players would someday attend college merely to prepare for a professional football career.

He had no way of knowing that the fifty former Ohio State players who had played in the NFL by 1939 would grow to 365 by 2008, or that a league that served only as seasonal work for its players would someday pay its stars many times more than what the nation's president received.

Carr did know his hometown. After the Tigers folded, the former newspaperman never tried to put another pro football team in Columbus. He had come to an awareness during his last few years as manager of the Panhandles and had seen nothing to change his mind in the years since: Columbus was a college football town.

chapter nine

God's own
plan

Columbus was already at war,
even before President Wilson asked
Congress for a declaration
of it against Germany on April 2,
1917. On the *homefront*, it was
a silent, suspicious war, a war
of wary hellos and penetrating
glares. It was a secret war
of distrust of the German man
you shared an assembly line
with at the Buckeye Steel Castings or
the Wagner brewery or even of that
seemingly nice German-American
family across the street. Some places
in the United States weren't ready

*Chic and the boys
of 1917—eight wins, one
tie—ushered in a new
dynamic, one that said
winning almost everything
wasn't quite enough.*

for war, or at least they hadn't spent much time pondering it. Columbus had. Like some of the other Midwestern cities surrounding it, Columbus's population had once been comprised of approximately forty percent German immigrants. Although the number of native Germans had shrunk significantly through the years, that didn't stop others from doubting the loyalty of second and third generation German families, especially those who still lived in households where more than one family member could still speak the language. The war seemed closer to German-American families than it did most of the others.

The newspapers read like daily installments of a serial horror story. Everyone knew what those heinous Huns were doing to our allies, and sometimes, even to peace-loving neutrals like us. Did your neighbor Frederick sympathize with the Kaiser? He said he didn't, but how could you be sure? Yes, his family had come to Columbus in the 1880s, or at least that's what he told you. But how did you really know? You had only known him for a few years, since you moved in next door to him on Jaeger Street. Did he have family in the German army? Where did his loyalties really lie? Was there something sly about that smile of his, something deceitful? He said the right things, but what *was* he thinking?

President Wilson had been re-elected in 1916 on the promise of holding America out of the conflict, but deep down, no one believed it was a promise he could keep. It was a confusing, frightening, exciting time to be alive. The daily routine continued uninterrupted, but an undercurrent of tension flowed just beneath the surface, and part of that tension was having German neighbors, co-workers, and friends.

When a German submarine sank the passenger ship *Lusitania* with over 1,900 aboard in 1915, normally-tolerant Columbus citizens looked at their German neighbors even more closely, and all over the country, American patriotism surged. President Wilson eventually got Germany to agree that it wouldn't sink any more passenger ships without providing for the safety of those on board, but that act was rescinded by Germany in January of 1917.

A few weeks later, the public learned of a secret German communication to Mexico promising U.S. territory to Mexico in return for support for the German cause—the so-called Zimmerman telegram—and America reacted with widespread fury. Neutrality no longer seemed a viable option, and it became harder for patriotic Columbus citizens whose families had come from countries such as England, France, Italy, and Ireland to view in the same trusting way the German families with whom they shared the city's streets.

When the United States officially declared war on Germany on April 7, 1917, life in America abruptly changed. And because of its German background, Columbus experienced tremors of change that were unknown in other places. In the campaign against all things German, streets with German names were Americanized. Germania Street became Stewart Street. Kaiser became Lear. Schiller became Whittier. Bismarck became Lansing. Even Schiller Park—named for the German poet—didn't escape the purge. Tradition and poetry be damned, Schiller Park became Washington Park and Columbus was all the happier for it.

Some German-American families felt pressured to buy more war bonds than others in order to prove their support, and some families even changed the spelling of their names (including some whose sons had already enlisted in the army). A Swiss-German Columbus family named Riechenbecher took the Hun out of its name by changing it to Rickenbacker, which, in time, seemed especially ironic: Eddie Rickenbacker, who rose from a job sweeping floors at the Frayer and Miller car factory at Fourth and Chestnut to become America's leading race car driver, took his new name to the army and became the country's leading flying ace.

THE ANTI-GERMAN HYSTERIA affected even some of the city's wealthiest families. The daughter of the late George Parsons, who acquired massive land holdings in the Columbus area as a director of a local bank and railroad (he gave his last name to the street that for years served as the city's eastern boundary), had the property she inherited from him confiscated by the federal government. Amelia Parsons had participated in the city's only royal wedding when she exchanged vows with Bavarian Prince Alexander Ernst zu Lynar at Trinity Episcopal Church in 1871, and the government considered her property German-owned. It didn't matter that she had grown up in a sprawling mansion on the city's east side or that her maiden name was printed on street signs up and down Parsons Avenue.

Harley is an English name, so Chic escaped the prejudice, but it was impossible for a young man of his age to be unaffected by all that was going on around him. Sales of liberty bonds boomed, and a giant wooden platform was set up on the Statehouse lawn to elicit donations for the war chest. Those who contributed were given a chance to throw a ball at heads stuck through portholes atop painted images of the German crown prince, the Kaiser, and Field Marshal von Hindenburg. Congress passed the Selective Service Act in mid-May, and all males between the ages of 21 and 30 had to register, ages that were later expanded to include males between 18 and 45. General John J. Pershing, presented with a standing army of 108,000, asked for a million men, then revised his request upward and asked for three million.

THE EFFECT ON THE OHIO STATE CAMPUS was immediate. Students began withdrawing from school to either enlist, go into defense work, or go back to family farms and help increase food production. The first Officers' Training Camps opened in May and hundreds of Ohio State students traded their textbooks for rifles and artillery simulators.

Ohio State president William Oxley Thompson attended a conference in Washington, D.C., where a plan was formulated to start six "ground schools" to give preliminary training for men in the U.S. Army Signal Corps, which then included aviators. The ground school at Ohio State became the School of Military Aeronautics, and the first squadron of new cadets, Squadron A, reported on May 21. On June 11, Squadron D began work on aircraft engines. The Armory became a barracks, and a cadet mess was set up in the Ohio Union. The Ohio State campus was now part military installation.

In the midst of the war-related chaos, Harley's future was a mystery. Only a week after the win over Northwestern in November of 1916, there were reports that Harley planned to transfer to Pitt. The report was apparently started by a member of the Pitt athletic committee who saw Harley at the Pitt-Penn State football game, made a not-so-educated guess, and spread the word. It was no secret that Harley had been visiting relatives in the area for Thanksgiving, so maybe it was simply a matter of wishful thinking on the Pitt official's part. No matter how it began, the rumor launched itself.

The report received considerable play in newspapers around the Midwest. Pitt coach Pop Warner said he was a little squeamish about it because "it might be interpreted that Pitt is importing its players." There was talk that if Harley did transfer, he would have to sit out a year, not because of NCAA regulations—non-existent in those days—but because of a one-year residency rule. Harley emphatically denied it in the *Ohio State Journal*. "There is nothing to it," he said, "absolutely nothing doing."

The reports were cause for some concern, for Chic was no longer just a local phenomenon. Shortly after Walter Eckersall named him to his All-America team, Walter Camp, who originated the idea of a national all-star team in 1889, selected Chic for his prestigious team. As the first Ohio State player ever named by Camp, it was natural to wonder if Harley might be interested in moving on. The OSU program had risen from relative obscurity but it might not *stay* risen; why not move on to one with more tradition and prestige?

The questions persisted: Was Chic really thinking of transferring to Pitt? Had he joined the service without telling anybody? Two OSU football players, quarterback Howard Yerges and end Clarence MacDonald, had joined a naval reserve unit that summer and were awaiting orders. Why not Harley?

HARLEY LEFT COLLEGE IN THE SPRING with many male students when the governor issued an order offering credit to students who intended to either join the armed forces or perform service beneficial to the war effort. In the early part of the summer, he worked for the Lazarus department store in Columbus, then left town for points unknown. Finally, on September 14, the day before Wilce's team was supposed to report for its first practice, the *Dispatch* announced in a banner headline that Harley had been "found" on a potato farm in northern Michigan. The sub-head offered an ominous warning: *His Return Not Yet a Certainty*.

Harley was vacationing on Platte Lake near Beulah, Michigan, it so happened, a guest of George Siebert of Columbus. The boys, the story said, had been hunting and fishing for three weeks. There were hints in the story that Harley had to make certain his academic eligibility. Just a day after he returned from the potato farm, Harley issued a statement to the *Dispatch* in the form of a letter from his Chicago home.

"Much as I regret having to pass up this year's football, I'm afraid I wouldn't feel right by going back," Harley wrote. "I honestly am crazy to get into the service and have my decision made. I am going to apply for the aviation service. It appeals to me as the most interesting branch and the one for which I am best fitted."

Harley had applied but not yet been accepted. While he was home in Chicago and St. John was in Chicago on conference business, the two met and talked.

Chic

St. John convinced Harley to return to Columbus and continue those talks. St. John's message was convincing: If the aviation corps were going to take its time calling Ohio State's star football player, the school would be able to use him on the gridiron in the meantime.

PRACTICE HAD ALREADY STARTED, although that didn't seem to matter much. Only twenty-one players participated in the first practice, and Harley, Yerges, and MacDonald were not among them. Classes began on September 18 and Harley wasn't enrolled, but he was in town. He showed up at practice, slipped on a pair of football shoes, pulled a sweater over his regular clothes, and threw a few passes and booted a few punts. The team was up to forty players now, including Harley, who enrolled two days later, his academic eligibility still not assured.

Harley's trouble stemmed from some difficulty he had with an American history class. He participated in a team scrimmage on September 26, just three days before the season opener against Case, and his academic problems were announced in a newspaper headline: *Schweitzer Will Start at Right Half if Harley is Still found Unable to Gain on 'American History.'*

Harley apparently did, because he was declared eligible for the game, and he experienced American history firsthand that same day. Orville Wright, who with his brother Wilbur had invented the first successful flying machine, was OSU Professor Thomas French's guest for the Case game. French had gone to high school with Orville Wright in Dayton.

Wright's impending visit provided a nice diversion from the talk of Harley's academic woes. Once football started and Chic was on the team, his academics were of little concern to the press or the public. It was quickly apparent that the fans were no longer much interested in games against lesser competition outside of the Western Conference, though. Case, Ohio Wesleyan, Northwestern, and Denison were easily disposed of by respective 49-0, 53-0, 40-0, and 67-0 scores. The Case game drew 3,500 spectators. Ohio Wesleyan lured 4,600. Northwestern drew 8,000, probably on memories of the last season's game, but later in a downpour, only 2,000 showed up for Denison. Even some of the opponents admitted they weren't up to snuff. Both Case and Ohio Wesleyan demanded shorter periods to make the final scores seem more respectable.

How important did a football game seem when the country was at war? Some

American troops were already in frontline trenches. The Columbus Barracks was serving as a mobilization and training center for troops, and the State Fairgrounds had been commandeered by the Army. The teaching of German in local schools was on its way to being banned. The city's last German-language newspaper, *Westbote*, was in trouble and in less than a year, it would be gone. A war that once seemed to affect only other people was beginning to affect everyone.

THE WAR ENCROACHED ON FOOTBALL in curious ways. Indiana coach Jumbo Steihm scouted the Buckeyes' 67-0 win over Denison and told reporters that Ohio State appeared to be one of the teams that had been "helped" by the war. Steihm thought Wilce could field three full varsity elevens, while the war effort had left him only sixteen players, many of whom were sophomores. It sounded like an early excuse for a poor showing in the following week's game against OSU at Washington Park in Indianapolis. It also made Wilce's decision to start Fred Schweitzer in place of Harley—a plan supposedly hatched to allow OSU to tire out the Hoosiers before Harley entered the game—seem all the more strange. If the Hoosiers were that weak, why try to tire them out before Harley got in? It raised the question of whether Wilce may have been disciplining Chic for some reason, particularly in light of his ongoing academic difficulties. Harley entered a scoreless game in the middle of the second period and ended up scoring all four touchdowns in a 26-3 OSU romp.

Unlike MacDonald, who never made it onto the team that year, Harley and Yerges still had not been called to service. The soldiers on campus were a constant reminder to the players of where many of them wanted to be. Gym classes had been cancelled because the gymnasium was being used as a barracks. After October 1, the Ohio Union was closed to the student body and open only to aviation students until it could be expanded (it was in November). There was nearly a fifty percent decrease in German class attendance, while attendance in French was "overflowing."

With the daily influx of war news, playing football must have seemed a trivial pursuit. On the day of the Denison game, the first American artillery troops reached the trenches on the French front. The next day, the Columbus Area Liberty Loan committee announced that the city had nearly doubled its original quota and had subscribed to almost $12 million in bonds. The war was a priority

in all phases of life; the "big three" of the football-playing eastern schools—
Harvard, Yale, and Princeton—had even decided to cancel the season, and those
who had gone ahead and played came under criticism. Advocates cited the benefits
from exhibition games played to raise money for the war effort and the improved
morale of the soldiers who followed the games.

The players had mixed feelings. The day before the Indiana game, twelve
American sailors were killed in friendly waters in the foundered launch of a picket
boat for the battleship *Michigan*. On the day of the game, three Americans were
killed in a German raid on a trench in France, the first American casualties of
the war. Just as the Buckeyes were reaching the pivotal point of the season—a road
game at Wisconsin and a home game against Illinois—the war heated up, and the
daily news reports demanded their attention.

What kind of news was it that the Buckeyes were going to wear gray jerseys for
the first time in several years? The Wisconsin jerseys were virtually the same scarlet
color and former OSU quarterback Lou Pickerel had once thrown a pass directly
to a Badger defender by mistake. But the players awoke in Madison that day to the
news that President Wilson had ordered the re-classification of the draft status of
9,000,000 men. Those who had been exempt from the draft because of marriage
or profession could now be drafted. *That* was the news of import.

THE PLAYERS SOMEHOW MAINTAINED THEIR FOCUS. The Badgers' new field, Camp
Randall Stadium, had opened the week before and the Wisconsin fans were
excited to get a chance to see Harley run. The more than 6,000 fans saw something
quite different. The Badgers bottled Chic up on the ground, but he beat them
with the pass. After Wisconsin's Eber Simpson drop-kicked a 43-yard field goal to
give his team a 3-0 lead, Harley faked a kick from the Badgers' 44 and threw a pass
to Shifty Bolen, who was hit near the goal line and bulled his way in. Later, Harley
found Howard Courtney with a 32-yard pass to the Wisconsin two, and Yerkes
sneaked in on the next play. Harley drop-kicked a 40-yard field goal in the fourth
quarter to give Ohio State a 16-3 win. The gray jerseys had served their purpose,
after all.

Back in Columbus, several hundred fans gathered outside the *Dispatch*
building at the northeast corner of Gay and High listening to a guy with a
megaphone announce the results of each play as they were telegraphed to the

newspaper office. A large scoreboard allowed the fans to follow the movement
of the ball up and down the field, and they watched, seemingly spellbound by a
contraption that allowed them to get instant results from a game played hundreds
of miles away. War or no war, the Buckeyes were undefeated. If they could beat
Illinois in a battle of unbeatens the following week, they would win the Western
Conference championship again.

The rumor made it back to town almost as fast as the team did. Howard
Yerges, OSU's three-year starting quarterback and the man who called the plays,
would probably be called to the navy before the end of the week. Yerges told
reporters he had received no official word from the government but he expected
to be called at some point and he couldn't be shocked if it happened this week.
Western Conference title or not, the war came before football. Everyone knew that.

As the week wore on and Yerges received no notice, it became clear that he
wouldn't have to leave before the Illinois game. The newspaper reported that
several members of Yerges's unit had had been ordered to report on Monday, so
Ohio State fans breathed a sigh of relief. If he weren't required to report until
Monday, he would miss only the two benefit games with Alabama Tech and Camp
Sherman. That was a palatable sacrifice.

THE LARGEST CROWD EVER TO ATTEND an Ohio State football game was expected.
Extra bleachers were added at both ends of the field and boxes were constructed in
front of the grandstands to hike Ohio Field's capacity to 14,000. The reserved seats
were gone by Tuesday, and the players, coaches, and administrators were flooded
with ticket requests. Athletic director L.W. St. John received a call from Chicago
White Sox catcher Ray Schalk, whose team had won the World Series a month
before. He asked if St. John could save him two seats, one for him and outfielder
Oscar "Happy" Felsch, and the OSU athletic director complied. Schalk and Felsch
were among baseball's biggest stars, and baseball was still the most popular sport
in America. Three years later, Felsch would be one of the infamous "Black Sox,"
banned from baseball for fixing the 1919 World Series. Now, though, he was a
hero.

If Schalk and Felsch came only to see Harley, they weren't disappointed. In
a game where both teams boasted an array of stars, Chic continued to add to his
legend. By contrast, Illinois' two biggest stars, end and future Chicago Bears owner

George Halas and halfback Dutch Sternaman, had little or no impact in a game that was widely hailed for its intensity.

Harley kicked a field goal in the first quarter to give Ohio State a 3-0 lead and a tense defensive battle of brutal hits and vicious tackles followed. Sternaman twice attempted field goals and both times his kicks were wide. Then, in the final quarter, Harley faked a punt and passed to Sam Willaman for a 10-yard gain. He ran for two yards, then completed a two-yard pass to Pete Stinchcomb. He completed an 11-yard pass to Willaman, then ran two more yards to the Illinois 15. After Willaman ran for no gain, Harley engineered the play of the day.

He started to his right as if to pass to Willaman, then turned suddenly and threw the ball laterally to the wide open right tackle, Howard Courtney, who had an open path to the end zone. Harley kicked the extra point to make it 10-0, then

Behind Chic's sleight-of-foot, Ohio State won its second consecutive conference title, even though the war in Europe dampened the jubilation.

added another 29-yard field goal later to seal a 13-0 victory.

On the Illinois sideline, coach Bob Zuppke seethed over Harley's touchdown pass. He had seen Harley execute the same play against Wisconsin the week before, hitting right tackle Howard Courtney who carried to the two-yard-line, and he had prepared his defense to specifically stop that play. So when Ohio State ran it, it should have played right into the Illini's hands; instead, it went for a touchdown and Zuppke stomped around the sidelines like a petulant child. But as it happened, Zuppke thought the play at Wisconsin went to left tackle Hap Courtney. So as the play developed, the Illini were all over Hap while Chic passed to his wide open brother on the other side. In a case of mistaken identity, Zuppke cost his team a touchdown and allowed the Buckeyes to put away the game.

Chic

In the jubilation over Ohio State's second consecutive Western Conference championship, the war intruded, as always. On the same day, a corrected report indicated that nineteen Americans—rather than two—had died when the Germans sunk a steamship known as the *Rochester*. An American soldier charged with murdering a French girl was shot by firing squad. Howard Yerges learned he would report to the navy on Tuesday. In addition to Yerges, Fritz Holtkamp and Dean Richmond left on the morning train for Norfolk, Virginia, where they would go into active duty in the naval reserve hospital corps.

The war that had shadowed Harley and his Ohio State teammates all season stepped directly in front of them. The soldiers on campus, the horror stories in the newspapers, and the anti-German sentiment around town had served as season-long distractions but the players had been working toward a goal—the opportunity to win another conference championship. Now that they had the title and some of their friends had packed their gear, vacated the Athletic House, and started off to war, Chic and his remaining teammates began to lose interest. Two games—both benefits for the army—remained on the schedule and practice sessions suddenly seemed like exercises in tedium. Their passion for football waned.

Wilce found it hard to motivate his players. The war had always been the story, but it didn't have to share the stage with football any longer. Regardless of what happened in these last two games, regardless of how well they played, most of the players would soon be in the service.

The game in Auburn, Alabama, against Alabama Polytechnic Institute—better known as Auburn—was for the benefit of nearby Camp Sheridan and it ended in a scoreless tie; Harley was pulled early in the second half with a badly swollen right hand thought to be broken. Even with Harley hurt, Yerges gone, and center Kelley Van Dyne and guard Charlie Seddon injured, the offense had several scoring opportunities, but suffered in part because of indecision over which plays to call. Yerges's leadership was sorely missed. Though the tie was a blotch on the team's perfect record, it didn't seem important. But with the benefit against the Camp Sherman military team from Chillicothe, Ohio, to be played at Ohio Field on Thanksgiving Day, it was suggested that maybe Yerges could get a holiday leave and call the signals for OSU that day.

The game against Camp Sherman, a team of former college players now in the

— OHIO STATE —
— WESTERN CONFERENCE CHAMPIONS —
— 1916-1917 —

DICK BOESEL·FB· CHICK HARLEY·LH· PETE STINCHCOMB·RH·
HOWARD YERGES ·QB·
PEABODY·RE· HOD COURTNEY·RT· SEDDON·RG· KARSH·LG· VAN DYNE·C· HAP COURTNEY·LT· SHIFTY BOLEN·L

*This unassuming lot of boys laid the foundation for what would
become the country's preeminent sports program.*

military, showed how immersed in war the country was. One thousand soldiers
from central Ohio were brought by train from Chillicothe to participate in a
parade from Union Station to campus on Thursday morning. The eight blocks
of marchers were preceded by a fifty-piece military band, and thousands of local
citizens turned out. A military drill before the game received equal billing with the
football. Patriotic songs took precedence over school fight songs. The game was
almost secondary.

Almost. Wilce, stung by the showing at Auburn, had driven the team hard
in practice. Yerges made it home on leave, and after sitting out the second half
at Auburn, Harley badly wanted to play. Trainer E.G. "Doc" Gurney had done
everything he could to make sure Chic's hand was healed well enough to grip the
ball. Both Van Dyne and Seddon were also cleared to play.

The military men wondered if they could stop Harley and some suggested that the Buckeyes would have just as much trouble with Camp Sherman halfback Nelson "Nocky" Rupp, a former Denison star who would play for the NFL's Dayton Triangles and the Chicago Staleys after the war. But the military team, clad in drab olive uniforms, was no match for the Buckeyes, who suddenly seemed determined to prove that the game in Alabama was a fluke.

Unfortunately, the next day's big story was not Ohio State's 28-0 victory over Camp Sherman, but Georgia Tech's 68-7 win over Auburn. In the South, the result served as conclusive proof that Tech, not Ohio State, was the best college team in the land, a claim that quickly proved to be a sore point in Columbus.

"There is no doubt that the Auburn game would have been a walkaway with Yerges and Van Dyne on hand," Harvey A. Miller wrote in the *Dispatch*. "But it has passed into history and has given Georgia Tech a lot of opportunity to crow over its 68-7 victory over the Auburn team on Thanksgiving afternoon. This big old world is large enough for championship lightning to strike in different places and do no harm to the rest of the earth. If the Georgians think they are the champion team of the United States, let them believe that. They ride the comparative score mule with the best of them and will not be in danger of being thrown from their mount until next year. . ."

The Georgians' bragging, nonetheless, continued to sting. While most of the Ohio State players put football aside and looked to an uncertain future in the military, Wilce found himself trying to answer critics who claimed that his unbeaten team wasn't as good at it appeared to be.

"The team is strictly legitimate in every way," Wilce wrote in the *Ohio State Monthly*. "Every member of the team is an Ohio boy. Not one has ever played football on another college team. Every one is eligible scholastically. The freshman rule was not suspended at this University on account of the war. Ohio State and Georgia Tech cannot be compared, as their eligibility standards have too little in common."

Even in 1917, a conference championship and an 8-0-1 season didn't always satisfy. It was a new concept in Columbus but one that would now become imbedded in the fabric of Ohio State football: Winning almost everything was no longer enough.

war is hell

War is hell. Everybody knows that now. A lot of people, mostly older people, knew it in 1918. Only the young didn't know. They were too inexperienced, too naïve. Until a friend, relative, or neighbor died, the deaths in the newspapers were mere ink on paper, without the violence or gore. The *newsreels* were fascinating—but monochrome and distant. Their horrors provided something to chat about when there were no more movies, dinners, or games to discuss, but they

Chic and his teammates of 1917 would soon be influenced by the war in Europe. By the next season, Chic himself would be in flight school.

might as well have been shot on Mars. The explosions weren't real. The bullets weren't real. The people who died weren't real. For young men of military age—dying age—none of it would be real until they got there. The war reports haunted the Ohio State football players from the day they showed up at school. Some of their former teammates had already been called overseas, and the news from Europe came with guilt: If my friends are risking their lives for our country, what am I doing practicing football? Boys who once thought football was life-or-death important began to understand that death had its own impertinent reality.

Chic and some of the other boys who had tried to enlist for specific training, hadn't been called, and now questioned whether they had tried hard enough. By the time of the Illinois game, most of the Ohio State players were talking about what they would do as soon as the season was over.

As the Thanksgiving Day game against Camp Sherman approached, Chic and most of his teammates knew that when the final play was run it would be the last they would see of football for now, if not forever. They were anxious to head off to the military, and no more enlistments would be permitted after the draft formally began on December 15. Most of the players wanted to control their own destiny, and most of them had already checked out their options. Enlistment might mean flying a plane, serving on a ship, or being part of a hospital unit. The draft almost certainly would mean infantry duty, maybe even on the front lines.

Chic was anxious to join. Flight training interested him immensely and it was part of the reason he had been uncertain of his plans over the summer. But it was also more difficult to get into than most of the other branches of the service, which may explain why he hadn't been quickly called. But the climate had changed in the intervening months, and his enlistment seemed almost certain.

Jack Wilce and Lynn St. John had other ideas. They had an appearance planned at the Hamilton County Alumni Association meeting at the Hyde Park Country Club the day after the Camp Sherman game, and they asked Chic to come along, enticing him with a couple of days of hunting in the wilds of southern Ohio after the Cincinnati meeting, a kind of final fling before he set off for the army. So while Wilce caught a train for Pittsburgh the next day to see Pop Warner's Pitt squad face Camp Lee in another one of their military exhibitions, St. John and Harley went hunting. As soon as they got back to Columbus, Harley

Chic was named football captain for the 1918 season but his old heroics would have to wait. He—and most of his teammates— would be playing on a new field. And more than one of them would not return.

applied again to become an aviator and went to Dayton to take an examination.

In the days that followed, a steady stream of Ohio State athletes enlisted. Dwight "Chief" Peabody went the same route Harley did. Hap Courtney was trying to get into the hospital unit where Howard Yerges was serving. Hap's brother, Howard, was accepted into the aviation division at Dayton and was already on his way to Cincinnati for a physical examination. By December 9, nearly half of the school's athletes from the previous two academic years had either entered military service or were in the process.

No man's departure meant more to Columbus than that of Chic Harley. On December 10, the *Dispatch* ran a two-column photo of the sweet-smiling Chic under the caption, "At 7:30 tonight, at home or elsewhere, let's drink to him."

In light of all the men entering service, it seemed curious to focus solely on one football player, but the paragraph beneath the photo did its best to explain: "No finer boy ever set foot on the campus of Ohio State University. No greater athlete has ever developed in Ohio. None has ever done so much for Ohio State. So, at 7:30, whether by ourselves, with our wives, with our friends, our children, our sweethearts, let's all drink to the success of 'Chic' Harley, whom we know will come back hailed as the premier Ace of the American flying corps."

If the photo demonstrated the attachment the city had for its favorite son, Harvey A. Miller reprinted a tale in his column in the next day's *Dispatch* that showed the widespread nature of Harley's following.

"ONE OF THE SWEETEST TRIBUTES PAID the man of Ohio came from a trio of children in a Woodlawn Avenue home," Miller wrote. "A friend of ours happened into that home just a few minutes before 7:30 and saw a pretty little procession, all gravity, coming across the room. Mary, about 5, Bud about 8 and Charlene about 12, were approaching the living room. Little Bud was bearing a tray with five small glasses and a bottle on it. In the bottle was sweet cider and our friend soon learned that Harley was to be toasted at 7:30.

"It was agreed that Bud being a 'man' should deliver the toast. Glasses were raised and Bud started out. 'Here's to Chic Harley. . . here's to Chic Harley. . .' Bud could get no further, for the job was too big for him.

"Then Charlene tried. 'Here's to Chic Harley, best athlete Ohio State ever. . .' and there her speech failed.

"The toast was passed to little Mary. She said: 'Here's to Shic Charley. . .' and Mary had finished her effort. Bud gathered thought and poise by this time and he went through with the toast. 'Here's to Chic Harley, best athlete Ohio State ever had and good-luck to him when he goes over to get the Germans . . . ' The ceremony was completed with raised glasses and with important mien. There was no frivolity about it. So we know of at least three tots who will follow Chic's career as a soldier and wish him Godspeed every minute."

Sometime during the previous two years, Harley had made the transition from football player to football idol. He probably didn't know it was happening; it was a subtle change. Football players are admired. Football idols are loved. Players are cheered. Idols are worshipped. There are many of the former and few of the latter, but idols have a magnetism that drew people to them, and Harley possessed an unlimited supply of it.

Ever since high school there had been an allure to him. Maybe it was because he was a small man in a big man's sport. Maybe it was because of the inviting grin. Or maybe it was because of his modesty. Away from the athletic field, he seemed almost unaware of his talents. People liked Chic because he was a football star, but they also liked him because he was an unassuming kid who treated everyone like a friend.

In more than twenty-five years, it was the first time Ohio State had an athlete with whom fans fell in love. It was the first time fans rooted for a player not just because he was representing their school but because of the player himself. So small children toasted him and sportswriters fretted over his safety when he went off to war. He was not so much a football player as a member of the family, and the public had a personal relationship with him.

AFTER HARLEY UNDERWENT HIS PHYSICAL, he went home to Chicago to await the call. While he waited, he was named 1918 team captain at the team's annual banquet at the Chittenden Hotel, an honor that was "vigorously applauded" even though the hundred or so who had gathered there knew he wouldn't be back. He did return to campus on February 1, but to enter the School of Military Aeronautics, an eight-week course that resulted in his assignment to Kelly Field in South San Antonio, Texas. He would finish additional preliminary flying work there while awaiting his commission and assignment overseas.

For Chic, Kelly Field was where his mental image of war and the reality of war began to merge. The base had been constructed a year and a half before on an empty patch of gently rolling prairie five miles south of San Antonio. With America at war, it quickly became a reception and testing center for recruits and a training center for pilots, mechanics, bakers and cooks, as well as engineering and supply officers.

This was where Chic Harley learned that war was indeed hell, even if his version of it was different from the one experienced by men in the trenches. Chic's celebrity made him a constant target of both his superiors and his peers. He was reminded repeatedly that being an All-American halfback "won't help you any here."

The weather was hotter and drier than he ever remembered in Columbus or Chicago, and he didn't think much of the base itself. He made friends, but he was no longer treated like the special person he was back home. He completed his preliminary flight training and was awaiting his commission when he found himself in trouble and was dismissed from service. It stemmed from an incident that Ohio State assistant athletic director Henry D. Taylor described in a letter to R.C. Oberdahn, a New Jersey man who requested information for a speech he was making on Harley to a local university club in 1940.

"One of the semi-comical exploits I remember well is in connection with his service in the flying school in war time," Taylor wrote. "He had enough hours to his credit that he could fly solo and got acquainted with a young lady who lived some forty or fifty miles from the base. Without asking anybody's permission, he deliberately flew over to see her one day. The fact of the matter is I think this was instrumental in the army discipline of discharge. . . ."

IT WASN'T COMICAL TO HARLEY. Great things had been expected of him, and he began to worry that he had let people down. The public had been anxiously awaiting word of his next heroics and instead he had acted foolishly. He was given a second chance and reinstated in the army a short time later but as punishment, he was forced to repeat his training. While those with whom he had come to Kelly Field finished their training and went off to battle, he was starting over.

He fell into depression and it grew worse when he received word that Fred Norton, one of his 1916 OSU teammates, had been wounded in an air battle near Toul in the St. Mihiel Sector of France and died two days later. He remembered Norton catching the kick-out in the mud that led to his game-winning extra point kick in the Illinois game. Norton was dead, and he, Chic, was still stateside, repeating training. In some indefinable way, he knew he had let Norton down.

Then less than two months after Norton died, Harley learned that Hap Courtney, his old East High and Ohio State teammate, had died of pneumonia on the transport *Louisville* while en route to France. This loss hit Harley even harder because Courtney had grown up on the east side of Columbus with him. The memories of high school came flooding back, and with them came deep concern for Hap's brother, Howard. Chic knew the loss would be devastating to him, and at the same time he wondered if Howard were safe. Once those disturbing thoughts gained entrance to his mind, others followed. He worried about all of his teammates. Were there more fatalities he hadn't heard about? Two were dead already. There was no telling how many more of them would die before the grisly war was done. In a hot, miserable camp a thousand miles from home, Chic's sunny visage became an unusually cloudy gray.

The Allies were finally winning the war, which was both good and bad for Chic. There were rumors of an armistice and he still had not completed his training. After all this time, it appeared that the chance to atone for his sins, to fight—maybe even die for his country as Norton and Courtney had—would be taken from him. He wanted the war to end, but he grappled with a swirl of emotions. By the time news of the impending armistice finally arrived, he knew that he would have to finish his training and receive his commission so he could be honorably discharged. If he weren't a hero, at least he wouldn't be a disgrace.

Some soldiers were already preparing to go home as Harley was being sent to Carlstrom Field in Arcadia, Florida, near Fort Myers. He was transferred to Souther Field in Americus, Georgia, which soon closed, and shipped back to Kelly Field in January of 1919, where new frustrations emerged.

"There are plenty of airships here to get time in, but the men learning are far too numerous," Harley wrote to St. John in a letter dated February 23, 1919. "There being 500 cadets—more than ever before—many Kee Wees taking flying instructions and student officers taking advanced work. Now what chance has a poor Kaydet? Anyhow, with good wheather (sic), I expect to get through soon."

But the four-page, handwritten letter wasn't intended so much to inform the OSU athletic director of his progress in air school as to discover whether he had a chance of returning to school and resuming his football career.

THE SCHOOL FIELDED A FOOTBALL TEAM IN 1918, but with the war in progress, only four players from the 1917 roster were registered in school. With Wilce ordering about his smorgasbord of players while wearing a military uniform (he was a member of the training corps), the team went 3-3 under trying conditions. Practice hours had been set by government officials according to training schedules (Ohio State's practice was set for 5-6 p.m., after military training and before mess) and teams were allowed only one overnight trip during the season. This late restriction forced Ohio State to change its October 26 game with Michigan to November 30, thus making it the first time it was played on the final Saturday of the season. This would not happen again until 1935, and the OSU-Michigan game has been the final game ever since.

Chic

None of it mattered to Harley, or to any of the former Ohio State players getting out of service. What mattered to them was the future, not an "unofficial" season they had missed. In his letter to St. John, Chic sounded as if he weren't sure he wanted to come back. The tone of the note suggested he hoped St. John would help him resolve his academic issues and ask him to return.

"I'm certainly glad to hear so many of the old gang will be back or are back now," Harley wrote. "They've all gotten more experience and should go great, especially (Pete) Stinchcomb—undoubtedly he has found his stride. I can't decide whether it's right for me to go to school anymore or not. Lord knows I want to and probably when fall comes around it will be hard to keep away.

"I've made such a mess of what college work I had and right now it's hard to see what I can get out of it, other than the pleasure of playing football. Of course, I don't know what I'd do—might play ball or fly for a while, though I'll admit there's not much of a future in flying. But then it's a gamble either way so I don't guess I'd better come back. I'll have some work to get off, won't I? And you know how I stand with some of the powers that be. What'll I have to do—go to summer school or can it be worked off next fall? I don't want to go to summer school as I must get a job when thru here—need lots of funds. So please let me know just how I stand, Saint. . . ."

THE TROUBLE IN TEXAS WAS BOTHERING Chic more than he let on. He had apparently put off writing St. John until he learned that news of his dismissal from service and subsequent reinstatement wasn't public knowledge, having never appeared in any of the Columbus newspapers.

"Again, I ask you to excuse me," Harley wrote. "I got very downhearted thinking that my affair was public scandal and wanted to drift away from everything. I didn't write anyone. But I've since learned that little C.W. (Charles W.) was lost in the excitement, hence I don't worry anymore.

"I haven't any Huns, no decorations, etc., etc., but have learned many lessons which will stick and best of all (am forever gloating over it) I've the honor of being the oldest Cadet in America—how's that! (not in years, but in length of service). . . P.S. Don't let any of those news hounds (the likes of Finn) put anything in the paper about me going to school. I think it's best for me to keep out of the papers—don't you?"

118

The worst was yet to come. Harley finished his training at the end of April and had started turning in his uniforms and checking his effects, preparing to be discharged when he was found asleep on his bunk by Lieutenant Art V. Wortman. The commander of the cadet squadron immediately confined him to the barracks. A few days later, Chic received permission from a cadet sergeant to leave the barracks for a short period of time and by chance ran into Wortman, who asked why he had violated his order. Harley said he had permission to be absent, and Wortman threatened to put him in the guard house. In the subsequent court martial proceedings, Chic was charged with behaving with disrespect toward Wortman, "smiling in a sneering manner while being reprimanded and by contemptuously saying to him, 'Can you do it?' or words to that effect."

An angry Wortman confined him to the guard house and preferred charges against him for showing disrespect for a superior officer, breaking his arrest, "lying asleep on his cot after 7:30 a.m.," and appearing "at the orderly room of his organization with his shirt not buttoned." After three weeks of confinement, Chic was tried on May 26 and sentenced to three months in the guard house.

He was devastated. Days from getting out and enrolling in summer school so he would be eligible to play football in the fall, he was confined to "Box B" at Kelly Field with no clear resolution in sight. His fear of disgrace back in Columbus returned. Depression set in. He began chain-smoking to calm his nerves. If his Ohio friends didn't know about his previous problem, they would surely find out about this.

THE LONGER HE SAT IN HIS CELL, the more desperate he became. His mind teetered between despair and anger; he felt that he had been singled out for punishment, and persecuted for insignificant offenses.

Others agreed with him. Mrs. W. F. Cunningham, head of the War Camp Community Service at the base, wrote St. John later that Wortman "did this to every cadet he could. I think he was jealous of the boys and wanted to show his authority."

Morgan Moore, who lived with Harley in Barracks 52, wrote to St. John that "the whole affair is a damned outrage" and said "it is a seemingly well founded rumor that the court went to his trial with the intention of giving him a long sentence. The boy does not deserve the punishment he is getting, and his companions in the guard house are most of them ignorant and dirty, coming from the lower strata of society and a number of them have every conceivable venereal disease. This alone is enough to drive him insane."

IN A LETTER TO ST. JOHN dated June 15, Harley confessed that he was in trouble again, even though the athletic director had already heard about it and was working to secure his release. Chic admitted he had tried to hide the news of his arrest from his family back in Chicago.

"After all that has happened, I haven't the heart to tell my people," Harley wrote. "I started to write you many times, had even finished a couple of letters, but tore them up, being ashamed to heap any more woes upon you and afraid that I might get in worse, as all mail is censored in the G.H. Everyone home is writing and wondering what happened. They wouldn't understand, mother especially would worry, thinking that it was just like being a regular criminal. Could you write them a few lines saying that everything will be OK in a short time?

"Had everything gone right, I'd a been in Columbus early in May—intending to be there to look over the ground and was seriously thinking of making up some credits in summer school. Now it looks like I'll even have to pass up that and be in a bad fix to begin next fall.

"I fear I'm getting in bad condition as I'm smoking like a demon—it's that or go cuckoo from worry. But now that I've heard that you're going to help me, I'll quit and take care of myself. It's not serious and I don't deserve it. . . Everything and everybody is so suspicious—one can't trust anybody the way I've been gouged on. Probably you'd better not tell anybody about this trouble.

"Just think, I was to be discharged in a couple days. My counsel left the field two days after the trial—before he told me that the C.O. had switched the court the last day in order to convict me. It's nothing but a frame-up. I hate to cry over spilt milk, but were you here to investigate, you'd agree."

The closing line above his signature was "Heap downhearted." He probably would have felt better had he known how hard school officials were working to secure his release. St. John wrote to a friend who was a member of the 313th Aero Squadron at Kelly, V.R. Billingsley, who gave him the names of all of the commanding officers at the base and noted that "some officers, presumably men from Western Conference schools, delight in the chance to hurt (Harley). . .

You would be surprised, Director, to know just how much of this smallness and meanness there really is in army life."

OSU PRESIDENT WILLIAM OXLEY THOMPSON and E. F. McCampbell, the dean of the college of medicine, wrote letters to the adjutant general of the army and other bigwigs above those in charge at the San Antonio air base. In one letter to Cunningham, St. John mentioned that he might go to Secretary of War Newton Baker, "a Cleveland man and we can reach him thru a number of influential political and financial men."

The flurry of letters seemed to help. Chic's jail time would have ended August 23. His prison officer recommended probation, which would have cut his sentence in half and allowed him to be discharged on July 9. Then on June 25, Harley sent St. John a telegram to inform him that he was to be sent to Camp Grant in Rockford, Illinois, the following day and was expected to receive his discharge papers "one or two days" later. In a note to St. John dated July 3, a frustrated Harley said he was still there awaiting his papers and getting no response from authorities at Kelly Field.

St. John put off a vacation in northern Michigan to deal with Harley's problems and finally headed north when he thought the troubled athlete was on his way home. But he wasn't, and with Chic now seemingly stuck in Illinois, Wilce asked Ohio Governor James M. Cox—soon to be the 1920 Democratic candidate for president—to write a letter to the commanding officers at Kelly Field and Camp Grant to help move the process along.

A campaign that seemed almost as exhaustive as the war effort itself finally accomplished its mission. Thanks to the Secretary of War, the governor of Ohio, the Ohio State University president, the school athletic director, the dean of the college of medicine, and who knows who else, Chic was finally discharged from the army.

War had been hell in a lot of ways, but both wars—his and the world's—had come to satisfactory endings. The threat from Germany had been extinguished, at least for now. And Harley's imposing stature had been confirmed by nearly every dignitary in the state of Ohio.

the new

war

The Dispatch called November 11, 1918, the "greatest Monday in the world's history," a bit of hyperbole probably not as outrageous as it seems. Massive celebrations erupted in major cities all over America, and after so much misery and *heartache*, it was a deliriously happy time. Even the most sensible people had reasons to go a little crazy. The war had claimed more than ten million lives in five years of fighting, and now the survivors were

*Chic's return to campus
in the fall of 1919 made
headlines, even if he wasn't
the biggest news.*

returning home. The shortages and the rationing would stop. The clouds of uncertainty everyone had lived under had moved on and now, for a time anyway, there were blue skies overhead.

The chamber of commerce arranged for an official celebration in Columbus at 2:30 p.m., but the official celebration was late to the party. Early-risers hit the streets before daybreak and the crowd kept building until it had swelled to more than 200,000. The stretch of High Street between Union Station and Mound Street turned into a mile-long mass of wildly happy people and the screeching sirens, shrill whistles, and piercing screams made it difficult to hear.

One by one, business and factory owners all over town declared their own holiday. Kilbourne-Jacobs Manufacturing Company employees found the gates closed when they arrived and work suspended for the day. It was the same at Jeffrey Manufacturing Company, and the Panhandle shops of the Pennsylvania Railroad, and scores of other companies. In almost every case, the workers headed straight to High Street. Female employees of the Columbus Dry Goods Company showed up wearing American flags. Ladies who worked at several of the city's leading stores—The Union, Boston Store, F.& R. Lazarus, Armbrusters—appeared waving banners bearing the names of their employers, all of which had locked their doors. For one day, money was superfluous. The war-imposed rules and sanctions would soon end. When the giddiness was over, business would again be good.

HAPPINESS ALSO RELEASED THE PENT-UP HATRED for both Germany and the Kaiser. It took the form of homemade signs and sneering placards, most of them carrying some variation of the same message: *There will be a new devil in hell soon.* Or, *The Kaiser has gone to hell. Where will the devil go?* Employees of the Clark Grave Vault Company paraded with a large steel truck-mounted vault marked *This is for the Kaiser.* A local funeral parlor resurrected a horse-drawn hearse from a storage shed and it carried a fat "corpse" wearing a German helmet visible through the side windows. Local No. 87 of the blacksmiths and helpers of The Hocking Valley Railroad shops followed a cage bearing the inscription *Uncle Sam's trained wild animals*, with men attired as the Kaiser, Hindenburg, and other prominent German leaders imprisoned inside.

The planned festivities seemed almost lost in the revelry. Politicians and civic leaders knew this wasn't their party. The day belonged to anyone who had lost

someone in battle, or had feared for the safety of a friend or family member, or
even feared for themselves. The day belonged to anyone who had purchased war
bonds or volunteered time to the war effort or made any kind of sacrifice, and that
included just about everyone, which is why Columbus was such a happy place.

The biggest parade came in February, in honor of the most famous Columbus
soldier of them of all, fighter pilot Captain Eddie Rickenbacker. When he returned
home, huge crowds greeted him at Union Station and every other railroad station,
big or small, between Newcomerstown, Ohio, and Columbus. As a famous race car
driver and American's foremost flying ace, Rickenbacker was toasted everywhere,
but he was especially revered in Columbus.

THAT WAS THE HAPPIEST PART OF THE WAR'S AFTERMATH. In other ways, the year
took an odd, sometimes uncomfortable form. A bitter debate raged over the peace
treaty and the League of Nations, and most Americans didn't want to hear about
it. Victory had created widespread euphoria, but it had also generated a growing
desire for isolationism. Americans had willingly sacrificed and now they were tired
of it. They stopped worrying about Europe and turned inward.

The anti-alcohol forces had grown considerably in recent years, though their
crusade was hardly new. The Women's Christian Temperance Union and the
Anti-Saloon League—based in nearby Westerville—had waged the fight against
alcohol since the 19th century, and around 1910 sentiment began to shift in favor
of a ban. A week before the armistice, with the end of the world conflict in sight,
Ohio voters approved Prohibition, which came just ahead of the ratification of the
Eighteenth Amendment that would make America dry.

In Ohio, D-Day was May 27, 1919. Beginning on that fateful Tuesday, alcohol
could no longer be legally served in bars, saloons, and restaurants. But because the
annual state-issued liquor licenses expired on May 24, that was the day most places
effectively went out of the liquor business.

In Columbus, the final Saturday turned out to be a wild but surprisingly
peaceful night. Under siege by a mad rush of customers, many downtown bars
and restaurants ran dry and closed early. In the saloons that didn't close, an army
of police officers kept things as quiet as could be expected on such a rowdy night.
As the saloons closed—the last at midnight—many posted signs advertising the sale
of bar fixtures and furniture beginning on Monday or Tuesday. For the regular

customers, these read like obituaries, for they felt as if they'd just lost a loved one.

For those who had licenses, there would be one final day of legal sales, and of the more than 5,600 bars and saloons in Ohio, 163 of them paid $305 for the annual license that permitted them to stay open for that one day. Nine of them were in Columbus, and one, the Hotel Deshler, at the northwest corner of Broad and High, advertised a grand final party—complete with marimba band—in its ballroom beginning at 8 o'clock on Monday night. The Deshler was the only hotel bar to remain open Monday; among the others, the door to the saloon of the Norwich Hotel at the corner of State and Fourth wore a wreath with black crepe bearing a card that read: *Sincerest regrets. Old John Barleycorn Died May 27, 1919.*

THE NINE OPEN BARS FIGURED to get their license fees back by welcoming thirsty crowds from morning to midnight, in some cases with a dramatic increase in liquor prices. The Kohn Company, 11 W. Broad, hiked its whisky prices from ten to twenty-five cents and doubled its beer prices to thirty cents, and the place was still packed all day. When local residents awoke the next morning, many with the hangover of a lifetime, they found themselves living in a different world.

Ads for non-alcoholic drinks appeared throughout the newspapers. Sterling Beverage, that "foody drink" made locally by William Fisher and Sons Company on Mound Street, was served in a beer bottle look-a-like with an advertising message that carried an obvious appeal to some: *Ohio is dry but need not be thirsty, for you'll never know the difference when you try Sterling. . . .* Hoster's, the former German Village brewery, advertised its gold top brands, Champagne Mist and Sparkling Burgundy, which were in fact, fruit and grape drinks. Even St. Louis-based Anheuser-Busch purchased ads for Bevo, the beverage. The ad's disclaimer—"Bevo is classified by the U.S. Government as a soft drink"—delivered the subliminal message that it was hard to tell the difference.

Several saloons followed the example set by the Bott Brothers on North High Street, which installed a soda fountain and a candy store and continued to serve "plain and fancy drinks of the soft drink variety" at the bar. In many cases, that was simply a ruse. It wasn't long before there were numerous complaints that many former saloons-turned-soft drink emporiums were selling liquor illegally. By the time Prohibition officially started around most of the country, Columbus had already developed a thriving cadre of bootleggers.

Chic Harley missed all of this—his time in the Kelly Field stockade began in May—and the average man on the street didn't miss him. Few knew of Chic's service problems and there was just too much going on in the summer of 1919 for people to think much about it. There was a heavyweight title bout between Jack Dempsey and Jess Willard in Toledo in July, not exactly a commonplace event in a farm state such an Ohio. The Ohio State Fair topped 100,000 in attendance on one day, and on that same day, President Wilson made Columbus his first stop in an early September speech-making tour designed to drum up support for the peace treaty. Columbus, for the moment at least, was too busy to worry about where Harley was and when he would return.

He was finally released from the stockade, discharged from Camp Grant, Illinois, and arrived in Columbus on July 17. He enrolled in summer school at Ohio State the same day and reportedly "got busy with his studies," which must have been heartening news to Jack Wilce, Lynn St. John, and other Ohio State athletic officials. But Wilce had also been busy. He had just finished his medical studies and appeared in full cap and gown to receive his degree at Ohio State graduation exercises in June.

HARLEY'S RETURN IN 1919 MADE HEADLINES in the Columbus newspapers, but away from campus, Chic wasn't even the biggest news in Ohio sports. The Cincinnati Reds owned that distinction; after a tough May, the Reds, between June 6 and August 26, compiled a sizzling 60-18 record and became the talk of the state. Interest in the Reds grew more and more intense and with good reason; an Ohio team had never played in the World Series.

The Reds drew 32,000 for a game against the New York Giants on August 3, at the time the largest crowd ever to see a baseball game in Cincinnati, and club officials announced that they were considering playing the World Series at The Speedway in the northern Cincinnati suburb of Sharonville. The Reds' board of directors reasoned that the race track could be configured to accommodate 100,000 fans.

If Prohibition hadn't been in effect, this curious proposal might have created doubts about the directors' sobriety, but it only demonstrated rampant enthusiasm for the team—not only in Cincinnati but around the state. (The Reds' appearance in the World Series generated the kind of interest around the state that the

Cleveland Browns' first appearance in the Super Bowl might cause today.)
Club officials finally came to their senses and determined that with the installation
of temporary bleachers, Redland Field could be expanded by 9,000.

The World Series was still a couple of weeks away, and Harley and his
teammates were still a week from their first practice when the encampment
of the Grand Army of the Republic brought an estimated 90,000 visitors to town.
Organizers called it the largest encampment of Civil War veterans since 1904—
likely the last for many of them—and the newspapers seemed determined
to interview all of them.

The *Dispatch* ran individual photos of five elderly black gentlemen—Henry
Frazier, W. H. Carter, Robert Daniels, Branville Duckery, and S.S. Dennis—in
Union soldier hats under the headline *Fought to Establish Freedom of Race.*
There was a front page picture of 74-year-old Jason Soles, one of six soldiers
who carried Abraham Lincoln from Ford's Theater to his deathbed across the
street on the night in 1865 when he was shot by John Wilkes Booth. Soles's
presence underscored the encampment's urgency. The other five members of the
Pennsylvania light artillery company who had helped Soles carry Lincoln's body
were dead.

With the town teeming with war heroes, few noticed when Ohio State
began football practice in the middle of September. There was still no doubting
that the old days of anonymity were gone. Two days after the OSU upperclassmen
reported, 205 freshmen came out for the team. *Zam-blooie!* the *Dispatch* campus
correspondent "Wahoo" wrote in the September 18 edition. (In 1920, the
newspaper identified "Wahoo" as graduating Ohio State student and football
player Fritz Holtkamp.)

"All Ohio State University football records went to smash with a resounding
thud Wednesday afternoon when 205 freshman athletes registered for the yearly
squad. Assistant coach George Trautman was simply swamped in handling the
new men, but the broadest grin that ever graced the blond coach's face never left.
It is an Ohio State record and from all information gained from old-timers at the
Athletic House Wednesday evening, it is a Western Conference record . . . When
Dr. Wilce was told of the freshman squad's size, he beamed with pleasure as well."

Ohio sports fans were still distracted. Preparation for the football season in the local newspapers still ranked below the Reds' best-of-nine World Series with the Chicago White Sox. The public hungered for news of Reds outfield star Edd Roush, not Chic Harley. They wanted to know if the Reds could solve Eddie Cicotte's knuckleball, not whether Harley and Pete Stinchcomb could run over Ohio Wesleyan in the season opener. OSU and OWU were old rivals, having played nineteen times since that first historic meeting in 1890, but the Buckeyes had beaten the Methodists fifteen times in a row and by a combined score of 106-0 the past three years. The outcome of the game was no mystery and there was little interest in it.

TWO DAYS BEFORE THE GAME, with the surprising Reds ahead of the favored White Sox two games to none, the OSU football team's upperclassmen, in a unanimous vote, named Harley captain. News of Harley's election shared the *Dispatch* sports pages the next day with the Reds and a Michigan story that carried an intriguing headline: *Fielding H. Yost Unsure of Winning Conference Title.*

Most Ohio readers must have seen the headline and smiled. Three games stood between Ohio State and its game at Ann Arbor, and if the game had been that week, it might have trumped interest in the World Series. Ohio State had no choice but to play its schedule—Ohio Wesleyan, Cincinnati, and Kentucky were its first three opponents—but football talk in Columbus and most of the state centered on one thing: This might be the year when Ohio State finally beat Michigan.

the biggest
game

A few minutes after the 1910
Ohio State-*Michigan* game
in Columbus, a taxi driver was
heading north on High Street just as
the crowds were coming the other way.
"What was the score?" he asked
a boy in the crowd.
"Three to three, Ohio State,"
the happy boy replied.
That's how it was in those days.
A game that would become one
of the greatest rivalries in collegiate
sports wasn't much more
than a schedule-filler for Michigan,
an early version of today's intrastate

*In the 1919 Michigan
game, Chic was flawless.
The Michigan coach came
to his dressing room
afterward and said so.*

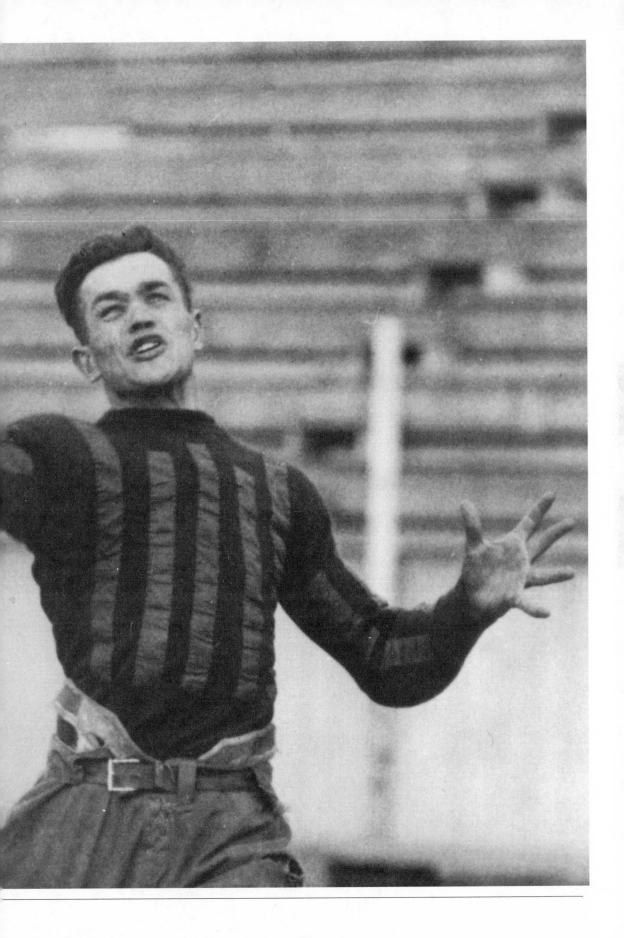

"rivalries" between Ohio State and Bowling Green, Toledo, or Kent State. For most of the first twenty years, Ohio State-Michigan wasn't The Game but a game, and usually not much of one at that. Some years—a lot of years—it wasn't much more than a way for the Michigan players to get out and stretch their legs.

The two schools didn't meet every season. When they did, they didn't play on the last week of the schedule as they do now. They weren't rivals; it's impossible to have a rivalry when one team never wins. Ohio State players and coaches dreamed of the day they would finally beat Michigan and that's all it was then: a dream.

Michigan ran an elite football program. Ohio State ran a program that was ambitious but ordinary. The Wolverines wanted to be the best team in the nation. The Buckeyes wanted to be the best team in the state. Michigan was serious about football. Ohio State was serious about becoming serious about it someday. Their aspirations were different and so were the levels of their commitment. In the burgeoning, increasingly popular world of college football, Ohio State was a scrawny kid. Michigan was a fully-developed bully.

When the two schools met to play football for the first time in 1897, Michigan already had a proud history. It had been the scene of impromptu games on campus since the early 1870s, and it had fielded a varsity team since 1879. Ohio State had fielded a team all of seven years. Michigan was a football pioneer; it played Racine College at White Stocking Park in Chicago in 1879 in the first intercollegiate football game west of the Alleghenies. While it was ten years later than the first collegiate game of the sport called rugby-football—Princeton vs. Rutgers—it was still eleven years before OSU's first official game in 1890.

Many Ohio State students were still unaware of the sport's existence when Michigan had gone east in 1881 and played Harvard, Yale, and Princeton during a whirlwind week that ranked as an ambitious, first-ever attempt at an intersectional college football schedule. Ohio State wouldn't meet any of those early football powers until it traveled to Princeton in 1927, long after those schools' greatest glories had passed.

It was a strange way to start a rivalry, for the two schools didn't have a lot in common. In 1889, Michigan's 2,153 students was the largest enrollment of any college in the nation; Ohio State had 415 students and wouldn't reach 1,000 for another eight years. In 1894, Michigan traveled to Ithaca, New York, where the

*The 1919 OSU game was an unusual one for the great
Michigan coach, "Hurry-Up" Yost. Harley baffled his Wolverines,
and the OSU-Michigan game became truly a rivalry.*

Wolverines lost to eastern power Cornell 22-0, but in a return game three weeks
later in Detroit, they drew 14,000 fans and beat Cornell, 12-4. The Buckeyes were
playing mostly in front of their families and friends. Michigan's win over Cornell
was big news, the first win for a "western" school over a school from the east. So
while Michigan was winning games against impressive national rivals in front of
thousands of followers, OSU was struggling to beat Kenyon, Ohio Wesleyan, and
Otterbein in front of a few hundred fans.

FOR MICHIGAN, THE EARLY GAMES AGAINST Ohio State were mostly a matter of
convenience. The formation of the Western Conference in 1896—with seven of the
strongest Midwestern programs—gave the Wolverines at least three or four games
each season against the top teams in the region. They usually played a game or two
against one of the reputable eastern teams, which left a few spots for tuneup games
with schools such as Ohio State, Case Western Reserve, and Ohio Wesleyan. The

Michigan game was the highlight on OSU's early schedule because it was the only Buckeye opponent with a national presence; their other games were against Ohio teams. The Michigan game represented OSU's one chance to step up in class.

Few in Columbus ever expected the Buckeyes to do it, though. Even two days before Ohio State's first trip to Michigan in 1897, a *Dispatch* account conceded that the Buckeyes' still-to-come game with the Columbus Barracks—the military installation later known as Fort Hayes—"will in all probability be the feature of the season in local football affairs." It may have been an inadvertant acknowledgment of the inevitable. After Michigan whipped the Buckeyes 34-0 in Ann Arbor, fans back in Columbus were actually satisfied with their "good showing." OSU wasn't in Michigan's league, literally or figuratively, and the two schools didn't meet again until 1900.

This time, the unbeaten Buckeyes pulled off a huge upset—the 0-0 tie—that may have been the highlight of the school's first eleven years of football. No less an authority than Chicago coach Amos Alonzo Stagg, witness to the contest, declared that OSU was a coming factor in Western football. As much as he knew about football, the legendary coach missed the mark by about fifteen years. The local papers reported that OSU outplayed the Wolverines and downplayed one factor that might have contributed to it: the game was played in miserable weather conditions, sleet having started just before the opening kickoff.

IT WAS FOOL'S GOLD TO BUCKEYE FAITHFUL. Fielding Yost arrived at Michigan in 1901 and the gap between the two programs grew even wider. Michigan had changed coaches not because the Wolverines had been tied by Ohio State—as unimpressive as that was—but because it had lost to its *real* rival, Chicago. When Yost was hired away from Stanford by Michigan athletic director Charles Baird, beating Chicago had been one of his prerequisites. "You've got to beat Chicago," Baird said. Beating Ohio State was a given.

By 1900, Yost had coached five teams to championships—Stanford, the Stanford freshmen, San Jose Normal (later San Jose State), and Palo Alto Lowell and Ukiah high schools. He had won everywhere he had been, including Ohio Wesleyan, Kansas, and Nebraska, and when he got the job at Michigan, the 30-year-old Yost asked a speedy halfback he had coached at San Jose Normal to come with him. Willie Heston balked at first, but finally changed his mind. Thus began an incredible five-year run that saw Michigan go 55-2-1, the first four with Heston as one of the game's brightest stars. From 1901 to 1905, Yost's famous "Point-a-Minute" teams averaged 49 points per game. That was less than the 70 minutes that comprised a game in those days, but Yost offered a plausible explanation: The 119-0 win over Michigan Agricultural College (later Michigan State) in 1902 was stopped after thirty-six minutes, the 128-0 win over Buffalo was stopped after fifty minutes, and the amazing 130-0 win over West Virginia lasted just thirty-six. In the Buffalo game, Michigan had 1,261 rushing yards, a figure made only slightly less incredible by a rule that allowed the scoring team to receive the ensuing kickoff.

That game against Buffalo was played during Yost's first season at Michigan, two weeks before the Wolverines visited Columbus for the first time. In light of some of Michigan's other scores in 1901—the Wolverines beat rival Chicago only 22-0—Ohio State's 21-0 loss seems quite respectable, and it must have seemed so to those in Columbus, too. That "Point-A-Minute" team became so famous that officials at the Tournament of Roses Parade in Pasadena, California, invited the Wolverines to play in its first Rose Bowl game. Michigan traveled across the country to meet Pacific Coast champion Stanford and beat the west coast team so badly—the Wolverines were up 49-0 when the Stanford coaches asked to stop the game with eight minutes left—that disappointed Rose Bowl officials decided to replace the following year's game with a chariot race. It was sixteen years before the annual parade was again followed by a football game.

THE ROSE BOWL SHOULD HAVE BEEN A CLUE that the Buckeyes weren't as close to the Wolverines as their 21-0 loss seemed to indicate, but Ohio State hired a new coach in 1902 and he quickly stoked the fires of the wannabe rivalry. The week before OSU visited Ann Arbor, the Buckeyes' new coach Perry Hale took a look at the results of Michigan's five previous games and told reporters that the Wolverines hadn't yet played a hard team. Maybe he said that because he was just coming off a successful playing career at Yale, or maybe it was because of his Ohio State team's 4-0 start, or maybe it was simply because he wanted to pump up his troops. But the Michigan wins—88-0 over Albion, 48-6 over Case, 119-0 over Michigan State, 60-0 over Indiana and 23-0 over Notre Dame—look pretty good from here. And afterwards, they looked pretty good from there, too. In a day when touchdowns counted for five points instead of six, Michigan was ahead of Hale's Buckeyes 86-0 when the game was stopped midway through the second half, an act of mercy. After the game, OSU captain Buck Coover was seen leaving the field weeping.

Such was the state of the Ohio State-Michigan "rivalry." Michigan had an All-American as early as 1898 and Willie Heston would be accorded that award in 1903 and 1904. No Ohio State player had even been considered for such high honors. Other than Michigan's first-ever visit to Columbus in 1901 when the game drew a record crowd of over 8,000, the Buckeyes routinely played before crowds that numbered in the hundreds. Michigan played a 1902 game against Wisconsin that drew 25,000. Later that season, unbeaten Michigan traveled to Minneapolis for a game against unbeaten Minnesota and drew a crowd estimated at between 25,000 and 30,000, called the largest crowd ever in the "West" for a football game. Michigan played its home games at Regents Field, capacity 15,000, until 1906 and sometimes that wasn't big enough; Ferry Field had a capacity of 18,000 when it opened and in 1914 it was expanded to 25,000.

THAT 86-0 BEATING IN 1902 brought the Buckeye faithful back to reality. They were practically joyous over Michigan's 34-6 victory in Columbus in 1904, partly because the Buckeyes had a 6-5 lead early in the second half. The fans considered that a moral victory and *The Lantern* apparently did, too; its headline said all one needs to know about the state of the one-sided "rivalry" at that point—*Wolverines Return Home Humbled by Score–Practical Victory for Varsity.*

Michigan left the Western Conference in 1907 over new rules designed to give more faculty control to athletics. It strongly objected to three of them—a maximum of five games, the abolishment of training tables, and a maximum of three-year varsity participation by athletes. (One former player, Horace Prettyman, was on the Michigan football team from 1882 to 1890.) The school wouldn't return to the league until 1917, and because of a "non-intercourse" rule that prohibited conference teams from playing Michigan after 1910, the Wolverines dropped off the Buckeyes' schedule when OSU started Western Conference play in 1913. So as the Ohio State program began to improve under Jack Wilce, the two schools no longer played each other.

The 1919 game wouldn't be the schools' first meeting since those one-sided days; Michigan had re-entered the conference and returned to the OSU schedule in 1918 while Harley and most of his 1917 teammates were in the service. The

Wolverines' 14-0 victory fed the perception of a still-superior Michigan program, even if it didn't prove much of anything. That wasn't the Harley-led Ohio State team that had won two Western Conference championships.

The history, however, was undeniable. In fifteen meetings since 1897, Ohio State had never beaten Michigan. Its signature moments were those two early ties. In twenty years, only three Scarlet and Gray football players had scored a touchdown against Michigan—William Marquart (1904), Millard Gibson (1908), and Chelsea Boone (1909). The aggregate score in those fifteen games was 369-21.

It was the accumulation of Ohio State failure that made the 1919 trip to Ann Arbor seem so special, that and the incredible 1916 and 1917 seasons in Columbus, which had convinced fans that OSU had grown up. There could be no doubting that Harley's arrival on campus in 1915 had changed things. As soon as Harley was on the team, the Buckeyes commenced beating teams they had never beaten before. There was no way to be certain if Michigan would become another one of those teams, but everyone in Columbus was itching to find out.

WHEN TALK TURNED TO FOOTBALL IN COLUMBUS that fall, it always centered on one game. While the OSU players prepared for the season opener against Ohio Wesleyan, local newspaper accounts focused on how the team stacked up against Michigan, the fourth game of the season. As odd as that seems, the local press knew its audience. Football interest had never been so high and it all centered on an afternoon in Ann Arbor.

School officials tried to capitalize on the surge of interest. For the first time ever, Ohio State took season ticket orders for all five home games, and no individual was permitted to purchase more than four tickets. In the past, only mail orders for homecoming games had been accepted. Ticket orders for the Michigan game were accepted with season ticket orders, and sales were brisk. It was the game everybody wanted to see.

Reporters and editors couldn't suppress their enthusiasm. On the Sunday following the Buckeyes' 46-0 win over Cincinnati, the *Dispatch* sports section offered the pictures of eight Michigan players in a diagonal line down the middle of the page with the heading, *Ohio State Will Know the Worth of These Michigan Players Two Weeks From Today.*

Kentucky, a worthy opponent, was next on the schedule and it was as if

Wildcats didn't exist. On the Thursday before the Kentucky game, the *Ohio State Journal's* lead headline was about OSU-Michigan—*Wonder If Yost Men Will Play Aerial Game Against State With Their Top Three Aviators*—and John A. Ward wrote a long story about the threat of Michigan's passing attack without ever mentioning Kentucky.

On the Tuesday before the game, Wilce put up a sign on his bulletin board in the Athletic House that showed where his sentiments lay: *Eight more practice days till Michigan.* Wilce had his OSU troops practicing for Michigan during the week of the Kentucky game, a daring approach that would be successfully used later by Woody Hayes.

LOOKING AHEAD BORE NO CONSEQUENCES. More than 7,500 fans watched Ohio State hammer the Wildcats 49-0, and most of the spectators were dreaming of Michigan. While the game was being played, tags were sold in the Ohio Field stands to raise money to send the OSU band to Ann Arbor. Based on press reports, the sale's success was almost as much a highlight of the afternoon as the football. So many tags were sold that the band's trip was guaranteed and there was money left over to buy balloons.

As the game approached, Harley became the focal point both in Columbus and Ann Arbor. Fielding Yost fretted over how his team could stop him, and Ohio State fans devoured reports out of Michigan detailing the famous coach's concerns. Although Wilce's popularity had grown dramatically since his arrival as an assistant coach from Wisconsin in 1913, Harley was the basis for most of Ohio's optimism. Ohio State fans believed the Buckeyes would finally beat their northern "rival" because of Chic Harley's talents, and gamblers in Ann Arbor agreed. Most were reluctant to take Michigan without receiving odds.

Dispatch sports editor Harvey A. Miller had been writing about these games since the early days of the century, so he knew intimately all the dark places this series had been. Over the years, Miller had been captive witness to most of the annual beatings, and he had written dozens of stories about Michigan's domination. If he gushed about the upcoming game a little more than the others, it might have been because this was a day he had anticipated longer than most of his newspaper counterparts: "Saturday, October 25 will be the supreme day in Ohio State football of a period covering more than a quarter of a century! It will be the culmination of a long time of athletic relations with Michigan and the proof of what often has been hinted on this page—that with Michigan back in the conference there would be a rightful rivalry between these two institutions, and that Ohio State and Michigan would play an annual game that would be as important as the Minnesota-Michigan or the Chicago-Michigan battle.

"After years and years of development, a Scarlet and Gray eleven will go into Ann Arbor a favorite, as the odds asked by some Michigan supporters indicate. That was almost an idle dream in the old days."

All of the games that came before were of a different breed. The Ohio State-Michigan rivalry did not exist before October 25, 1919. On this date, the rivalry entered the world with arms and feet flailing, creating all the noise and commotion of a newborn infant. *This* meeting was the true ancestor of the ones that would come later. It was the first chapter in a new book with Wilce cast as an early-day version of an icon who would become The Game's principal author, Woody Hayes.

WILCE DISPENSED WITH HIS USUAL ROUTINE of a light practice on Monday and—shrouded in secrecy—gave his troops a stiff workout. Many visitor practice "passes" weren't honored, and the *Ohio State Journal's* Walter Chamblin said that the squad practiced "behind gates closed tighter than prison doors." While the public was never permitted to watch the Buckeyes practice, Chamblin made it clear that Wilce was taking no chances. Even the privileged few who were allowed to watch practice were kept under tight surveillance. That kindly old mathematics professor who had attended every Ohio State home football game for the past ten years might be a spy.

"Three men watched the only open gate," Chamblin wrote. "It was a vigil more strict than the 'watch on the Rhine.' A canvas was stretched around the iron fence at the south end of the field to prevent wandering eyes from gazing in from the street.

"At intervals along the north, east and west exposures, trusted students kept guard. But the search for spies went even further just before a certain play was put in progress and persons within the field were forced to again show their passes."

Wilce trusted reporters more than most modern coaches. Local press types were allowed in to watch and they even described the "secret" workouts in some detail. But then, reporters in that era weren't required to be as objective as they are now; Fritz Holtkamp, the *Dispatch* student correspondent known as "Wahoo," was a member of the team. Besides, it wasn't really news to anyone that Wilce was working his players hard.

"At 6:30, the players were sent to the showers, tired, but able to trot at a good clip," Wahoo reported. "The freshmen were through for the day, but an announcement awaited the varsity squad. 'Back after supper' said the coach, and 8:45 o'clock found the men again on the field, not however in football togs of hard practice but in civilian clothes, running signals under the lights until 9:30 o'clock."

UP IN ANN ARBOR, Yost was doing the same thing. *Dispatch* correspondent Tom Sargent reported that after conducting "secret" afternoon practice sessions, Yost assembled his squad at 7:30 nightly and that "so many new plays have been added that some of the huskies have been completely swamped with new signals, but the coach is pounding them into the heads of his boys every evening."

Ticket sales in both cities were remarkable. Ohio State had already sold two 500-ticket allotments and requested another. Michigan officials were expecting the largest crowd in school history, anticipating that more than 28,000 would try to squeeze into Ferry Field. Yost told the Michigan papers that "there is more interest in this game than any other I have known here," an impressive statement given the teams he had played and the places he had been.

Wilce could have made a similar statement about Columbus. Three thousand people jammed into the Armory on Thursday night for what was called the largest pep rally in school history. Johnny Jones, a "300 horsepower" freshman cheerleader from East High School who would one day become a well-known Columbus newspaper columnist, helped ignite the crowd, and then Dave Warwick, known as the "original" OSU cheerleader, and Professor George W. Rightmire spoke briefly. The noisy building fell silent when Chic Harley entered, then erupted in wild cheering.

"I never realized what a Michigan game was before tonight," Harley said. "That is, I never thought it was more than a Wisconsin or an Illinois game. This crowd sure made the team feel like fighting harder than ever. That's all."

Fans cheered the players when they boarded the train for Ann Arbor the following morning. When the team arrived about 5:30 p.m., people were pouring into Ann Arbor from all directions, using all manner of transportation to get there. Two trains brought OSU rooters from Columbus, although most Ohio State students came by automobile. A passenger steamer from Cleveland to Detroit on Friday night was so crowded with OSU rooters that they doubled up in the berths.

If the Ohio State players didn't totally understand the magnitude of the game before, they did now. When they reached the Hotel Allenel, the venerable five-story downtown structure at the corner of Main and Huron, it teemed with hundreds of Ohio State rooters. The crowd seemed to grow by the hour. The lobby resembled a busy casino without the slot machines; it was jammed with fans when the team arrived and it remained that way until just before game time. The mob was a mix of students, gamblers, fans, dignitaries, and former players, and the bodies seemed in constant motion, pushing and shoving and mingling their way to nowhere in particular, most just happy to be part of something with this much energy.

SOME OF THE FACES WERE FAMILIAR FACES, faces that might summon a name from memory and might not, faces that were nonetheless recognizable to many OSU fans. They had seemingly made the trip here by time capsule . . . *Millard Gibson* . . . *Tommy Jones* . . . *Maurice Briggs* . . . *Cy Snyder* . . . *Bunny Olds* . . . *Mule Elder* . . . *Clement Cook* . . . *Howard Courtney* . . . *Buckeye Hobt* . . . visitors from Ohio State's football past. The mob spilled out into the streets surrounding the hotel, and although it was easier for the shuffling bodies to move outside, the atmosphere was no less electric. The cacophony of voices both inside and out rendered some of what was said inaudible, but there was no mistaking the topic; the talk was all about the game. Ann Arbor belonged to Michigan, but the Hotel Allenel was Ohio State country. The Buckeyes had never beaten Michigan, and the mob in this lobby and on this street corner was here to witness history.

Ferry Field was about a mile south of the hotel. The Buckeyes went there in a stream of motor cars on Saturday morning, and they found the scene on South State Street to be just as wild. The streets around the field resembled those around their hotel, only the bodies in the dense crowd were multiplied by a hundred. Temporary bleachers had been erected, but it was by no means certain they would be able to accommodate everyone. The crowd continued to swell until just after game time, when two airplanes carrying more spectators landed not far from the playing field. Even the press box was crowded: telegraph operators had been hired to transmit play-by-play from the game to more than twenty newspapers. A game had turned into The Game, at least for one day.

THE GAME DIDN'T BEGIN WELL FOR THE BUCKEYES. Pete Stinchcomb fumbled the opening kickoff and Michigan's Archie Weston recovered at the OSU 20. That could have been disastrous, but the Buckeye defense kept the Wolverines from scoring, and late in the first quarter, Iolas Huffman blocked a Michigan punt and teammate Jim Flowers recovered in the end zone. Harley kicked the extra point to give Ohio a 7-0 lead.

Michigan got on the scoreboard in the second quarter with a 37-yard field goal by Clifford Sparks, but Ohio State's offensive display was yet to come. Midway through the third quarter, after holding the Wolverines on downs at the OSU 34, Stinchcomb ran 24 yards to the Michigan 42. On the next play, Harley zipped around right end Willard Peach, sidestepped Ernie Vick, Archie Weston, and Cliff Sparks, and streaked to the end zone. His extra-point kick made it 13-3. This was what an estimated 5,000 Ohio State rooters had come to see.

At that point, Yost finally unleashed the passing attack that Wilce had been worried about—and the Buckeyes were up to the challenge. Michigan tried 16 passes, 12 to tall, lanky star end Duke Dunne, and didn't complete one. Harley intercepted two of them and Stinchcomb one.

Harley also averaged 42 yards on his 11 punts, so Michigan's anxiety about him was well-founded. The pre-game suspicions of many were true: Chic's presence meant more than any so-called Michigan "jinx." Stinchcomb, a budding star in his own right, had also offered more than a hint that things might not be that much different when Harley was gone.

In the Michigan locker room afterwards, Yost confided to a small group of Michigan alums how he had been coaching his men to stop Harley for the past two weeks, "but we couldn't do it." He later explained why.

"Harley's change of pace, straight-arming, and shifting of the hips as he shook off three tacklers in making his run for a touchdown was as pretty a piece of work as I ever saw any player do," Yost said. "Harley threw off my best tacklers when making that run."

Yost had never gone to the opposing locker room following a Michigan loss. This time, he did. He asked if he could make a short speech to the victorious

Buckeyes and a surprised Wilce invited him in.

"You deserve your victory," Yost said. "You fought brilliantly. You boys gave a grand exhibition of football strategy, and while I'm sorry, dreadfully sorry, that we lost, I want to congratulate you. And you, Mr. Harley, I believe you are one of the finest little machines I have ever seen. Again, I want to congratulate Ohio State."

With that, "Hurry Up" Yost spun around and made a quick exit. The Michigan-Ohio State relationship he had known would never be the same again.

more than a
game

The line outside the Lazarus store
at High Street and Town was a visible
sign of how much things had changed.
Starting beneath the large canvas
awning that stretched the length of the
High Street side of the
store, hundreds of men lined
up two-, three- and sometimes
four-abreast up High north to State,
where the line turned the corner
and kept going west. The human
column began to form on Monday
night, long before the announced
9 a.m. Tuesday sale of 3,000
general admission tickets

*The pressure throughout
the 1919 season was
unremitting on Chic.
At left, his teammate
Pete Stinchcomb.*

Chic

to that Saturday's Ohio State-Illinois game. Almost a month had passed since the historic win over Michigan, and OSU wins over Purdue and Wisconsin heightened the focus on this game, which could mean a third unbeaten season and third league championship in the three years Chic had played. All reserved tickets had sold out early, mail orders had been returned with money refunded, and this was the last, best chance to see the season's final game. There was no other way.

Actually, there was one. A "Mr. Gammil" placed a 3 x 5 ad in the *Dispatch* sports section: *Football Tickets, I would like to buy—pay liberally for SIX SEATS in Box 11, East Bleachers, Saturday's Football Game, OSU vs. Illinois. Call Mr. Gammil—Citz. Phone 5352.*

BEFORE THE MICHIGAN GAME, Mr. Gammil would never have sprung for an ad that size to buy tickets to see the Ohio State football team play. Before 1916, there was no reason to purchase any kind of ad. A fan could purchase all the tickets he needed to any game. But the old, understated Ohio State football was gone forever. The Tuesday after that 1919 game in Ann Arbor, Harvey A. Miller was writing about the new U-shaped stadium that had been proposed at Ohio State and how the $500,000 it supposedly would cost was an eminently safe investment. "When Illinois comes here November 22," he wrote, "a crowd of 25,000 would be willing to look in but no more than 18,000 likely will be accommodated."

The lines at Lazarus, the Schoedinger-Marr store, and Hennick's restaurant seemed to prove Miller's point. The crowd at Schoedinger-Marr was so desperate for tickets that two showcases were broken by overzealous buyers, and the store had to stop the sale and clear the store. Herb Hennick noticed an unusual number of young men hanging around in his restaurant about 8 o'clock Monday evening.

He asked if they had already finished their studies for the night and they said they were waiting for football tickets to go on sale the following morning. About fifteen of them had congregated there by 10 o'clock, including some freshmen fraternity pledges who had been sent by their frat brothers to get tickets. But some of the overnighters were described as middle-aged men, including one guy who brought a thermos full of coffee to get him through until morning.

If the hysteria over the game seemed a bit outrageous, it had grown steadily since Chic Harley burst on the scene as a sophomore. And the win over Michigan had turned football into a Columbus obsession. In a city that barely acknowledged

Pete Stinchcomb was the other OSU back, overshadowed by Chic Harley yet a great back—and an All-American—in his own right. Here, he carries against Illinois in 1919.

the sport twenty years before, it had become more important than baseball, more important than politics.

Even a conference championship wasn't enough. A week after Ohio State beat Michigan, reporters asked Lynn St. John about the possibility of the Buckeyes meeting Colgate for "the championship of the United States," should both teams finish unbeaten.

"No chance," the Ohio State athletic director said.

OSU ATHLETIC OFFICIALS were against lengthening the season. They believed extra games were a hardship for players who must continue training beyond the end of the regular schedule. But the fact that reporters were talking about the possibility—both in Columbus and on the east coast—shows how little the human thought process has changed over the decades. Of course it would be nice to win that conference title. But proving that your team was better than all the others would be even better.

While the press busied itself with such fanciful notions, the Buckeyes had other things to worry about. Michigan may have been the game everyone had circled on the schedule, but it wasn't the last one. The players had to win three more games to finish unbeaten, no easy feat after beating a rival in what was supposed to be the game of the year. Miller, ahead of his time again, wondered in print how long it would be before Ohio State and Michigan would meet at the end of the season rather than in the middle.

"Of course when Michigan was full grown as a football institution, Ohio State was still a babe," Miller wrote. "Naturally, Minnesota or some other big rival was the traditional foe. All of that has changed now. When the needed stadium is finished at Ohio Field the time will have arrived for this important alliance for a closing date. And what an attraction it will be to lead up to!"

For now, though, Purdue, Wisconsin, and Illinois closed out the schedule, and the latter two, at least, would be tough.

JACK WILCE SURPRISED EVERYBODY by not starting Harley against Purdue, going with C.J. (Jack) Farcasin instead. If Harley were being punished for some indiscretion, it wasn't written about at the time and 55 years later Farcasin claimed not to know the reason

"For some reason. . . the right half job was mine," Farcasin told the *Columbus Citizen-Journal's* Tom Keys. "After a scoreless first half, Harley came in and on his first carry ran 40 yards for a touchdown. But we were called for a holding and penalized. On the next play there went Chic again. . . a touchdown. If ever there was a perfect football player, he was it."

Farcasin's memory is accurate in describing Harley's talents; on the game itself, his memory is a little blurry. Harley actually scored a 30-yard touchdown the first time he had the ball, shaking off four Purdue defenders, including two who appeared to have a hold on his legs, and then had two touchdown runs called back later. The details are unimportant; all that matters is that the Buckeyes won 20-0 and moved one week closer to another unbeaten season.

Only two games stood between Harley and the end of his college career, and professional football teams were already bidding for his services. Between the Purdue and Wisconsin games, Vernon "Mac" McGinnis of the Akron Pros offered Chic $500—a sum that would be equivalent to almost $6500 today—to play with his team the Sunday following the Illinois game. Probably to avoid being roundly criticized by Ohio State rooters in his home state, McGinnis hinted that if Harley wanted to play basketball or baseball later in the school year, he didn't want to get in the way of that, and oh, by the way, he would like to have a shot at Harley's services next fall after he was out of college.

News accounts were vague, although the Akron Pros apparently wasn't the only professional team to contact him. In a day when players could join a pro team immediately after their final college game, this was a way for both a player and a team manager to make a few fast bucks, especially with a high profile player such as Harley.

Chic had received star treatment since he was a high school sophomore; the attention he got now rivaled that of any famous athlete, actor, or war hero. When the team left Union Station on Thursday night train for Wisconsin, the *Ohio State Journal's* Walter Chamblin estimated that 5,000 people showed up to send them off, and as always, Harley drew most of the cheers.

"Cries of 'Yea, Chic' filled the air," Chamblin wrote. "'Harley, Rah,' 'Team, Rah,' 'Coach, Rah' came on top of each other."

The thirty-one players walked single file through the "howling throng" with Harley, "a broad grin spread from ear to ear," safely tucked in the middle of the group.

"Dozens of girls patted him on the back as he passed by," Chamblin wrote. "Many grabbed his hands. Cries of 'It's up to you, Chic' greeted him."

CHIC AND HIS TEAMMATES made it on the sleeper that had been reserved for them and many of the students tried to force their way onto the car's platform, but the doors were quickly closed. In the days before rock stars, this may have been as close to idol treatment as any human being had ever received.

As much as Harley appreciated the affection, the idea that it was indeed "up to him" may have begun to weigh on him. The final three games invite questions of whether Harley was beginning to experience emotional problems that would plague him later, and whether Wilce had noticed any behavioral change that might have resulted from it. After not starting against Purdue, Chic started at Wisconsin but carried the ball very little for the first three quarters. Wilce could have been reacting to a statement by Wisconsin coach John Richards—Wilce's predecessor at Ohio State—that the Buckeyes are "a one-man team," or perhaps it was a way to confuse the scouts sent there by Illinois coach Bob Zuppke. Then again, maybe something else was going on.

Chic

Harley still managed to be the hero of Ohio State's 3-0 win, scoring on a drop-kick in the fourth quarter that was set up by his own 70-yard punt. In the fourth quarter, he also ran wide and threw an apparent touchdown pass to Pete Stinchcomb, but the play was called back because the referee said Harley was not the required five yards behind the line of scrimmage, as the rules of the day required. Even so, Harvey Miller called Wilce's strategy of not unleashing Harley until the fourth quarter "peculiar," and it still looks that way almost ninety years after the fact.

Perhaps Wilce was simply trying to take some of the pressure off Chic. The coach admitted years later that his star running back had done some things during the 1919 season that seemed a little strange to him, so he must have sensed that something was occurring that wasn't quite right.

BEFORE THE WISCONSIN GAME, Harley was quoted in the *Ohio State Journal* as saying that he believed "Wisconsin and Illinois are much stronger than Michigan," so he knew a loss was possible. A loss wouldn't be easy for any of the Buckeyes, but after three years of winning every game, the thought of a loss to Illinois in his final game seems to have bothered Harley most of all.

At a pep rally in the gymnasium the night before the game, Harley "broke down" after he said a few words to his supporters. Farcasin remembered that on the night before the game, Harley couldn't sleep.

"He walked all night," Farcasin said. "I'm sure he had his final high school game in mind, when East lost to North."

Harley apparently had other things to think about as well. Chamblin reported that during practice on Thursday Harley "was limping a little in one leg, but it is thought that he will be primed for the fray before Saturday." Because this was the first and only time any of the local newspapers referred to the injury, it seems likely that he injured his knee or leg during practice and after it was first reported, Wilce might have asked the local reporters to stop writing about it. Harley obviously knew he wasn't 100 percent, which may explain why he was so nervous.

Most Ohio State rooters were unaware of the injury. The latest edition of *The Sun-Dial*, a campus humor magazine once edited, illustrated, and written by Harley's old East High schoolmate, James Thurber, came out the day before the game and had a cover photo of Chic carrying the ball. A Saturday morning story in the *Ohio State Journal* that reported on plans to start a fund-raising effort for a 50,000-seat stadium, noted that it "may possibly be known as Harley Field."

The Buckeyes had won every game they had played with Harley in three seasons. He always delivered when the team most needed it—he asked for a clean shoe as a sophomore and kicked the game-winning field goal against these same Illini. It seemed preposterous to even consider the possibility of him failing now.

So while a restless Harley walked the campus area streets on Friday night, his mind a muddle of anxious thoughts, most of Columbus worked itself into a frenzy. There was dancing to Young's Famous University Orchestra in the Victory Room of the Neil House, impatient milling in the lobbies of the Deshler, Southern, and Chittenden hotels, a pep rally at the Armory, crowds of students in Marzetti's and Hennick's, and who knows how many out-of-town visitors thrilled to be ordering sundaes—*wink, wink*—in some of those "converted" Short North saloons.

THE CITY FILLED UP WITH PEOPLE THAT FRIDAY. The Illinois football team practiced at Neil Park. Harley's father and most of his brothers and sisters came in by train from Chicago, although Mom was back home nursing one of Chic's brothers. A small army of newspaper reporters converged on Columbus, including three from Chicago and former Ohio State football coach Jack Ryder, now writing for the *Cincinnati Enquirer*. Former North High coach Earl Prugh brought his entire Troy High School squad over from the western part of the state. A large contingent of former OSU stars and coaches, including former Buckeye coach Al Hernstein and recent star Howard Courtney, now a high school coach in Toledo, descended on the city from all over the Midwest. Frank Crumit, assistant coach George Trautman's brother-in-law, was among the hundreds of alums who came back for homecoming. Crumit was just another face in the crowd, but he had written a song, *Buckeye Battle Cry*, especially for the Illinois game and heard it played for the first time at the 7 p.m. pep rally.

When Columbus crawled out of bed on Saturday morning, it was obvious there had never been a day quite like this one in the city's 107-year history. Hundreds of people lined up at the Ohio Field ticket windows, many before daybreak, hoping that they could secure one of several hundred standing room tickets that St. John had said would be put on sale at noon.

Because of the cold November air, some of them started small fires on the sidewalk, and the warm glow from dancing flames gave the area a surreal appearance.

As the black sky turned a pale blue before sunrise, a remarkable scene came into focus. The temporary bleachers that had been erected at the south and north ends of Ohio Field now nearly encircled the playing surface, leaving only narrow spaces for fans to reach their seats. It was a radical transformation, and little Ohio Field wore the changes like a hobo who had been given a new suit. The plain two-sided stadium suddenly seemed like an uncomfortable, ill-fitted offspring of the famous Yale Bowl.

Dozens of fans perched like birds in the trees near the field. Faces began to fill the windows in the houses facing the north end field along Woodruff Avenue, and one of the homeowners even erected a small bleacher in his front yard to hold all of his friends. A special train from Akron carrying sixteen carloads of the city's businessmen and alumni arrived Saturday morning, including approximately a hundred passengers without game tickets. They were forced to pay scalpers between $15 and $25 for tickets, and they were probably grateful to do it. Some fans were said to have paid as much as $50 for a ticket, unheard of in the day of the five-cent movie. In today's dollars, those desperate fans shelled out approximately $650.

And yet, in the football hysteria of the moment, the buyers obviously considered it a bargain. Less than a month after the biggest game in Ohio State football history, it suddenly seemed as if the Buckeyes were about to play an even bigger one. There was no way to know for sure, but it seemed foolish to take the chance.

RESTLESS FANS MOVED FROM HIGH STREET to their places inside Ohio Field and the static-charged air seemed to move with them. The spectators yelled encouraging shouts to the families of some of the Ohio State players, sang along with the band, and erupted in a loud cheer when little Chic Harley Aquila, son of Ohio Field groundskeeper Tony Aquila, appeared on the field in a scarlet and gray outfit. Most were certain the Buckeyes were going to win, for since Harley had been on the team, they always had. They were sure Chic would be terrific, even though they couldn't account for the nervous internal churning which seemed to say all that certainty was no such thing.

And from the game's outset, Harley wasn't terrific. He wasn't as quick or as shifty. He didn't seem to be making those sharp Harley cuts. There was no Harley magic or daring, no Harley verve. He was like a housefly made sluggish by the cold winter air, a creature that had somehow lost the knack for its customary evasiveness. His runs were stopped one, two, three yards from the line of scrimmage. In the first quarter, the Buckeyes got a big scoring chance when Dutch Sternaman lost a fumble at the Illini 29-yard line. But three Harley runs netted a total of five yards, and Chic missed a field goal try.

The crowd shifted uneasily. Some of the fans had read somewhere that Chic had been limping a little in practice. As the game progressed, there were more than a few nervous whispers in the stands. Surely, Harley wasn't hurt. That couldn't be what they were seeing now. He seemed to be limping a little—well, no, maybe that was just the imagination—but there was something. . . something. . .

NEITHER TEAM WAS ABLE TO MOVE THE BALL. They took turns punting. Defense dominated. Later in the period, a Harley pass was intercepted. Illinois was forced to punt again. The Buckeyes' offense continued to sputter, then took a 15-yard penalty that forced Chic to punt from behind his own goal line. He got off a booming kick and Bob Fletcher caught it and was tackled immediately at the 50 and it seemed that the Buckeyes had escaped from serious jeopardy.

But on the first play, Sternaman raced around the left end, and the Illini interference lined up perfectly. One, two, three Ohio State players were blocked and suddenly Sternaman broke into the clear and went 50 yards for a touchdown. Harley was one of the last players blocked—yes, a tentative Harley—before Sternaman reached the end zone. The extra-point kick was missed, but the fans in Ohio Field were stunned. Illinois led 6-0.

After that, defense on both sides dominated until almost the end of the third quarter. Finally, Harley broke free and returned a punt to the Illinois 37 and the crowd exhaled for the first time in over an hour. Pete Stinchcomb gained one yard. Harry Bliss tried a sweep and was stopped for no gain. Harley's pass fell incomplete on third down. Then on a fourth and nine, Chic fired what one writer called a "wonder pass" cross-field to Clarence McDonald, who caught the ball near the sideline at the two-foot line. On the next play, Harley went off tackle for a touchdown and there was pandemonium on North High Street. Chic's extra-point kick hit the inside of the upright and went through, and the Buckeyes had a 7-6 lead.

Harley still wasn't Harley, though. His runs weren't crisp and his passes were off the mark; the Buckeyes completed only two of 13 passes and most were attempted by Chic. The Ohio State offense continued to misfire, but as the fourth quarter unfolded and the two teams traded more punts, it appeared as if the lead would hold up.

The Buckeyes moved the ball close enough to the Illinois goal in the middle of the fourth quarter for Lloyd Pixley to try a 43-yard place-kick that would give Ohio some breathing room. Instead, the attempt was blocked and it nearly turned into a disaster. Sternaman grabbed the ball and raced 23 yards, and after another abortive series, the Illini lined up to try a 33-yard place-kick for the lead. Regular kicker Ralph Fletcher was hurt, so Dick Reichle would be kicking in his place. It was a break for the Buckeyes, but it didn't cut the tension—this kick could determine the success of Ohio State's season. Reichle got the kick off, it cleared the line of scrimmage and . . . missed. OSU's 7-6 lead was intact.

THE SENSE OF RELIEF WAS ONLY TEMPORARY. The Buckeyes still couldn't move the ball. Illinois defenders were all over Harley and Stinchcomb, and Chic's passes weren't close. But the Illini backs weren't going anywhere either, Illinois was behind, and time was running out. Finally, after a Harley punt pushed Illinois back to its own 20, a desperate Coach Zuppke instructed halfback Larry Walquist to throw on every down. After two long passes to Chuck Carney moved the ball to the Ohio State 20, it appeared that there might be time enough for only one more play.

The Illinois players didn't seem aware of how much time was left—the field judge kept the time on the field and there was no visible game clock as there is today. Illinois seemed to be taking too much time in getting a play called. Seeing that, Zuppke quickly grabbed the player closest to him, Clarence Ems, and sent him in for Wayne Middleton at guard. Under the rules of the day, that stopped the clock until the ball was snapped, and by doing so, the Illinois coach may have saved the game.

Eight seconds remained as Ems carried in Zuppke's instructions. Bob Fletcher, brother of the regular kicker, was to attempt the first place kick of his career. It was a gamble, but given his team's offensive struggles, it seemed a better option to Zuppke than a pass. One swing of the leg, one kick, would determine the Western Conference championship.

For the second time in the fourth quarter, nervous Ohio State fans watched as an Illinois player's kick sailed over the line of scrimmage toward the goal posts. They craned their necks and stood on their toes to get a better look. Some covered their eyes. Some begged fate for a favor—*oh, please, please, please, please*—and many prayed to a scarlet and gray God to make the ball curl right or left and . . . it went through. It may have been a long shot, but Fletcher's 30-yard kick sailed between the uprights with five seconds left, giving Illinois a 9-7 lead.

THE OVERFLOW CROWD, so certain of victory only seconds before, was stunned. The game wasn't finished, but Harley couldn't hold back his tears. The Buckeyes had a chance for one more play, and Harley was crying as he threw a pass that fell incomplete. The field judge approached the referee, told him the game was over, and Harley's tears turned into a torrent. His college football career was over, and it had ended in defeat.

While the Illinois players celebrated their dramatic victory, an eerie silence fell over the huge Ohio Field crowd. Many fans sobbed, as much from the sight of their heart-broken hero as from their own anguish. Some of the spectators turned away, shielding their eyes from an agonizing scene of the school's greatest athletic hero leaving the field sobbing like a grief-stricken child. The band began to play *Carmen Ohio* and fans began to sing, their attention temporarily diverted from the players and their sorrow. Teammates tried to calm Chic, but he was inconsolable. He seemed unable to stop weeping, and so his teammates surrounded him tenderly and led him off the field and toward the Athletic House.

"I can't recall a game when he wasn't personally responsible for a victory," Farcasin recalled later. "And when we lost Chic's final game, we couldn't get him out of the dressing room until midnight. He cried. He thought he had let us down."

Center Fritz Holtkamp, writing under his own name in the *Dispatch*, said it was Chic's nature to give credit to others and take all the blame himself.

"Chic Harley. . . was as wonderful in defeat as he had been after his many victories," Holtkamp wrote. "The only difference was that in defeat he took all of the blame for the loss, while in victory all his praise was for the other man."

The team was toasted and cheered at the homecoming banquet at the Armory that evening, but Harley wasn't there. Whether he was still back in the dressing rooms in the Athletic House, as Farcasin suggested, or with his family, there was no doubting how he took the defeat. In Columbus, the cruelty the loss inflicted on Harley made it all the more painful for everyone else. It seemed almost unfathomable that fate would treat him this way.

"HE'S GONE," JOHN A. WARD WROTE in the *Ohio State Journal*. "It was the irony of circumstance that his last game should have been his poorest. That his only defeat should have been his last. That his physical condition should have tripped the drive in those wonderful legs in his final appearance as a Western Conference star.

"It was all the blind injustice of destiny. The inevitable crisis which every superman of football must face as long as there is sand left in the hourglass.

"During the three years of his activity on Western Conference gridirons, Harley has overshadowed every halfback in the West. Today, the starlight of Ohio's most famous football player shines forth with all its accustomed luster. America today knows no greater halfback than Captain Charles W. Harley of Ohio State.

"It was against Illinois that he first sprung into the beacon rays of stardom. It was against Illinois that he concluded his college football career with the cheeriest embers of defeat smoldering about him. Fame is a jealous friend.

"Illinois befriended Chic and Illinois betrayed Chic.

"Like the dawn he came. Like the night he departed. It is natural. It was true to life. Inevitable."

Inevitability comes in many shapes, though, and here was another one: After drawing an estimated 20,000 fans for the Illinois game, after hearing St. John say that he might have sold 55,000 to 60,000 tickets if he had the seats, the Ohio State board of trustees met three days later and signed a resolution giving St. John the go-ahead to begin the process of building a new football stadium.

Chic Harley had lost a game, but he had won something bigger than a game.

dreams of the shoe

If Chic Harley was the school's football Messiah, Thomas E. French was its prophet. Before Harley was even a student at *East High* School, the engineering drafting professor had an astonishing vision. He saw Ohio State's small-time, so-so football program playing its games in a concrete, horseshoe-shaped stadium. This was 1908. The athletic board French served on recommended substantial improvements to little Ohio Field

The one-time med student, St. John (left), wanted a stadium three times bigger than the biggest crowd to ever see an OSU game.

—substantial as in the erection of wooden bleachers on the east side to increase capacity from 4,200 to 6,100—and French was dreaming of a "magnificent concrete stadium." In those days, even major league baseball teams hadn't made the move from wood to concrete and steel; Philadelphia's Shibe Park and Pittsburgh's Forbes Field would start that trend the following year.

Nonetheless, in explaining the improvements to little Ohio Field in the *Alumni Quarterly*, French risked publicly identifying himself as one of those academic eggheads without a shred of common sense by penning these words: "It is hoped that this is only the beginning of the final Ohio Field. The fence will be continued around the entire enclosure, with perhaps behind the bleachers a concrete wall paneled for bronze tablets to be left by future classes; and with the continued splendid financial management and the support of the alumni the dream of a magnificent concrete stadium in horseshoe shape may be realized sooner than anyone would expect."

The truth is, no one but French expected it. Ohio State's membership in the Western Conference was still five years away. Jack Wilce was still playing football for Wisconsin. Lynn St. John was still coaching and finishing up his bachelor's degree at Wooster College. Harley, Pete Stinchcomb, and most of the other players who would make the program famous were still a bunch of kids whose only glory had come on their local sandlots.

From a hundred years away, it isn't hard to see what French saw, crazy as it must have seemed to every man, woman and child he passed on the Columbus streets. The kind of stadium he was dreaming about did exist, just not in the Midwest. Out on the east coast, then the blinding sun in college football's expanding universe, similar stadiums had begun to sprout. Harvard built a concrete U-shaped stadium in 1903 that seated 50,000, the first of its kind for American intercollegiate athletics. Yale followed with a massive bowl-shaped structure in 1908, upping the seating capacity to more than 70,000. Palmer Stadium, a 45,000-seat horseshoe-shaped stadium at Princeton, was a realistic dream that would open six years later.

By comparison, the "substantial" improvements French and his associates had gotten approved for Ohio Field show how much of a football backwater Columbus was. For $30,000, an ugly board fence at the field's south end was replaced with an iron railing, bleachers were erected on the east side, and the south end of the

THE OHIO STADIUM

*An architect in the OSU architecture department drew plans
for a horseshoe-shaped stadium as early as 1918. After the
1919 season, sentiment for it floated heavenward.*

structure was extended ten feet, making the area about 800 by 500 feet.

The fence—a few notches below magnificent in the architectural pecking order—caused a stir. Eight feet high, it ran 172 feet along High Street and 400 feet across the south side, up to the grandstand on the west side. "OHIO FIELD" was spelled out on top in colored tiles. Flagpoles were erected to display visiting team colors as well as those of the Buckeyes.

There were eight covered gates on the south side with turnstiles that registered the number of fans who came through. On the southeast and southwest corners of the field, there were two sixteen-foot gates. Along the south curve of the quarter-mile track surrounding the field was a four-and-a-half foot railing on which brown canvas was hung during games to cut off views from the outside.

It was an improvement, but Ohio Field wasn't the Yale Bowl. But other than French, no one could even see the day when there would be a need for it.

To THIS POINT, THERE HAD BEEN NO REASON to believe French was a visionary. Born in Mansfield, Ohio, in 1871, he had worked as a draftsman before entering Ohio State in 1891. In school at OSU, he continued his work as a draftsman, and when he graduated in 1895, he was immediately given a teaching job. That was, incidentally, the year Harley was born.

French's wife died in 1903, five years into his marriage, leaving him to raise an infant daughter. He seemed determined to fill the void by plunging deeply into university business. He was bright and ambitious; he would later write a textbook, *The Manual of Engineering Drawing*, which became an educational best-seller, and he also designed and drew the OSU seal. His brother, Edward, had been captain of the football team in 1896, and early on, Thomas devoted a great deal of time to the school's loosely-organized athletic programs. He helped recruit volunteer coaches. He helped schedule games with other Ohio schools. He was an advocate for teams in all sports, and it wasn't long before he was called to serve on the university's athletic board.

His ideas might not have mattered much if William Oxley Thompson hadn't become president of the university. Thompson, a Presbyterian minister, also had a vision but it didn't start with football. Since moving from the Miami University president's office to the same position at Ohio State in 1899, he was determined to raise the school's stature. The land grant institution he took over had 1,100 students and was derisively called the "college of the cornfield." He saw it growing into one of the great universities of the Midwest. French's vision of athletics fit the president's plans for the university as a whole because Thompson could also see into the future. When he retired in 1925, there were more than 14,000 students on campus and it was the fifth largest school in America.

The other man who gave credence to French's idea was Lynn St. John. St. John attended Ohio State in 1900 at the age of 23 and played football one season before being called home due to a death in his family. He coached at Fostoria High School the following year, then went to the College of Wooster, where he both coached and attended school at the same time.

St. John planned to become a doctor, and he took the athletic director's job at Ohio Wesleyan with that in mind. Delaware, Ohio, was close enough to Columbus for him to commute to Ohio Medical College, and he did that from 1909 to 1911. When Thompson decided to reorganize the school's athletic program, St. John had a chance to end all that wearisome travel. Thompson created a new athletic board and made French its chairman. The hiring of year-round coaches with faculty status was part of the reorganization, and after French brought in John Richards as athletic director and football coach, St. John was hired as football line coach, head basketball and baseball coach, and athletic business manager. St. John wouldn't have to commute from Delaware to Columbus, but he discovered he didn't have time to continue medical school.

When Richards resigned early in the winter of 1913, French and the other board members promoted St. John to athletic director without even asking if he were interested. Saddled with all this new responsibility, St. John gave up his dreams of a medical career.

St. John also wasn't afraid to think big. He was just a little later to the game than French was. Once the school joined the Western Conference in 1913, St. John, too, started to see the day coming when Ohio State would need a bigger stadium. If he didn't share French's 1908 vision of a concrete horseshoe, his mind started working overtime in 1916 after Chic Harley began to perform his feats on the football field.

French was still ahead of St. John, but not for long. In a speech to the Columbus Chamber of Commerce in 1915, French, now the school's faculty representative to the Western Conference, said he could foresee the day when more than 50,000 would attend Ohio State football games. The idea still seemed far-fetched, but now it came across as more exaggeration than fantasy.

"It was in 1915 that the first preliminary notion of some kind of stadium began to develop," French wrote in the *Columbus Dispatch* stadium edition on Ohio Stadium dedication day in 1922. "The increasing interest in football and the demand for seats was overtaxing the capacity for Ohio Field and the temporary expedients were reaching their limit.

"We had bought circus seats, most uncomfortable things, as those who had to sit on them well remember, had rented movable stands and built standing platforms until all available space had been filled, and Director St. John said in desperation, 'We've got to tear down this field and build a larger one.'"

This is where Harley and his teammates came in.

"When the 1916 season came, with seat orders totally over twice the possible number that could be crowded in, some real action was started," French wrote. "After proposing and abandoning various schemes for rebuilding on the old field, there was advanced by the director the idea of building a bowl in the adjacent woods and keeping the old field for track and baseball."

AFTER HARLEY AND HIS TEAMMATES won the Western Conference championship in 1916 in front of record crowds, the trustees met in February, 1917, and "looked with favor" on the 40,000-seat bowl-shaped stadium. They even dedicated the woods to the west of Ohio Field for that purpose. Thompson embraced the concept and the plan gained momentum, but when he saw the plans and realized that the stadium would be ten feet taller than the new library and cover ten times the area, he had second thoughts. Thompson also worried about how the growing use of automobiles would impact the campus on game day. He asked university architect Joseph Bradford to find another location; Bradford proposed the Olentangy River flood plain at the northwest corner of the campus, bottom land used by the school's college of agriculture to grow corn and other crops.

All the while, the interest generated by Harley and his teammates was making the whole idea seem less and less ludicrous. French asked architecture department colleague Howard Dwight Smith to draw up plans for a horseshoe-shaped stadium as early as 1918, and after the 1919 Illinois game, almost everyone got behind the idea. St. John was now more convinced of the need for it than French was, and when French had Smith design a 50,000-seat horseshoe-shaped stadium that could also accommodate a 220-yard running track, St. John wanted to make it 60,000. The young athletic director might have been late to the bandwagon, but now he was driving it.

It would be interesting to know why St. John thought a 50,000-seat stadium—which would have dwarfed most of its 1919 counterparts—wouldn't be large enough. An overflow crowd of 17,000 was by the far the largest crowd in school history. There was no compelling evidence that a 60,000-seat stadium would be needed at any time in the future. St. John said after the Illinois game that "between 55,000 and 60,000 tickets could have been sold," but it sounded like the words of a man laying the public groundwork for his own grandiose dream. If demand doubled from where it was in 1919, a 35,000-seat structure would easily accommodate the crowds. He was proposing a stadium to hold a crowd more than three times larger than the largest crowd the program had ever drawn.

Perhaps St. John was simply being carried away by his own ambitions. But given his career as one of the nation's foremost athletic administrators, it seems more likely that he had a better view of the future of college football and its place in Columbus than almost any of those around him. As with Thompson and French, St. John also seemed to have a window on the future. The university didn't have just two visionaries now, but three.

THE TRUSTEES GAVE THEIR APPROVAL of a new stadium on university land, but they refused to pay for it. Thompson lent his support, but he wanted the public to finance it. He didn't want to ask the legislature for favors; he wanted to save them for academic projects. So privately, Thompson, St. John, and French hatched a plan that would include a public campaign to raise the money to finance construction. The campaign would begin with a Stadium Week celebration the following October.

Construction of a stadium might have happened without Harley, but it wouldn't have happened this way and certainly not this soon. In Madison, Wisconsin, Camp Randall Stadium was erected in 1917 with an initial capacity of 10,000. Michigan, the Midwest's oldest and strongest football power, was making plans to expand Ferry Field from 21,000 to 42,000, which it did in 1921.

THE OHIO STADIUM

*When a model of the proposed stadium was unveiled in late 1920,
there was a collective public gasp—the magnificent structure would seat
63,000, nearly 20,000 more than the famous coliseum in Rome.*

Chic

A 60,000-seat stadium in Columbus, where Ohio State football teams had struggled to draw even 10,000 fans less than ten years before, seemed crazy to those without the vision, which included just about everybody but French, Thompson, and St. John.

So the principals tried to keep the actual capacity of the stadium a secret for as long as possible. They didn't want the growing momentum halted by some spoilsport asking why his money was going to build a pie-in-the-sky boondoggle.

In the meantime, Clyde Morris of the school's engineering department was sent east to look at other stadiums built mostly with concrete, a relatively new material. Most concrete buildings were less than twenty years old, so it was difficult to ascertain how well it would hold up beyond that. Morris looked at the stadiums at Harvard and Yale, New York's Polo Grounds, and seven-year-old Palmer Stadium at Princeton, which had some crumbling concrete. Morris dismissed the Princeton's problem as an isolated case; he determined that it was the result of a poor mix and not the material itself.

French pulled out the plans Smith had drawn up for a horseshoe-shaped stadium in 1918, and St. John again convinced French that bigger was better. Consequently, he asked Smith to build it as large as possible, which in this case, meant 63,000 permanent seats. The stadium's south stands, on the open end of the horseshoe, was years away.

ONLY THE MOST IMPORTANT PIECE OF THE PUZZLE—the financing—had yet to fall into place. Just eleven months after people had climbed trees and telephone poles to see Chic Harley's last game against Illinois in Ohio Field, the campaign for a massive new stadium went public with a campus-wide ox-roast and carnival supposedly designed to celebrate the school's fiftieth anniversary.

Simon Lazarus, owner of the Lazarus department store, was in charge of publicity, and he intended to make sure everyone in the state knew about it. He invited representatives from every Ohio newspaper to attend the carnival—October 16, 1920—piquing their interest with the promise that something truly newsworthy was going to be announced. Those who came were glad they did. A model of the proposed stadium was unveiled and the public gasped. This would be a big event not only for Columbus, but for any city. The Colosseum in Rome seated just 45,000, and Ohio Stadium would seat 63,000. The public was being asked to donate $1,000,000 for construction, but this structure would be as impressive as any stadium ever built.

"Stadium Week" commenced two days later, with more than 3,000 Ohio State students dressed in athletic garb marching down High Street in a parade witnessed by an estimated 100,000 people. Across High near Gay, a giant transparency stretched across the street bearing the message, *Boost Ohio Stadium, It's for Columbus.* The parade culminated in students doing calisthenics on the north lawn of the Statehouse.

On another day that week the OSU infantry and artillery regiments marched downtown, and on yet another day campus fraternities and sororities paraded fifty-one floats with themes promoting the stadium campaign. Music, stunts and short pep talks were given at noon and 5 p.m. each day on the west side of Statehouse. Newspapers ran story after story. A huge electronic horseshoe outside the Deshler Hotel showed how much money had been raised.

On "Ohio State Day," November 26, 1920, subscriptions reached $923,775, of which alumni and citizens in Columbus had contributed $544,500. On January 20, 1921, just over three months after the campaign started, organizers announced that the goal of $1,000,000 had been met.

The board of trustees still had to approve the plan and now that the 63,000-capacity was known, one influential member of the board made it clear that he would fight it. Dr. Thomas Corwin Mendenhall, the first member of the original 1871 faculty and the sole surviving member of that group, said that the new stadium would be much too large and would never be filled. He insisted that it not exceed 35,000 seats. He was also worried about the reliability of concrete and proposed that the stadium be made of brick.

On August 3, 1921, a thousand men with shovels marched to the stadium site on the Olentangy River flood plain and broke ground with Ohio Governor Harry L. Davis before a crowd of 2,500. The new facility was targeted for completion by October 1, 1922, an amazing timetable considering the scope of the structure that was planned. Seating capacity would be 63,000. It would be built with concrete.

the Bears and
Chic

The ordinary boy who became
the extraordinary boy who became
the extraordinary man was ordinary
again. Transitions of that sort are
never easy and this one was no
different. The transformation
from extraordinary to ordinary
must have been painfully difficult
for a man with the increasingly
fragile emotional makeup
of Charles W. Harley. Chic
Harley the *idol* became
Chic Harley the student, and
he had never been much of a
student. He became Chic Harley

*After OSU, George
Halas wanted Chic to play
for the Chicago Staleys.
The pro game of the
1920s was a different
game, though.*

the basketball player, and he had never been much of a basketball player. He possessed extraordinary athletic ability but few basketball skills. Some of his former football teammates were much better basketball players than he was and it showed on the court at the one-year-old Ohio State Fairgrounds Coliseum, where the team had moved from the Armory for the 1919-1920 season. It was the only year Harley played varsity basketball at OSU.

"He played at it," said Andy Nemecek, one of the athletes who played and excelled at both. "He got a letter, but Chic never played very much. He was a drawing card. He'd probably play two or three minutes a game. But Chic was never a basketball player."

BASKETBALL WASN'T A PRIORITY, either for Harley or the school. The move to the Coliseum was an improvement—the Armory seated only 2,000 and the end wall was just a few feet from the basket—but St. John gave up coaching the team that fall and assistant football/basketball/baseball coach George Trautman took over. Trautman was more a football and baseball coach than a basketball coach; even his son, George M. Trautman Jr., described him as "a fill-in." Trautman would become well-known later as the president of the National Association of Professional Baseball Leagues, baseball's minor leagues, and his major contribution to Ohio State athletics outside of the years (1911-1914) he played three sports there was bringing football star Pete Stinchcomb with him from Fostoria, Ohio, where Trautman had coached him in high school.

Harley, Nemecek, basketball captain Clarence MacDonald, and even Trautman didn't pick up a basketball until the football season was over. And while Harley practiced with the basketball team, "at least a dozen different schools" contacted him about coaching football. His late nephew, Richard Wessell, once said he had a letter addressed to Chic from the University of Tennessee offering him the coaching job there. None of the schools were named by the newspapers, but in a day when star athletes sometimes became—without experience—head coaches, there is no reason to doubt the reports. The offers didn't seem to matter to Chic, anyway. Finishing college was paramount to any kind of college coaching career and he was behind in his studies.

Professional football teams also continued to contact him. In his time at Ohio State, Chic said that he had no interest in playing professional football, which was often the norm for college players in that era. Pro football players didn't make much money and the game could be rougher and more physical than its college counterpart; Chic knew that from seeing games of the local Panhandles. He might also have known from first-hand experience.

In the 1979 book, *Halas By Halas*, then-Chicago Bears owner George Halas recalled how a semi-pro club in Taylorville, Illinois, that would become part of a major scandal involving players from the University of Illinois and Notre Dame in 1922, had been "regularly serviced by players from Ohio State University" years earlier. "The 1919 stars," Halas wrote, "were two gentlemen who, despite an abundant application of facial adhesive tape, were recognized as being Chic Harley and Pete Stinchcomb, on their way to All-American greatness."

This may or may not be true, but it's certainly plausible. The early history of pro football is littered with incidents of college players picking up a few extra bucks on Sunday by playing under assumed names for pro teams, and as Taylorville showed two years later when it stocked its team with nine Illinois stars in order to win a game with nearby Carlinville, it wasn't a stickler for rules. When the Taylorville-Carlinville scandal broke in January of 1922, the Taylorville coach even charged that quite a few Western Conference athletes had played pro ball under assumed names, including Harley. Lynn St. John quickly responded, telling the *Ohio State Journal* that he was quite sure that it never happened. His fast denial sounded good, but he couldn't possibly have known for sure.

WHETHER HARLEY AND STINCHCOMB SNEAKED into the Taylorville lineup in 1919 or not, Chic seemed more interested in finishing college in 1920 than he did in playing pro football. That was confirmed in May when he accepted an offer to join the Ohio State coaching staff. It seemed like a perfect fit for both him and the university. He had considered professional baseball—the Columbus Senators had offered him a contract and reportedly the St. Louis Browns were interested in him—but he was still living at the frat house and hadn't finished school. By coaching, he could make a modest living while he kept at his studies.

"Certain it is that Harley has a bunch of little tricks up his sleeve which he will impart to the Scarlet and Gray candidates next fall," the *Dispatch* reported. "It is expected that he will devote considerable of his time to the freshmen in the art of running with the ball, drop-kicking, and all those other tricks in which Chic as a performer was without comparison. He will also assist in other sports as they come along."

It sounded better than it was. Like many an outstanding athlete, Harley's "tricks" were more the result of his own incredible athletic skills than any technique that he could impart to an incoming freshman. The cuts he made were cuts other players couldn't make. Those long punts weren't an acquired skill; he had been booming them since high school. He could run faster, kick farther, and throw with more accuracy than all of his teammates because he was a gifted athlete. These weren't tricks; they were pure athleticism.

His coaching stint turned out to be one-year deal. Harley gradually decided he wanted to play football, not coach it, and pro teams continued to contact him. But pro football at this point still wasn't so much a career as a lucrative hobby, so the offers presented him with something of a quandary. He didn't know if he could afford to quit school to play probably a dozen football games at maybe $100 a game. As much as he might want to play, Chic needed some kind of plan, some kind of situation that would offer him more.

THE OPPORTUNITY HE NEEDED came from an unexpected source. One of Harley's former college rivals, ex-Illinois player George Halas, approached Chic about joining a professional team he had charge of in Decatur, 172 miles south of Chicago. The team's owner, A.E. Staley, had hired Halas in 1920 to come to Decatur and manage, coach, and play on the football and baseball teams that represented the starch company bearing his name. Staley wanted to build the football team into one of the best in the country, to improve employee health and morale as well as spread the name of the A.E. Staley Company across the United States, and Halas's first season with the Staleys had been better than even he expected. The football team had gone 11-1-1, played several games before large crowds in Chicago, and drew 10,800 for a season finale against the unbeaten Akron Indians that had been arranged to decide the "world" title.

Halas was doubly excited by the team's prospects and wanted to make the Staleys even better. Because of his Western Conference background, he naturally thought of Harley. Chic was playing for older brother Bill Harley's Logan Squares semi-pro baseball team that summer in Chicago. Bill saw an opportunity for both himself and Chic, one that would not only bring his brother closer to his family in Chicago but might make it possible for him to actually earn a living from pro football.

Two of the stars on Ohio State's 1920 team, halfback Pete Stinchcomb and guard John Taylor, were also interested in playing pro football, and Bill Harley saw a way to help them while he worked out an arrangement for him and his brother. (Taylor was an irrepressible type, known at Ohio State for occasionally pitching his helmet onto the sidelines and playing a few downs bareheaded.) After some negotiations, the Harleys agreed to a deal on July 21, 1921; they would in effect become managing partners of the Staleys with Halas and Edward "Dutch" Sternaman. They would share profits and losses, and they promised to bring Stinchcomb and Taylor along.

"The new man I sought most for the football team was Chic Harley, a 165-pound All-American back at Ohio State," Halas wrote. "He could pass, kick, and run. His brother Bill offered to supply the team with Chic, Pete Stinchcomb, also an All-American, and John R. Taylor, an aggressive guard known as 'Tarzan,' in return for a percentage of the profit. I accepted. I had no idea of the problem I was creating for myself."

Ironically, Chic might later have said the same thing, even though it seemed like a dream deal at the time. Decatur called itself "The Greatest Little City on Earth," and the players could earn a good living at the starch plant when they weren't playing football. The three Ohio State players were also happy to be going to a team that included an impressive lineup of former college stars, one that had proclaimed itself "world champions," even if officials of the first-year American Professional Football Association (soon to be called the National Football League) back in Canton declared Akron the champion based on the fact that the Indians had lost no games to the Staleys' one. (The NFL doesn't recognize either as champion today.)

Bill Harley went along as the team's business manager, a position which enabled him to keep an eye on the Harleys' financial interests, and all seemed well. The playing field adjoined the factory and had been built for baseball, but Halas remembered it as being "soft as a mattress." He said the "team accommodations were comfortable, with good showers, lockers for each man, and a room for blackboard sessions." With the strong team Halas assembled, this seemed to be pro football nirvana.

Things were different behind the scenes. After the team opened the season with a 35-0 win against Waukegan, a warm-up for a huge game with the powerful Rock Island Independents, Staley called Halas to his office and told him that he thought he should take the team to Chicago. The starch business had taken a turn for the worse, Staley didn't think the team had a long range future in Decatur, and he didn't see how the company could continue to underwrite the expenses there. The five games the Staleys had played in Chicago the previous year had turned the club a nice profit; the first game in Chicago had made more money than three games in Decatur combined. Staley told Halas he would give him $5,000 of seed money, cash to defray the costs until the gate receipts started coming in. In return, all Halas had to do was continue to call the team the Decatur Staleys for the rest of the season and print advertisements for the company in the program. At the end of the season, the team would belong to the four partners.

The Harleys had to be happy when they learned of the move. Not only were they going home, but their payoff from the prior agreement figured to be much larger in Chicago than it could ever be in Decatur. Their agreement gave them each one-fourth of the profits, so the deal Bill Harley struck seemed better now than on the day he made it.

HALAS WENT TO CHICAGO and worked out a deal with Bill Veeck, president of the Chicago Cubs, for the use of Cubs Park, which was later renamed Wrigley Field. He rented ten rooms for $2 per week at the Blackwood Apartment Hotel, 4414 North Clarendon Avenue, which was within walking distance of the park. Then he went back to Decatur, gave his team the news and got ready for the game against Rock Island, the last game that would be played there.

There was an American Legion convention in town and many of the visitors were eager to see the game, so the Staleys doubled the seating capacity of the field to 3,000. Even with the increased capacity, seats were still at a premium. Before the game, scalpers littered the streets and the fans who paid a hefty price for their tickets weren't sorry they did. Harley was a star, setting up one touchdown with a nice pass and passing for the other one in the Staleys' 14-10 win.

Chic was riding high. Bill Harley had gotten him a writing deal with the *Ohio State Journal*. He would pen a series of articles three times a week during October on how to play football, "so as to prove of practical value to players and coaches who wish to follow proven methods during the current gridiron campaign." With three Ohio State stars on the team, the newspaper also printed a short story on every Staleys' game. Local coverage of Halas's team was nearly as good as that for the fading Columbus Panhandles, who had brought in the OSU trio's former teammate, Harry Bliss. Bliss wasn't Harley, though. Local fans were more interested in the Staleys.

With such an auspicious start, it was impossible to foresee the disaster ahead. Pro football was a much different animal than the college game, which Harley and other former Ohio State players soon learned.

"Those were rugged days, especially for the linemen," Tarzan Taylor recalled years later. "If you didn't play the entire sixty minutes, you were considered a sissy. Why, for part of that '21 season we operated with only one substitute lineman, Lou Usher, an All-American from Syracuse, and he played every position in the line."

There was none of the old college rah-rah. Mistakes weren't tolerated. If a player screwed up, he heard about it from his teammates in language that would send grandma into apoplexy. If Harley had received special treatment at Ohio State, it was clear from the outset that he wouldn't receive it here.

If anything, his reputation and his ownership deal made him more of a target for the other players. He was getting more money than they were, so he got more grief for his failures. But then, all the players faced some form of ridicule if they didn't perform.

"If you played a bad first half, it wasn't safe for you to come into the clubhouse," Taylor said. "You'd be berated as a yellow so-and-so and take such a verbal beating that you'd go out for the second half all fired up. I missed a tackle one day, and as soon as I stuck my head inside the dressing room door, the boys began leveling on me. 'So you were a star on that great (1920) Ohio State team, huh? Why, you bum, what do you know about football? No wonder Ohio State blew the (1921) Rose Bowl game.'"

At first, this didn't seem to bother Harley. Two weeks after the team left Decatur, the Staleys won their first game in Cubs Park before 8,000 fans, beating the Dayton Triangles 7-0 in a dull game where Harley's kicking was one of the features. The Staleys' next game with the Canton Tigers was rained out, and the following week, Chic's troubles began.

About a hundred Buckeye fans who had come from Columbus to see Ohio State play Chicago on Saturday stayed over to see the three former Buckeyes play against the Detroit Tigers, and as always, Harley was the center of attention. But instead of being the star, Harley was hit hard, suffered fractured ribs, and had to come out of the game. Stinchcomb scored one touchdown on a quarterback sneak and Sternaman, Halas's former Illinois teammate, scored on a 25-yard run in a 20-9 Staleys win. Harley hadn't done much and he must have heard about it. When he missed the next two games, both wins by the Staleys, his standing with the other players became even more tenuous.

Stinchcomb and Sternaman were playing well, doing many of things that had been expected of Chic, and the Staleys were winning without him. This couldn't have set well with Halas and Sternaman, on the hook for part of their profits to a guy who wasn't playing. The other Decatur players probably saw Harley as an overpaid prima donna who wouldn't play through pain. To make matters worse, Chic had apparently started exhibiting traits that indicated he had problems more serious than his injured ribs.

Jack Wilce's daughter, Dorothy Krause, recalls her mother talking about how Harley began to show signs of mental illness that year with the Staleys.

"I remember her talking about this," Krause said, "that one of the tragedies of Chic's first year in pro ball was the beginning manifestations of his illness, when he would drop the ball and did things that would not be a Chic Harley thing and would get him booed. That was the beginning, I think. People were expecting this great person to do all these magical acts, and the poor thing was suffering."

With Harley still out, Stinchcomb scored on touchdown runs of 85 and 30 yards against the Cleveland Tigers in Chicago on November 20. Four days later on Thanksgiving, Chic wore a steel plate to protect his ribs and returned—as a sub—in a 7-6 loss to the Buffalo All-Stars, a loss that shattered a seven-game Staley winning streak.

HARLEY SHOULDN'T HAVE BEEN USED; his ribs weren't healed, and after he was on the field a few minutes, he had to come out of the game. He tried to re-enter later and the player he was supposed to replace refused to come out for him, and he had to return to the bench in embarrassment. The humiliation Harley felt by this snub, in front of 10,000 fans, seemed to haunt him for the rest of the season. He began to ask brother Bill and his other family members why his teammates would treat him this way.

Meanwhile, back in Columbus, all talk was of a Grid-Grad charity football game on Ohio Field two days later that Harley, Stinchcomb, and Taylor planned to play in. The trio arrived on Friday and worked out with the Starbucks team of former Ohio State stars including Nemecek, Shifty Bolen, Howard Courtney, and Honus Graf, and the *Ohio State Journal* reported that Chic "raced back and forth over the gridiron." He also "tried his toe at drop-kicking, and just like in other days, the ball glided over the bar."

This was the old Harley, which must have been a little befuddling, if not downright exasperating to his Staley teammates. Even with the great Jim Thorpe in town, Harley was the center of attention, and the newspaper remarked upon how good he looked:

"There is no apparent change in Harley's appearance; in fact, he stands in the backfield with his hands on his hips, unexcitable-like, as in Western Conference days."

HARLEY MUST HAVE EXPERIENCED a sense of relief to be back in Columbus, among old friends who appreciated him. A photo of him in the *Ohio State Journal* with Eddie Casey, a former Harvard halfback who won a place on Walter Camp's All-American team with Chic in 1919, shows a fit, smiling Harley, one who seemed to be enjoying himself. He didn't exhibit many of his old talents in the game itself, but the field was a sea of a mud and the newspaper reported that it was clear he hadn't fully recovered from his broken ribs.

Back in Chicago the next day, Stinchcomb was again the star, breaking free for a 45-yard run in the Staleys' 20-0 win over the Green Bay Packers. If Harley played at all, news reports didn't mention him, and it was the same the following Sunday when the Staleys beat Buffalo 10-7, with Stinchcomb making two impressive 30-yard runs.

Chic had become a non-factor. His lower standing on the team was eating at him, a situation apparently exacerbated by the riding he endured from some of his teammates. It seems likely that Halas was now looking for a way to get out of

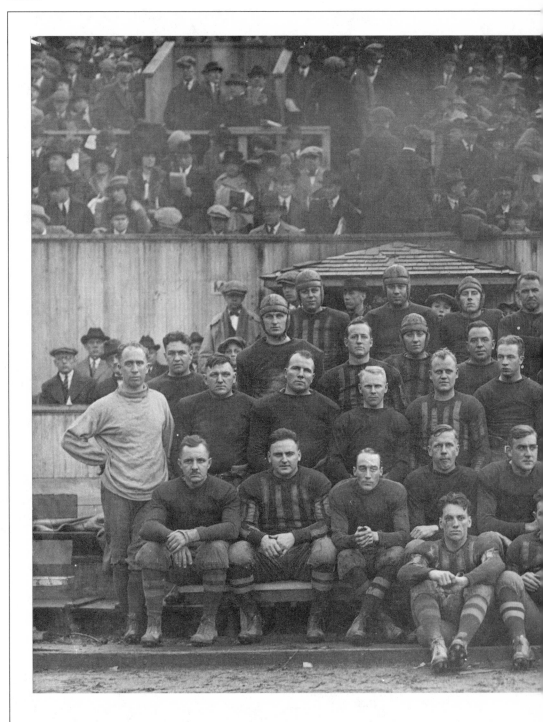

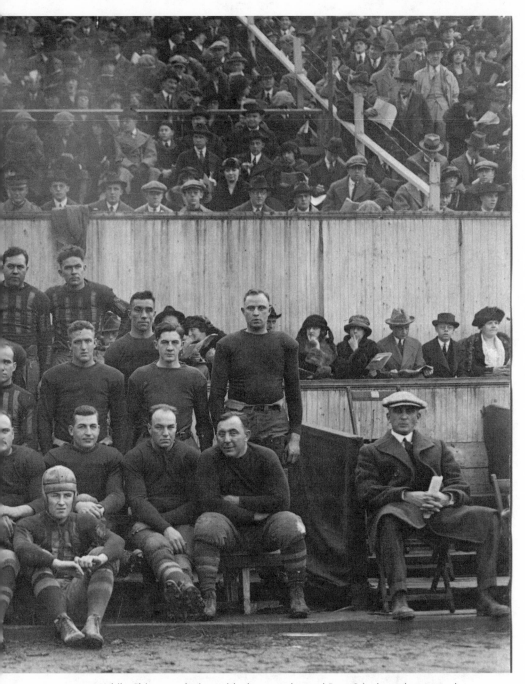

While Chic was playing with the pros, he and Pete Stinchcomb returned to Ohio State for the 1921 Grid-Grad Game. That's Chic, front row, middle, with Stinchcomb to Chic's left. At far left is George Trautman, one of the OSU assistant coaches who coached Chic's team in the grad game.

the deal he had made with Chic and his brother, Bill. Owners had to watch every expenditure closely to make a profit, and Chic was an increasingly unnecessary expense. Another sixty or seventy years would have to pass before rich team owners routinely accepted the risk of guaranteed contracts.

Harley's anxiety grew. He became moody and withdrawn. His ribs were still bothering him. He was a substitute for the first time in his life and he didn't know how to handle it. He began to complain to family members that his teammates were against him, which some undoubtedly were. Many of the players didn't like him, probably for good reason. As the tragic story unfolds, the image of an increasingly despondent Chic begins to fuse with one of a desperate, chain-smoking Chic in the army guard house in 1918. It begins to merge with that of the sobbing, emotional Chic who wouldn't leave the Athletic House until midnight after the 1919 Illinois defeat. Chic had always been sensitive and impulsive, but now his behavior seemed to go beyond that. He was having trouble holding himself together. Something was wrong.

"My dad was always talking about the Staleys, who became the Bears, and how they wanted Chic because they wanted a marquee player," said Bob Harley, grandson of Chic's brother, Bill. "There was always a lot of jealousy among the players, even including some of his former Ohio State teammates. Just not blocking for him, doing things that would make him look bad, and Halas, being a U of I guy.

"Those are all just hearsay things; unless Chic were standing here or my grandfather were standing here, they could substantiate them. By the same token, my grandfather saw it with his own two eyes, in terms of them trying to humiliate Chic. Him being sent out onto the field and maybe a player refusing to come off the field and sending him back. The rules were you could do things like that. It was a tragedy."

CHIC ENTERED THE GAME as a fourth quarter sub for Stinchcomb at quarterback against the Canton Bulldogs on December 11 and threw a 25-yard touchdown pass in a 10-0 win. But he was again a non-factor in the last game of the season, a scoreless tie with the Chicago Cardinals.

Chic slipped out of the park unnoticed, and when Bill Harley asked the others where he had gone, no one knew. Bill stopped by the Blackwood Apartment Hotel and he wasn't there. He hadn't gone to his parents' house. Bill and the family waited, and when Chic still hadn't turned up a couple of hours later, they began a frantic search. They checked all of the places he was known to frequent. They searched the streets and the alleys, becoming more worried as the evening turned into night. Finally, they found him at the corner of State and Madison streets in the heart of the city.

A man powerful enough to raise a 63,000-seat concrete horseshoe from a campus cornfield was sitting on the street corner, crying like a baby.

the stadium
rises

sixteen

The irony makes you squirm.
It pokes and prods until it pricks
even the most callous heart, until it
forces even Chic Harley's adversaries
to see the abject cruelty in the contrast.
On the east side of the *Olentangy*
River on the northwest corner
of campus, workers swarmed
over the ground like determined
locusts, forging steel, positioning
beams and mixing concrete,
building a massive monument to
Harley's football accomplishments
at Ohio State. And all the while
this was happening on that

Even as the stadium
was dedicated, Chic's
behavior was becoming
more unstable, and
he was in and out
of various hospitals.

once-deserted flood plain, something—damaged brain cells, angry chemicals, defective genes—was working just as hard to dismantle the information-processing control center inside Harley's brain.

The contrast is vivid, the irony almost vicious. Ground had been broken for the school's new concrete stadium in August, 1921, and the rapid demolition of Harley's mental health followed it by less than two months. About the time the enormous football palace began to assume its famous horseshoe shape, the official part of Harley's long, tortuous journey into mental illness began.

Hard, wearisome days followed that depressing night on a Chicago street corner. Chic went home with his parents and tried to pull himself together, and he finally returned to Columbus with the idea of getting back in school. He still wasn't well. More incidents must have followed because sometime in early January, Bill Harley and father Charles came to Columbus and persuaded him to accompany them to an unnamed sanitarium in Ishpeming, Michigan, for treatment of what the *Chicago Tribune* called a "partial nervous breakdown."

There is no indication why they decided to take him all the way to such a remote location in Michigan's Upper Peninsula to seek treatment, unless they were hoping to keep Chic's problems out of the newspapers. That didn't happen. In a brief, two-paragraph item, the *Tribune* reported that "it is said that rest will banish the trouble."

If that were an unduly optimistic appraisal, it is only because neither Chic nor his family had any clue what was wrong. The details of his early problems are sketchy. In the 2005 book, *Papa Bear, The Life and Legacy of George Halas*, author Jeff Davis claimed that the Harleys' partnership with Halas and Dutch Sternaman was dissolved because of a medical examination they required of Chic nine games into the season. The Staleys' ninth game would have been against Buffalo on December 4, a game in which the Tribune had him listed in the pre-game lineup:

"The deal collapsed nine games into the season," Davis wrote, "when, in a physical exam Halas and Sternaman demanded for the partnership, doctors discovered that Harley was infected with syphilis. This was before the penicillin cure was discovered, and the disgusted Halas and Sternaman cancelled the deal."

The syphilis story has been around for years, and evidence indicates that it is little more than a persistent urban legend. In the mid 1970s, one of the authors remembers asking an aging reporter about Harley, and after a couple of minutes of praise, the man lowered his voice to a whisper and said, "You know that his mental problems came from a case of syphilis, don't you?" In an interview with an elderly fan for a column in the 1990s, the scene was replayed to the reporter in exactly the same manner, down to the whisper.

When Davis was asked if he had any documentation for the syphilis story, he said that the information had come from "a Halas associate" whom he couldn't name and admitted he "probably should have checked out the story" but didn't.

Given Halas's interest in dissolving the partnership with the Harleys, having this story told by one of Halas's associates adds an intriguing element to the mystery. Even if Chic weren't inflicted with a debilitating venereal disease, if his mental problems stemmed from a high school or college head injury or from something that had occurred while he was under contract to the Staleys, rumor seems the perfect way to get public sentiment—and maybe even the courts—on Halas's side. It would mean that Harley's problems were his problems, that he didn't suffer from emotional issues because he was encouraged to come back too soon from his broken ribs or because of intentionally poor blocking by some of his vindictive teammates. It would mean that the Staleys, i.e., Halas and Sternaman, had done nothing wrong.

THERE IS NO WAY TO KNOW WHETHER HALAS or Sternaman was the source of these rumors, but it seems almost certain that rumors are all they were. In the Ohio State University archives is a small mountain of letters spanning the decades and written among Harley friends, school officials, and doctors at various sanitariums. Syphilis isn't mentioned in any of them. A succession of doctors diagnosed him as suffering from dementia praecox, a mental illness not associated with the venereal disease and one that was eventually categorized as a form of schizophrenia.

When Chic was admitted to the Veterans Administration Hospital in Danville, Illinois, in 1938, he was given a thorough physical and mental examination, and the proof is written plainly on two lines on the second page of the clinical record marked Laboratory Examinations: Both the "Complement Fixation Test for Syphilis" and the "Precipitation Test for Syphilis" are marked "negative," with the names and initials of the doctors who performed the tests. The discovery of penicillin would eventually offer a cure for the disease, but the drug wasn't developed in 1938 and wasn't administered even to test patients until 1942. In effect, if Chic didn't have it in 1938, he didn't have it in 1921.

Bob Harley, grandson of Chic's older brother Bill, doesn't believe the syphilis story for another reason.

"The funny thing about that syphilis thing, nobody in our family knew or ever said anything about that," Bob Harley said. "The only time I ever heard that as a rumor, I happened to be looking at a book on football history and there was some stuff on Chic and it mentioned in passing the syphilis story. I said, 'What?' We'd never seen or had any evidence of that being part of his illness. I even asked my mother and she was aghast. She said no one said anything about that, and there was never anything about people hiding it."

Harley played in the Staleys' final two games after he supposedly had the examination, and in either late December or early January, Halas told Bill Harley that he didn't plan to honor the partnership. Harley subsequently went to Chris O'Brien, owner of the Chicago Cardinals, and asked for his permission to operate a different franchise in Chicago in 1922, separate from Halas and Sternaman, if the league would allow it. He also apparently made inquiries about locating a pro football team in Milwaukee, ninety miles up the road.

DUTCH STERNAMAN'S LITTLE BROTHER, Joey, was a member of the Staleys' team in 1921, and the version of the story he told to Richard Whittingham in the 1984 book, *What A Game They Played,* indicated that he didn't think Chic was even at the heart of the decision to cut the Harleys out.

"They brought in Chic Harley, an All-American from Ohio State, a big shot, one of the biggest names in the game then," Joey Sternaman said. "Along with him was his brother, Bill, a real egotistical fellow. Hell, he wanted to take over the whole thing but Dutch and George were not about to let him do that. 'We're not going to take him in,' Dutch told me. 'That Bill is just too bossy.'"

Bossy or not, Bill Harley planned to fight for what he believed rightfully belonged to him and Chic. He planned to attend the American Professional Football Association's annual meeting on January 27, 1922, in Canton, Ohio, and ask the league to either award the Staleys' franchise to the Harleys or give them a Chicago franchise of their own.

In the days before the meeting, Chic was released from the Michigan hospital and returned to Chicago. Family members still had no idea about the extent of his troubles; they undoubtedly thought his problems stemmed from exhaustion and stress from his injuries, and they apparently were told no different by the medical personnel in Ishpeming. Bill wanted Chic to accompany him on his trip to Ohio. He must have figured that his younger brother could help make his case before owners of the league that would soon be called the NFL.

Chic wanted to visit friends in Columbus, so they left a day early, and the Harleys were luncheon guests of Pete Stinchcomb and his wife, Ann. While he was there, he told the *Ohio State Journal's* Russ Needham that he was unable to account for recent newspapers stories that reported he had been a patient in a sanitarium.

"I haven't been in a sanitarium," Chic said, "and I don't expect to be."

It would be interesting to know what he told the owners of the other APFA teams in the Cortland Hotel in Canton the next day. The owners surely had some idea of what had happened with Chic. Or at least they knew what they had been told by Halas, who was there to request a transfer of the franchise from A.E. Staley to the Chicago Bears Football Club, i.e., Halas and Sternaman. If he or Sternaman had found a way to get the Harley-syphilis story out there among the other owners—and they were permitted to sit in on the all-day meetings with the other owners and the Harleys weren't—that might have sealed the deal.

IN HIS AUTOBIOGRAPHY, Halas made it sound as if the Harleys' appearance at the meeting and their business there was a surprise to him:

"Unexpectedly, Bill Harley produced a startling demand for one-third ownership because of our agreement of the past year," Halas wrote. "He obtained a lawyer and went to court. He came to the Association meeting and asked that the Staley franchise be given to him. The executive committee telephoned Mr. A.E. Staley. He said he had transferred the team to me the previous fall. The company, he said, was quitting all athletics.

"The members debated all day and into the evening. In the end, they decided to vote on whether the franchise should be given to me or Bill Harley. Eight voted for us. Two for Harley. The Chicago Bears were born!"

Bill Harley felt that Halas and Sternaman were trying to pull a fast one, and the evidence indicates they were. In a lawsuit Bill Harley filed against Halas and

Sternaman, he alleged that there had been a deliberate attempt to injure Chic and that the partners had attempted to shut him out of the decision-making process, and many of those charges must have surfaced in the Association discussions. Bill Harley's anger must have been roiling.

It's not surprising the owners chose Halas and Sternaman; the owners knew them better and at that point, they offered more stability than the Harleys did. Chic still wasn't well, and a day of meetings where his own health was a major topic of discussion likely put even further strain on him. Given the bizarre events that followed, his presence in Canton may have done the Harleys' cause more harm than good.

Chic apparently went back to Columbus, where, according to *Time* magazine, he became "morose and pugnacious," traits totally out of character for the pre-Staleys Harley. His condition deteriorated rapidly. His friends grew worried and paid for his admission to an Asheville, North Carolina, sanitarium, and he went there and seemed to improve. He was released, returned to Columbus, had another relapse, and went back to his parents' home in Chicago.

The Columbus-Chicago shuttle emphasized just how sick he was. He didn't belong in either place, but in a hospital. Chic's father wrote a letter to Lynn St. John dated May 7, 1922, indicating that Chic must have been involved in some kind of ugly incident at home, because Chic quickly went back to Columbus and Charles Harley was happy he had gone. His worried father "was glad to hear that you have Charles in (your) charge and hope you'll send him back soon to Asheville, as I think and so does his mother that he can get well quicker their (sic) than any place else. . . Mother and I would love to see him, but not like to have the same experience as the last time. If you can talk him out of the idea of coming to Chicago, do it. . . "

St. John couldn't. He had a long, frank discussion with Chic about his situation, and he wasn't sure how much of it mattered. Chic seemed determined to keep moving, probably so he wouldn't have to go back into the hospital. He immediately left for Detroit to see his friend Dan Carroll and said he intended to go to Chicago from there. St. John wrote to Chic's father ten days later and admitted "the only alternative would have been to forcibly restrain him and none of us felt that we were quite justified in doing this at this time."

The way Chic was spiraling downward, St. John must have known that it might soon come to that. Harley always seemed caught in the same disturbing chain of events: Treatment, improvement, relapse. Treatment, improvement, relapse. The minor details changed from event to event, but the framework was always the same. Improvement was temporary.

This time, Chic bought a car for $250, even though friends had advised against it. They worried he wasn't stable enough to safely drive it, but before they saw him again, he had sold it.

"He does not look well and acts strange," his father wrote to St. John. "He told me he was going back to Asheville because you wanted him to, but wanted to go back to Columbus first. . . We encouraged him all we could about going South, but he insisted in coming back to Columbus."

St. John saw Harley in Columbus shortly after that, and it was obvious to him that something needed to be done. He had a conference with two local psychiatrists and they all decided the best thing would be to get Chic voluntarily committed to the Dayton State Hospital and placed under the care of Dr. E.A. Baber. Harley agreed to a "voluntary" commitment of sixty days. But St. John cautioned the family that the next step was to have him "legally committed," a prospect no one wanted.

NERVES WERE GETTING FRAYED. Some of his friends—probably Bill Havens, Russell Paul, and Ray Pennell—drove him to Dayton from Columbus. The doctors cautioned that he not have visitors for at least thirty days, but two friends ignored the request on July 4 and created a small storm when they complained that he wasn't receiving proper attention. The irritated director of the Department of Public Welfare told St. John that Harley was receiving the best treatment possible and "the Superintendent is questioning the advisability of allowing young men from Columbus the opportunity to visit with Harley in the future." His friends backed off.

Irony shadowed Chic throughout this agonizing ride. His horseshoe-shaped creation at the northwest corner of campus was standing tall now, and workers were busy installing seats and putting the finishing touches on the inside. Doctors in Dayton had been working just as hard on Harley's psyche. One of them reported progress "in the last three weeks since he has been put on straw baling," and said that he not only "seems to enjoy it," but "looks better than he has at any time since Asheville."

Unfortunately, baling straw doesn't cure dementia. The same doctor spoke of transferring him to "Dr. (Henry A.) Cotton's hospital in New Jersey" when his voluntary stay in Dayton ended in early August, a move that figured to cost considerably more than care at a state hospital. In the days before medical insurance, Harley needed high-priced help that neither he nor his family could afford.

Friends and local businessmen stepped forward again, contributing more money to what was now called the "Harley fund." It had a balance of $695 on August 19, and Bill Havens wrote to Parry Forse in Trenton, New Jersey, and asked what it would cost to have Chic under the care of Cotton, widely known for his progressive ideas in psychiatry. After some discussion, the group was apparently ready to pay for the more expensive care when Chic voluntarily recommitted himself to the Dayton hospital for another sixty days.

The accelerating Harley merry-go-round is dizzying: Columbus. . . Asheville. . . Chicago. . . Columbus. . . Detroit. . . Chicago. . . Columbus. . . Chicago. . . Dayton. . . Columbus. . . Dayton. . . all in the span of seven months. And he didn't seem to be getting better.

IN THE MEANTIME, the widespread adulation of Harley turned into a murmur of confusing whispers. Though his problems never made the newspapers and few outside of Chic's circle of close friends and family members knew the sordid details of his ordeal, stories about his mental struggles still got around. The tales must have been twisted in the retelling, and regardless of the origin of the syphilis story, the "secret" got out. There seemed no other way to explain why a healthy young man with Chic's remarkable athleticism could suddenly land in a mental hospital. He was popular with the ladies; everyone knew that. It fed a perception that seemed to fit: here was a popular, good-looking athlete who couldn't control his sexual urges and had paid a high price for it.

As the city's giddiness over the nearly-completed stadium grew, the irony became more visible: While finishing touches were being applied to the concrete stadium that Harley's almost superhuman football feats had inspired, he was in a Dayton hospital trying to perform mental tasks that the average person took for granted. At a time Chic might have been giving interviews about the glories of the old days or the bright future the new structure seemed to promise, he couldn't have been more invisible if he were dead.

James Thurber was a reporter for the *Dispatch* by this point. In an insightful September, 1922, letter to former OSU classmate Elliott Nugent, who had moved to New York to pursue a career as a playwright and actor, Thurber wrote both of the stadium and of Harley:

"Too bad you can't be here to whiff the football air and to see the Stadium dedicated. It is nearly completed now, a wonderful structure, set down in the pastoral back eighty of OSU like a modernized Greek temple or a Roman coliseum born of mirage. Michigan plays here on October 21, dedication day. . .

"On football, I wonder if you have heard of the truly sad condition of Chic Harley. He has been in a bad way since last winter and is variously reported as hopeless, his case being diagnosed as dementia praecox by a number of examiners, although the Harley mind, unless known of old, might bother any medical man. At any rate, he has dropped out of life and is now in a Dayton sanitarium. . . "

There is no mention of syphilis in the letter, which surely Thurber would have known about if Harley had it. He was good friends with Finn, a Harley pal, and wouldn't have been reluctant to mention it to their mutual friend Nugent; this was a private letter between friends that Thurber had no reason to suspect would ever become public. Thurber and Finn doubtless discussed Harley's condition in their morning sessions in Marzetti's restaurant at 59 East Gay Street where *Dispatch* reporters gathered daily. He was about as aware of what was going on with Harley as anyone in town.

CHIC TOOK ADVANTAGE of his "voluntary" commitment and left the Dayton hospital on his own, in time to attend the Ohio State-Michigan stadium dedication game on October 21. He finally seemed to have shaken the irony that had been stalking him; in this historic moment, his old friends were heartened by his appearance. The house that Harley built— and Harley himself—were finally together in the same time and place, both seemingly built to last for a hundred years.

It was a cruel delusion. The old Chic made it to the stadium dedication and must have felt a deep sense of pride at the structure he and his teammates had created both in concrete and in public sentiment, but again the mental fixes didn't stick. After his brief moment of glory, the period between the dedication game and early December turned into the most volatile period of Harley's life and a nightmare for all of his close friends. A short *Time* magazine piece in 1924 reported that "friends told of Chic's 'cleaning out' restaurants and theaters and of his annoying the family of a former sweetheart by nocturnal demonstrations."

These demonstrations likely came at the expense of Bill Havens's family. Bill's son, John P. (Jack) Havens, said that "my father's sister (Louise) came pretty close to marrying Chic Harley." Louise Havens eventually married Harley's East High pal Russell Paul, and their grandson, Mike Paul, says that he has Chic's Varsity O pin.

"My understanding from my father was that they were pinned," Mike Paul said.

Like her brother Bill, Louise Havens must have known Chic from East High days, although Jack Havens said their relationship came "during college." No one remembers the trouble Harley seems to have caused the family, but given Harley's mental state and his interest in his former fiancée, it makes sense.

"My aunt said (Harley) was always infatuated with my grandmother," Mike Paul said. "But my aunt says my grandmother never totally returned that. One reason, according to my aunt, is that she always saw Chic as having some issues. She didn't know what kind of provider he would be down the road."

CHIC'S BEHAVIOR WAS BECOMING more unpredictable and he was growing increasingly uncooperative. In a December letter to Chic's father, St. John wrote that "we had all arrangements made for Chick to go with Russell Paul out to a ranch in Wyoming where he might have had most excellent care. Chick absolutely refused to go there."

Chic's public fits of temper were grist for the rumor mill, although the newspapers continued to shield him from public ridicule by effectively squelching stories about his outbursts. Finally, on the occasion of the second Grid-Grad charity game, his anxious friends decided that they had to do something and they had two local doctors "examine" him at halftime of the game. How much of an examination they conducted is debatable—Chic said later that it never happened—but they signed papers indicating that they thought Chic was "insane."

While the game was still in progress, Ned Giesy, an OSU student who had gone to North High School, immediately took the papers to court and signed an affidavit indicating that he believed Harley was insane and that "he being at large is dangerous to the community," a document that would allow Chic to be committed to the Dayton hospital.

Giesy's role in the affair is confusing, in part because there is no indication that he was among Harley's close friends. Giesy's sons, John and Dan, say that their late father often spoke glowingly of Chic as a football player, but never mentioned the incident or having had any kind of personal relationship with him. One intriguing possibility is that Giesy knew Chic from local pool rooms. Giesy was an excellent pool player "who was always playing at the College Inn" and Chic supposedly beat legendary billiards champion Willie Hoppe in a game at The Clock Restaurant (Bott Brothers) at 161 North High. Giesy also spent a lot of time at Hennick's restaurant, so he may have been either a witness or party to one or more of the incidents that led Chic's friends to seek the insanity order.

Harley must have been agitated when the doctors "examined" him at halftime of the football game. He had wanted to play, but some of the players wouldn't allow it, aware of his fragile mental state. Chic didn't take this rebuff well, and told those around him, "They won't let me play because they are afraid of me," a very un-Harley like response. He finally agreed to serve as head linesman at the football game, then threw the chains down after the third quarter because he said it became too cold.

HE WENT TO HENNICK'S AFTERWARDS to meet Bill Havens and Frank "Tee" Young, an Ohio State player who was captain of the 1924 team. They invited him to accompany them to the Athletic Club on East Broad Street for the Grid-Grad banquet and Chic readily agreed. But when he climbed into their car he found Deputy Sheriff Oliver J. Baxter sitting there. Baxter showed him the order and told him he would have to go back to the Dayton hospital.

Harley didn't argue, but as the car headed south on High Street, he began insisting he be taken to his rooming house to get his clothes. His companions consented and soon after he went inside, they saw him leap from an upstairs window, jump over a nearby fence and run—a dramatic, if peculiar demonstration of his legendary athletic skills.

He was finally caught, and after he was secure in the car again, he asked if he could go to the Phi Gamma Delta fraternity house to pick up a few more items. They kept closer tabs on him this time, and he seemed fine for the rest of the trip. He talked football in the car, greeted attendants at the institution, and went to his regular room without assistance.

Bill Harley was surely monitoring all this from afar. At a June meeting, he had been awarded a Toledo franchise in the league now called the NFL, and his Maroons had been more of a success on the field than at the turnstiles. The Chicago Bears, the new name of the Staleys' franchise that Bill believed had been stolen from him, had been crowned league champions, one of the few league teams to enjoy a profitable year. The Bears' success grated upon him. Two days after Chic's friends virtually kidnapped him and took him back to the Dayton hospital, Bill Harley filed suit in the Superior Court of Chicago against Halas and Sternaman, seeking one-half of the team's proceeds from the 1922 season.

The suit contended that Chic was an "unremitting object of attempts to belittle his playing ability, that the Staleys' line gave way in games of 1921 in order to let opposing players spill him, and that he was driven into a state of mental collapse by the 'freeze out' treatment which culminated in the team's refusal to accept his insertion in the second of the game with Buffalo. . .with 10,000 people looking on." It was Bill Harley's contention that the freezing out accorded his brother was calculated to divorce him from interest in the club, following his retirement as a player.

CHIC'S PROBLEMS WERE MORE BASIC THAN BILL'S; he didn't like being confined in a mental hospital at Christmas time. After he had spent little more than two weeks there, he took off on Christmas Eve without telling anybody. He went to Cincinnati—without his overcoat—where he met a friend who gave him railroad fare to Chicago. He went to Bill's house this time, afraid that someone might be waiting at his parents' house, ready to take him back to Dayton.

Even on these terms, the Harley family was happy to see him. He had planned to spend the holidays with them before he entered the hospital and he seemed more stable to them than he had before. He told his father that he shouldn't have left the hospital, but he "simply could not spend Christmas there and wanted to be home for the holidays." He was now interested in taking St. John's earlier offer to go to Colorado and work with a friend in the brisk mountain air.

Chic had fallen a long way in one year. He had been in and out of three different hospitals, and while confinement helped, he repeatedly relapsed. Even when he seemed calm, he couldn't be trusted to remain that way. The quiet, unassuming guy everyone knew, might instantly devolve into a belligerent brute with a lightning-like temper. Even when he seemed normal, he was prone to commit bizarre acts no one could explain.

St. John saw all this more clearly than Harley's family did. His January 2, 1923, letter to Walter Harley didn't offer much reason for optimism:

"At the time we made arrangements for Chic to go out West, it seemed possible for Russ Paul to go out there with him and in that way we might possibly have gotten along in pretty good shape. I do not believe it is practical at all for Chic to go out there by himself. . . It is my judgment that after Chic has been with you a time down there, you had better take him back to Dr. Baber. . .Chic may be with you at thoroughly frequent intervals for a short time, but until he demonstrates a good deal more stability than has yet been shown I believe he is better off in the hands of Dr. Baber and the people at Dayton."

Chic returned to the Dayton hospital on January 10. Doctors were pleased by what they saw. The three weeks in the hospital and the time at home had helped, and he seemed as normal as he had been in quite some time. After a thorough examination, the doctors decided that he could go back to Chicago and live with his family, at least for a while.

No one mentioned the word "cure."

journey into dark

There was no going back. For whatever reason, Chic Harley had started down a narrow road where U-turns weren't possible, a tapered path where the grade was gradual but always sloping down.

Sanity lay somewhere behind him. It often seemed closer than it was, but the image was a mirage.

He seemed to be normal and then he wasn't. He seemed to be improving and then he wasn't. He seemed to be the old Chic and then he wasn't. The unpleasant surprises, the unprovoked

At the age of 30, Chic played an exhibition game in Ohio Stadium, but his life was spiraling ever downward.

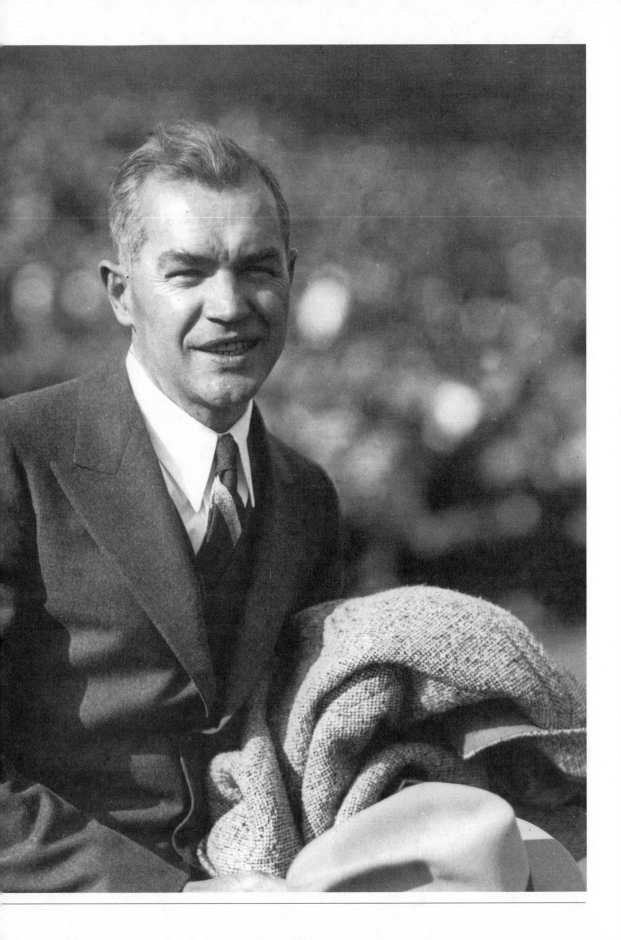

outbursts, were a jolt to those around him, and there seemed no certain way to keep them under control. Dementia praecox is a chronic psychotic disorder characterized by a rapid disintegration of the thought process, usually beginning in the late teens or early adulthood. The disorder is primarily cognitive—it generally affects attention, memory, and goal-directed behavior more than it does a sufferer's moods—but the diagnoses during the early part of the 20th century all seemed certain about one thing: it was a progressively degenerating disease from which no one recovered.

For a while—it was always just a while—things were normal. Harley seems to have lived with his family in Chicago for most of 1923 and 1924. At the urging of his brother, Bill, he decided to go to the Franklin County Probate Court in November of 1924 to have the declaration of insanity that had been lodged against him expunged from the court records. His attorneys alleged that the judgment recorded in December, 1922, following the Grid-Grad football game, was keeping him from securing the kind of employment he sought. While it doubtless hurt him, Harley's increasing apathy and poor judgment—symptoms noted by several physicians—seems a more likely cause.

THE TRIAL CREATED A SMALL STIR. Harley hoped it would prove he was the victim of do-gooders; mostly it brought his mental struggles before the eyes of an adoring public that had known little or nothing about them. He hoped to get his name out of the court records; instead, he planted doubt in places where none had existed before.

The Columbus newspapers had kept Chic's mental difficulties private. His friends and family knew of his travails, and in places such as Hennick's and Marzetti's his fits of temper were recounted in hushed tones, but it was an era when the private affairs of heroes remained private. Babe Ruth's off-the-field adventures would be the stuff of best-selling books only later; at the time the intimate details of a wanton personal life were known only to close friends and reporters. So it was with the mental health problems of Ohio State's greatest football hero. University officials quietly went about the business of raising money for his medical treatment, paying him as an assistant football coach when they knew he couldn't serve, contacting local businessmen for donations that would keep the Harley fund solvent, and doing everything in their power to ensure that his problems wouldn't become news.

Harley's attorneys tried to prove that at the time of the incident he was a resident of Illinois and not Ohio, hence the court didn't have jurisdiction to declare him "insane." They attacked the credibility of the physicians who examined him, and they tried to prove "fraud and misrepresentation" on the part of his friends, citing—among other things—the listing of "John Wilce" as his nearest living relative.

But it was difficult for Judge Homer Z. Bostwick to ignore medical evidence suggesting that the former star, known in the community as a quiet, unassuming man, had changed. The medical certificate listed Harley as "violent, dangerous," indicating that he had "an unhealthy suspicion of others, lack of judgment in ordinary matters, has been annoying others by attention at times. . . "

Finally, Judge Bostwick ruled that Harley was a resident of Columbus at the time of the incident, that he didn't have to be examined in court, and there were no misrepresentations and fraud that he could determine. He let the insanity declaration stand. He took exception to a statement by Harley's attorneys that he was "the victim of too many friends."

"The patient was in the hands of his friends—true friends—those who had seen him climb to the very zenith in athletic honors; sympathetic friends who were ready to co-operate with the court and medical witnesses to cause no unnecessary notoriety but quietly and speedily procure the hospital treatment deemed essential," Bostwick said. "In fact, to save the distinguished patient from all humiliation, and rescue him, if possible, from mental disease then seemed securely fastened upon him."

FOR THE NEXT SEVERAL YEARS, Chic bounced back and forth between Chicago and Columbus, and his mental health followed a similar cycle. He seems to have had difficulty holding a job, although years later, former OSU basketball player Mel Shaw remembered Harley, Jim Thorpe, and Pete Stinchcomb barnstorming with the Columbus Kinnears pro basketball team. The team, which also included

Chic

Johnny Miner, Deacon Lynch, and Bob Shea, was formed after Ohio State won
the Western Conference basketball championship in 1925 and played during the
winter of 1925-1926. It visited teams in Cleveland, Greenville, Oak Harbor, Port
Clinton, and Springfield, among others.

"Chic could get pretty mean," Shaw said. "The only guy who could really
handle him was Andy Nemecek. He always called Harley 'Charley.'"

Chic was pictured in the 1927 football program as an assistant coach, although
letters in The Ohio State University archives indicate that Lynn St. John was
looking for some way to justify paying for Harley's medical expenses and having
him as an assistant coach was one way to do that.

Harley stayed with members of his family off and on all through this period.
He was not listed in the Polk Directory of Columbus from 1924-1926, but in 1927
he was listed as a salesman living at the YMCA. He was not listed again until 1930,
when he was said to be a coach at OSU, but no address was listed.

ON NOVEMBER 28, 1925, HARLEY PLAYED in Ohio Stadium in an exhibition
game between the Varsity O Alumni and the Downtown Coaches, with the
$1 price of tickets being used to pay for a new trophy room in The Horseshoe.
Stinchcomb, Howard Yerges, and Swede Sorenson played with Chic on the Varsity
O squad and Chic's former East High teammate, John Vorys, a Yale grad, was
among those recruited for the other side.

Harley, now 30 years old, "thoroughly lived up to the hopes that drew better
than 5,000 fans to the contest," the *Ohio State Journal* reported. "Chic ripped
off several of the spectacular runs that made him famous and the Ohio Stadium
possible, one of his sprints being for a touchdown."

In 1926, the game was played again, only this time it was a tribute game to
Harley, a nice way of saying that athletic department officials had decided to use
it as a way to beef up the private fund set up for his health care. The *Ohio State
Journal* reported cryptically that receipts for the game were to "go into a fund, the
nature of which is generally known." Chic, who was being called an "assistant
freshman coach" at the school, did manage to play in the game, and Jack Wilce
appeared as a fullback on the other side.

A third and final game, this time against an Army team in 1927, drew a smaller
crowd of 4,000, and the only listed charity was the "Columbus Baby Camp," which

*Chic lived with his family (shown here with his father) for several
years, then began to wander. In the 1930s, he became increasingly
apathetic, negligent, asocial—and alone. By the early 1940s,
he was confined to the Danville hospital where he would spend
the rest of his life.*

was to receive five percent of the proceeds. There were supposedly other unnamed charities, and the "Harley Fund" was likely one of those.

The "coaching" stints didn't last. Chic's father, Charles, died in 1930, and "home" for Chic changed. Chic was living with his sister, Irene Bowling, and her family in Chicago by 1932, and his troubles persisted. St. John finally asked Dr. Earl Garver, a Columbus physician who had examined Chic back in 1921, to go to Chicago and offer an updated opinion of his mental health. In a detailed two-page letter to the Ohio State athletic director, Garver told of his meeting with Chic, his two brothers, and a group of his friends at the Sherman Hotel on December 6, 1935, for about three hours of "general conversation and observations." Garver said having friends around enabled Chic to lose his inhibitions, thus giving him more of an insight into Harley's condition than he would have received from a regular examination.

"My observations at this conference showed to me that Chic had deteriorated mentally to a considerable extent since my last contact with him," Garver wrote. "This was not surprising to me as it conforms with the usual course of Dementia Praecox. This mental enfeeblement is the chief underlying characteristic of the above mental disorder.

"Emotional indifference is noticeable. This characteristic coupled with deterioration of will power has a rather marked effect on his conduct. It begets a loss of the ordinary incentives to normal behavior and as a result he will sit more or less stupidly about, becomes somewhat negligent of person and dress, and impulsive actions, silly and senseless, often dangerous and destructive, are manifested.

"Chic now shows apathy, increasing loss of will power. In a transitory way, he may think of 'getting a job' but carries out no effort to obtain one. His dependency on others does not worry him to a normal degree. Animation, enthusiasm, and expression of strong feeling of excitement over thrilling events, etc., exist only to a slight extent. He is asocial, taking no interest in ladies, and really prefers most of his time to be alone. He shows peculiarities known as mannerisms. On one occasion, (he) went out in (the) yard, a rather public one, and knelt in the snow and prayed and his mother could not stop him. (He) has been observed giving the military salute to no one person or thing in particular. . .

"His future: His mental trouble is a slowly progressive one. The course of the disease is one of years. The time period in which he can get along out in society varies and sometimes depends upon the indulgence of his friends and associates. A time does come however when it is almost impossible for them to live and adjust themselves to outside life and it becomes necessary to institutionalize them. I believe Chic is nearing this period. He would in his present state resist confinement in an institution. This resistance gradually fades with the progressive deterioration. I believe his family now feels a rather urgent necessity to place him in some institution."

HARLEY LIVED WITH HIS FAMILY ANOTHER TWO YEARS. In 1938, he took up "the wandering habit," as Ohio State assistant athletic director Henry D. Taylor described it in a 1940 letter. His family took him to the Veterans Administration Hospital in Danville, Illinois, and placed him under the care of Dr. T. J. Walsh.

Except for visits with various family members and infrequent trips to Columbus for Ohio State football games, Harley would live in the Danville hospital for the rest of his life.

chapter eighteen

Chic, a love *story*

Chic Harley's life was a love story.
That became even more obvious
in the portion of it that remained.
As his days as an athletic idol
receded farther into the past, his life
evolved into a poignant tale of loyalty
and *friendship* from his childhood
buddies and college pals, friends who
could have easily forgotten him
and moved on, rationalizing
their memory lapses with excuses
about their own busy lives.
The nation's mental hospitals
are teeming with patients
awkwardly abandoned by those

*Chic was often invited
back to be with the team.
At right is one thought to
be a Francis Schmidt squad.*

close to them. Every ward has a patient whose illness became such a burden that his friends could no longer tolerate it, a patient whose conduct had annoyed, embarrassed, even sickened them. The initial plan is to make him well, but when that doesn't happen, patience thins. They are gripped by sadness and remorse, but lack of progress grinds away sympathy. Frustration turns into anger. Thoughts once deemed impossible became painfully real. *Get him somewhere, anywhere, where he is no longer a bother. Get him out of our life. There's nothing we can do. Put him away.* Out of sight, out of mind, out of conscience.

This never happened with Chic Harley. A man described by his friends as modest and shy turned into a volatile, unstable aggressor, and his friends stood by him. As his erratic episodes increased in number and severity, his friends remained steadfast.

They had known the old Chic, who treated every player on the squad equally. They knew the Chic who never bragged about his considerable accomplishments, the Chic who made up for his lack of words with an unassuming manner and a kind smile. Chic was too good to abandon. As he turned into someone who wasn't always as good or as congenial, they knew that the old Chic was still in there somewhere, and they refused to let the new Chic drive them off.

Joe Finneran, who roomed with Harley after his OSU days, spoke glowingly of his buddy until his dying day. He also told his nephew, Russ Finneran, that his friend scared him. "He said 'I was always kind of afraid of Chic,'" Russ Finneran said. "He said, 'Something could just set him off,' and that sometimes he could 'just get mad at somebody just like that.' Joe used to say, 'I was pretty handy, but I would hate to fight Chic.' He said it was apparently part of those mental problems he had."

THE LETTERS DEALING WITH THE "HARLEY FUND" in the Ohio State University Archives trace both Harley's mental health and the support of his friends. The men who were with him when his symptoms surfaced in the early 1920s frequently appear throughout the remaining years of his life. Ray Pennell was custodian of the fund in 1948, nearly thirty years after it was first established. Bill Havens, Chic's friend and brother of the former girlfriend whom Chic apparently targeted with the "nocturnal demonstrations" described by *Time* magazine in 1924, drove him to the Dayton hospital and visited him there, tried to get him into a better hospital

*A family reunion in 1948, as brothers Walter, Bill, and Chic
are visited by Congressman John M. Vorys. Chic's early
presence had been such that not only family but friends stood
by him forever.*

on the East Coast, and—decades afterward—visited him at Danville every chance he had.

"Dad just said Chic went off the deep end mentally," Jack Havens said. "I remember him and some friends going back and forth to visit him in the Danville hospital. He admired Chic. He thought he was marvelous. I think he probably spent a lot of time and effort trying to help him."

School officials did, too, which in some ways is just as striking as what his friends did. Some of this may have been for the same reasons. The school's athletic officials knew the old Chic and liked him as well as nearly everyone did; he generated a magnetism that is hard to define. But Lynn St. John might have also been acting out of gratitude; without Chic, the athletic program he ruled might never have come into existence. Chic was at the beginning of its growth, and he had made it possible for St. John to realize his vision. In a sense, St. John was the king of an empire Chic had all but created.

SHORTLY AFTER HARLEY ENTERED THE DANVILLE V.A. hospital in 1938, the Buckeyes had a road game at Illinois, thirty-five miles away in Champaign. Ohio State coach Francis Schmidt agreed to conduct the Buckeyes' Friday practice on the hospital lawn while Chic and 5,000 hospital patients looked on. It was a remarkable show of support for the fallen star. St. John and OSU line coach Ernie Godfrey stood on the sidelines and reminisced with Chic. St. John recalled a drop-kick Harley used to beat Wisconsin in 1919 and Godfrey remembered how he brought Chic's Arcadia Air School team to Camp Joseph E. Johnson in Jacksonville in 1918 and saw Harley score three touchdowns in an 18-0 victory. Harley, the troubled mental patient, beamed the whole time.

The next day in Memorial Stadium, Chic listened in on Schmidt's pre-game talk, was presented with a football autographed by the entire Ohio State team, and sat on the bench during the Buckeyes' 32-14 win. It was the first OSU game Harley had attended in four years, and an Associated Press photograph of a smiling, robust, dapper Chic receiving the football from co-captains Carl Kaplanoff and Mike Kabealo indicated all was well. But the team went home from Champaign and Chic went back to Danville, and his illness grew progressively worse.

School officials kept close tabs on him. The following spring, Henry Taylor inquired about the possibility of picking up Chic at the hospital and taking him to the Ohio State-Illinois baseball game in Urbana. But Dr. P.J. Walsh turned the request down, saying that Harley "had been more disturbed than he had been when you were here last fall," that in March and April of 1939 he had made five attempts to run away from the institution and had been transferred to "the elopers' ward" where he was watched closely at all times.

Walsh wrote that Chic "actively hallucinated, was frequently seen kneeling in the day room or on his bed and talking to imaginary voices. He also had a tendency to hide in corners where he thought he would not be observed by employees, no doubt with the idea of going though a door if he had an opportunity."

IN DECEMBER, 1939, THE FAMILY DECIDED that it wanted to have a party for Chic on Christmas Day, and OSU athletic officials arranged and paid for it at Danville's Hotel Wolford. It did not go well. In a letter to hotel manager Charles M. Stack, Taylor wrote, "Chic was pretty much embarrassed by the waiter service afforded for the dinner. One of the unfortunate parts of his malady is that he has an almost unbelievable inferiority complex and at best not being a hearty eater, his attention to and embarrassment by the presence of waiters seems to have rendered it almost impossible for him to eat anything at all."

Taylor detailed how he wanted dinner served right down to the menu, yet another sign of just how much Harley meant to those back in Columbus. Here was one of the school's top athletic officials fussing over what a hotel should serve the Harley family at a Christmas dinner ("a fruit cup, a large roast chicken or capon, celery and olives, mashed potatoes and dressing, possibly some cranberries, rolls and butter, and mince pie") and it had been more than twenty years since Chic had last appeared in a game at OSU.

Harley's world inside the hospital bore little relation to the world outside. When the Japanese bombed Pearl Harbor on December 7, 1941, and jolted the United States into World War II, Harley was a patient at the Danville V.A. Hospital. When the war ended in 1945 after an estimated seventy-two million casualties, Chic was still a patient. This was a period when Chic seemed to lose interest in all events large and small.

St. John and Taylor, the two OSU administrators who had devoted countless hours looking out for his welfare, retired. Schmidt, the popular Michigan-killing coach who had brought his team to Danville to practice in front of Harley, lost three in a row to the Wolverines and was fired. Paul Brown was hired out of Massillon High School, coached three years, and went into the service; Carroll Widdoes, Paul Bixler, and Wes Fesler were hired in rapid succession. While Chic was insulated from the anxiety, fears, and torment that gripped the world outside the hospital walls, it was hardly a blessing.

Friends and family members continued to visit him. The OSU Athletic Board sent a monthly stipend from the Harley Fund—$50 in the mid- to late-1940s—to his mother, Mrs. Mattie Harley, and his sister, Mrs. Ruth Wessell, who were living together in Chicago and apparently weren't in a good position financially. During times when Chic's condition improved, he would sometimes be permitted to leave the hospital and spend a few days with his relatives.

"I remember one time after the team played at Northwestern," nephew Richard Wessell said, "they took the whole team in a bus to Uncle Bill's house in Chicago because they knew Uncle Chic was there visiting. We had a monstrous party. I'll never forget it."

St. John sent Taylor on a visit to Danville in 1947 to see how Harley was doing and also make arrangements for the disposition of the money upon his mother's death. He found Chic "in particularly good humor and mental attitude" and said that he seemed "unusually coherent and logical in his conversation and attitude."

Taylor also had good news: "Chic at the present time is in the best condition I have seen him since he was confined to the hospital. Of course, he is under expert supervision and care, and with occasional jaunts to different sporting events, which his brothers or individuals at the institution take him, he seems to lead a pretty cheerful existence. . . The Superintendent and the Medical Officer agree that there is no optimistic outlook for a complete cure, but that he is getting the best of care and probably is as happy as he could be anywhere safely."

Mrs. Mattie Harley died on March 1, 1948. While athletic department officials were grappling with what do with the Harley Fund—$10,646.95 at that point—family members were trying to decide which, if any, of several new treatments might benefit Chic. There was an inquiry about "a prefrontal lobotomy" to a doctor in Charleston, West Virginia. There was talk of "electroshock treatments." In a July 6, 1948, letter to Ohio State assistant athletic director Oscar L. Thomas, the manager of the Danville hospital, Dr. George A. Rowland, recommended insulin treatments and said that preliminary studies had been started on Chic a number of weeks before.

"It should be clearly understood that chronic cases frequently do not respond," Rowland wrote, "but aside from the minimal physical risk, the treatment can do no harm. In a small percentage of cases, even of very long standing, very satisfactory results may be obtained. The other specific methods of treatment, viz., electroshock and brain surgery, could not be expected to produce any favorable change in your friend's illness."

Chic apparently wanted to have the treatments, although a letter from Ruth Wessel to Thomas dated August 2, 1948, indicates just how difficult they were for him. "There will be a series of forty to fifty insulin shock treatments," she wrote. "They are very severe. They start giving them about seven in the morning and they last until noon. It leaves the patient weak, but the doctor seems to think they help Chick. . . It sounds wonderful and each night I pray Chick can stand the treatments and that they will help him. One of mother's last wishes were that I do all I can for him. I hope I can grant her wish."

The treatments seem to have had the desired effect. His interest in Ohio State football suddenly picked up, and brother Bill and his wife took him to the Ohio State-Indiana football game in Bloomington on October 16, where they were joined by his former OSU teammate Leo Yassenoff. The trip went so well that they took him to the OSU-Northwestern game in Evanston on October 30 and the OSU-Illinois game in Champaign on November 13.

Chic wanted to return to a game in Columbus and see his old friends, and the family wanted to make sure that he was up to it. If he was, both the school and the city planned to demonstrate their affection for Chic in ways never accorded an athlete in Columbus, before or since.

Chic comes
home

chapter nineteen

Twenty-nine years had passed
since Chic Harley played football
at *Ohio State*, and as
with any time frame, observers
defined this passage by a personal
theory of relativity. Twenty-nine years,
a blink of the earth's eyelash,
can take many forms. It can seem
like a millennium to a college student
and the good old days to a 50-year-old.
To an octogenarian, it is only yesterday.
Harley's contemporaries were
in their 50s and Chic and his teams
were the basis for all their football
comparisons. His Buckeyes had

*It was quite a parade so
long after Chic's early fame.
Some 75,000 people came
out to cheer him, a fifth
of the entire city.*

won consecutive Western Conference championships—no other Ohio State football team had done that—and came within a field goal of winning a third. They had posted two unbeaten seasons and there had been only one other one at the school in the twenty-nine years since. Over the years, Ohio State had filled massive Ohio Stadium to see great football teams with great players play great games against great teams, but none had been able to duplicate what Harley and his teammates had done. And if they ever were able to duplicate it, they would not be able to match when Harley and his teammates had done it. In the minds of some—we're dealing in relativity here, remember?—that would always be enough to set it apart.

Ohio State's greatest successes had come when the 50-year-old men who ruled Columbus were young and impressionable, in the best days of their lives. Harley was their hero then and forever. Great players would follow him, but they would never be as good as he was. What other Ohio State player would ever have the impact on the program that Harley had? Chic built that concrete monster that sits hard by Olentangy and he created the monster program that plays within it. Another Harley? How?

Among his contemporaries, there was strong sentiment to rename Ohio Stadium for Harley, and it's a wonder it was never done.

"I remember Dad (Whit Dillon) saying he regrets never making a bigger effort to have it named for Chic Harley," Whitney B. Dillon said.

MANY OTHERS DOUBTLESS FELT the same way later. It just didn't seem like a pressing issue at the time. Former Ohio State football player Leo Yassenoff, a senior in 1915 when Chic was a freshman, dedicated his new University Theater on High Street to Harley in 1947 and put a relief statue of Harley kicking the ball on the façade of the building. The Harley Fund was still spitting out money to Chic and his family. Columbus sportswriters still wrote about Harley as if his marvelous runs had occurred only last week.

Local people knew his story, or at least they thought they did. Younger family members had grown up hearing about how Chic did this or did that, heard that he was the best football player the school had ever produced, and vaguely knew of the tragedy that followed. They knew that for whatever reason—war injury, blow to the head suffered while in high school, serious rib injury while playing for the Chicago Staleys or (*Shhh!*) something else—that he had lost touch with reality and been

More than a quarter of a century after his playing days, Chic found that he had not been forgotten in Columbus. Here, he is greeted by Governor Thomas Herbert and then-Columbus Mayor James Rhodes.

forced to spend most of his life in a mental hospital. And now they knew that his condition had improved and that for the first time in years, he was coming back to Columbus for the homecoming game with Michigan.

There was a certain small town giddiness to the anticipation, which hinted at a circus on the outskirts or the first day of the county fair. The advance publicity for the parade was stunning, although sportswriters cautioned for a week that Harley would be able to endure only so much excitement. They knew, or at least surmised, that he still possessed a fragile psyche.

"How is the subject of all this adulation going to take this rich menu served up by loyal Ohio Staters?" asked the *Ohio State Journal's* sports editor, Robert E. Hooey. "Some of his friends have been wondering about the wisdom of such a celebration. Will all the excitement be a good thing for him, since he has been out of the hospital for such a relatively short time? Might not the strain of playing the role of a conquering hero be too much, and effect the splendid progress Chic has been making along the long, tortuous road to complete recovery?"

The Columbus newspapers heralded the parade and reception planned for Harley with banner headlines all week, and Mayor James A. Rhodes—who would later serve four terms as Ohio governor—proclaimed Friday "Scarlet and Gray for Chic Harley Day." The city geared up for the kind of welcome that it hadn't accorded anyone since World War I flying ace Eddie Rickenbacker returned to his hometown in 1919.

THERE WERE SIMILARITIES. When Chic, his brothers Bill and Walter, and nephews Bill Harley and Richard Wessell arrived at Union Station, thousands of people were waiting for them, just as they waited for Rickenbacker. It all must have seemed at least vaguely familiar to Chic; this was the same place where 5,000 fans had mobbed him and his Ohio State teammates in 1919 as the team prepared to leave for a big game at Wisconsin.

With his brother Bill at his side, Harley climbed into the back seat of a convertible to lead a ticker-tape parade of five cars, twenty-one floats, the OSU marching band, and all the homecoming queen candidates down High Street to the Statehouse, and an estimated crowd of 75,000 cheered him—at the time, Columbus was a city of 375,000—on a gray, rainy day. Chic seemed a little stunned that so many people remembered.

"He was such a laid-back person," nephew Bill Harley recalled later. "As a young man, I remember looking at him and not believing someone could have done all that. He never talked about it unless you drew it out of him. During that parade, he was so taken that all the people remembered him that he cried."

The rain stopped when they reached the Statehouse and the sun peeked out from behind the clouds.

"Chic was in an open touring car," Wessell said. "There were maybe thirty, forty policemen trying to hold crowds back and the police couldn't do it. They wanted to get at Chic. We stood on the steps of the Statehouse crying. I'll never forget that."

After Mayor Rhodes and Ohio Governor Thomas J. Herbert welcomed Chic and the procession, Harley and his family were escorted to the Deshler-Wallick Hotel at the northwest corner of Broad and High, where they would stay.

Wessell remembered a steady stream of friends and acquaintances being

The old boys gather at an Ohio State game. And not just any Ohio State game but the one that made Chic legendary —Michigan. Bill, Chic and Walter Harley are sitting in section 18-a, on the Michigan side for the 1948 contest.

brought to their room to see Chic at the Deshler, and was especially struck by a touching visit from a woman believed to be Mrs. Russell Paul, the former Louise Havens, whom he described as "the love of Chic's life."

"It was a touching moment," Wessell said. "She went into a room with Chic and they talked for about an hour. It was sad. I could tell she meant a lot to him."

JUST ABOUT ALL OF HIS OLD FRIENDS came back to see him. Former Columbus Panhandles' player Joe Mulbarger, one of his closest friends at East High School, was one. Bill Havens was another. There were many former teammates, East High classmates, and Columbus businessmen who had been so quick to help when Chic needed it. Meanwhile, the local newspapers gushed and gushed, local sportswriters seemingly intent on educating the poor unfortunates who had never seen him play.

"Chic could run the 100 in around 10 seconds in a day when 10-second men were few and far between," Lew Bryer wrote in the *Columbus Citizen*. "He had as deceptive a change of pace when running with the ball as any I've ever seen. His dodging was superb and his straight-arming terrific. I've seen only one ball carrier I'd rate with him in Western Conference football. That was Illinois' Red Grange.

"Chic's offensive greatness didn't stop with ball carrying, however. He was a fine forward passer, a great punter, a fine drop-kicker, a fine place-kicker and a superb blocker whenever someone else carried the ball. On defense he was one of the finest safety men and punt receivers I've ever watched. To top that off he was a deadly tackler."

"Most of his running was wide," Russ Needham wrote in the *Dispatch*. "If you got him past the line of scrimmage, it was ten to one he'd go for a touchdown. On wide runs, he would put his hand on top of an enemy's helmet and pivot right around him. He would go at less than full speed as long as he could. Guys would tackle both legs and he'd still get away. The football was rounder in those days and Harley could throw it like a baseball. He was a quadruple threat. He could pass, placekick, punt, and run.

"Chic was an inspirational player like few who've ever lived. His teammates had unlimited confidence in him, knew he'd bring them through. In all but that last game he never failed."

Several radio stations interviewed him, and he must not have said much. When asked about the 1919 Michigan game, there was no flood of rich, colorful memories. "I don't remember any exact plays in the game," he said, "but I remember we beat 'em." This may have been in part due to his illness, although his nephew said that he understood that Chic was always that way.

"He was overly bashful," Wessell said. "But people tell me that he was like that during his playing days, too."

The next day, Harley sat in Section 18-A, Row 28, Seat 30 and watched Ohio State lose to No. 1 Michigan, 13-3, and on Sunday, he was the center of attention at the annual Captain's Breakfast. Then he quietly left town with his family, a smile permanently affixed to that older, but still familiar face.

It is probably not an exaggeration to say that the weekend was the high point of his post-football life, although the next twenty-six years were almost certainly better than the previous twenty-six, his dementia under control, if not totally cured.

"I saw him during the reunion of the 1916 team, the second reunion in Westerville," Dorothy Wilce Krause said. "He just looked so gentle and quiet. You can imagine this dynamo on the football field. This was just his mental illness."

HARLEY REMAINED A PATIENT at the Danville V.A. hospital, but his commitment was voluntary and he was mostly free to visit his family whenever he wanted.

"Sometimes he would catch the train on his own and we would meet him at the station," Wessell said.

In 1951, he was one of thirty former players elected into the College Football Hall of Fame's inaugural class. He deserved the honor every bit as much as the other famous names in the group—Red Grange, Jim Thorpe, Bronco Nagurski, Ernie Nevers, Don Hutson, Nile Kinnick, Sammy Baugh, and Amos Alonzo Stagg—although there were signs that his brief pro football career and life of hospitalization had already eroded the public's memories of him.

In an Associated Press poll on January 24, 1950, designed to pick a college football All-Star team for the first half century, Jim Thorpe was the runaway vote-getter, followed by Red Grange and Bronco Nagurski. Out of the 391 sportswriters and broadcasters who participated in the voting, Harley received only two votes.

Two years later, he returned to Columbus for Ohio State's football game with Michigan State and was honored at halftime for his Hall of Fame induction. The outpouring of sentiment didn't match the incredible display of five years earlier, but it did give his friends and admirers a chance to say the things that the AP voters apparently didn't know.

Pete Stinchcomb: "I played two years with Chic and he had more ability both for offense and defense than any player I have ever known. The records themselves prove this. In our modern times, he would be labeled Mr. Football. . ."

Former Illinois coach Bob Zuppke: "He was without a doubt the fastest, most capable and colorful figure of his days and always will rank tops among football immortals. The Big Four in my twenty-nine years of coaching in the order of their times are Harley, (Red) Grange, (Jay) Berwanger, and (Tom) Harmon."

BIG TEN COMMISSIONER TUG WILSON, who played against Harley while at Illinois: "A cool, poised individual possessing great speed and dodging ability, it was almost impossible to bring him down once he was underway with the ball. There was little he couldn't do on the gridiron. He could pass, kick and run, and with it all, had a fierce competitive spirit that inspired his teammates to great heights and made him a potential threat as long as he was in the game. He is truly one of the great backs of intercollegiate football. . ."

National Football Hall of Fame executive secretary George Little: "In the fall of 1912, while an undergraduate in the Agricultural College at Ohio State, I was assigned as a one-man official to referee six of East High School's scheduled games. Working behind this promising young sophomore, it was nothing short of inspirational to me to observe his all-around boyhood qualities as a future college gridiron performer. . . It was little wonder when, after returning from World War I to Columbus in 1920, I found prominently displayed on the walls of the Southern Hotel the photographs of Marshal Foch, President Wilson, General Pershing and . . . Chic Harley."

Harley's return gave his former coach, Dr. John W. Wilce, and OSU President Howard Bevis an opportunity to give long halftime speeches that explained just who he was and how much he had meant to the university. Wilce's speech was sprinkled with telling phrases that indicate how much he admired him:

"He was the answer to a coach's prayer, as an athlete and as a personality. . . Nature blessed him with the superb coordination, unusual speed, and superior enduring resiliency of a true All-American. . . He was a rare sportsman and an honestly clean player. . . Do not think that I try to exaggerate when I say that I do

222

not remember his committing a single personal foul, in spite of a great legitimate fighting spirit. . . The phrase 'ideal competitor' describes his seemingly intuitive ability to rise to heights of achievement in clutch situations. . . He led to victory at times over obstacles and opposition which would have defeated one of lesser talents or smaller spirit. . . It is sometimes forgotten that he was also excellent in track, basketball and particularly in baseball. . . He had the honest affection of his teammates and quickly earned the admiration and respect of his opponents. . . Characteristic of his personality was real modesty as to his own ability and achievements. . .While he was the true individual star of his great teams, to him it was the team that counted, rather than himself."

Ohio State President Howard Bevis's long halftime speech focused on just how much Chic had meant to the school as a whole.

"It takes a lot of people a long time to build a university," Bevis said. "Such building, as a matter of fact, is never done; it is a continuing process. . .

"There have been many builders of this University, and there will be many more. Among the names of the builders in the realm of inter-collegiate athletics are those of former President George W. Rightmire, who presented the argument which got Ohio State admitted to the Western Conference; of Professor Thomas E. French, generally regarded as the "daddy" of the stadium; of L. W. St. John, director of athletics during the period of major building, and of Chic Harley, whom we honor today.

"It is no exaggeration to say that in his way Chic Harley was one of the builders of the University, and as such he will always be remembered."

As time passed, that would become a matter of degree.

a passion for

OSU

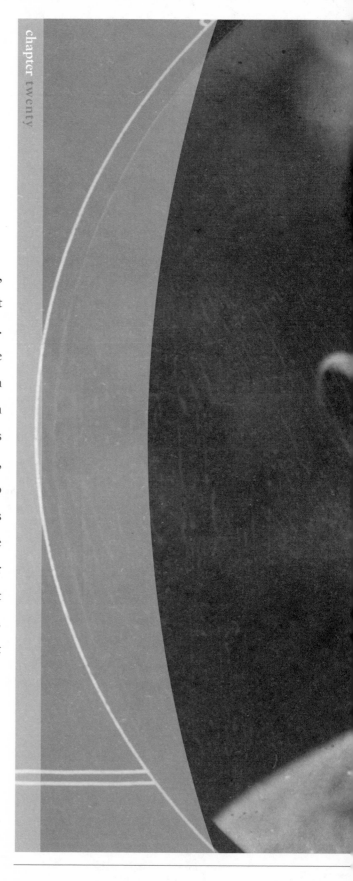

If Chic Harley had died in 1953, the *stadium* he spawned might well have been named for him. The idea sprouted in the newspapers around the state from time to time, flourished briefly, then withered and died. As much as his friends and fans loved him, it was an accepted practice not to affix the names of living heroes to public buildings, lest the honorees commit a crime or perform an act that the government considered embarrassing. As a man who had spent

Would the stadium have been built without Chic? Probably so, but not then, not so soon. And not so monumentally.

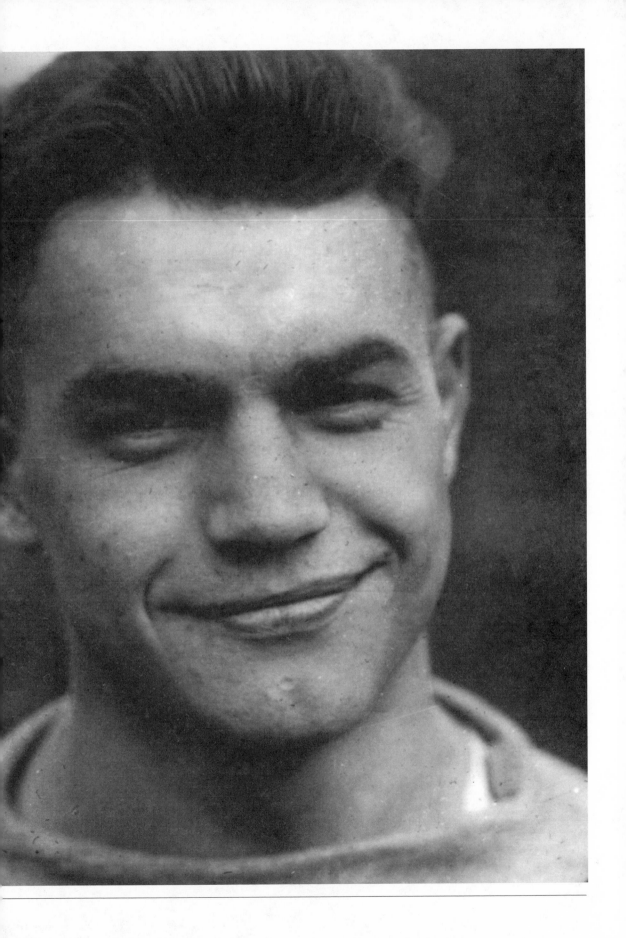

Chic

most of his life in mental facilities, even a docile Harley must have seemed an unacceptable risk.

It didn't seem to matter much in those days, anyway. His friends and admirers knew he had built the stadium. They remembered when Ohio State football teams couldn't fill the wooden bleachers at little Ohio Field, remembered the unexpected rush of fans in 1916 that came to see him play. They remembered the way it was when Ohio State was a rival of schools such as Case, Ohio Wesleyan, and Kenyon, and the way all that changed when a shy, smallish kid from East High School arrived. They remembered the way he performed feats on the football field that seemed extraordinary, the way the public came to adore him, the way he infused color and texture and drama into the relentless humdrum of their everyday lives.

They remembered and revered him, told tender stories that reflected their devotion to him, talked of how Ohio State football would never have become a religion if Chic hadn't written and spread the gospel, and then they . . . died. As one generation was slowly supplanted by another, Harley's exploits moved deeper into the past. New heroes came and went, and the more there were, the less special the old ones seemed. Time was as much Harley's enemy as mental illness. Time erodes fame until it gradually loses its luster, and then layer after layer of it is stripped away until all that's left is a name.

Chic Harley. Yeah, I've heard of him. What did he do, anyway? Wasn't he a football player or something?

HARLEY WASN'T THE ONLY ONE TO SUFFER this cruel ignominy. His coach, Dr. John W. (Jack) Wilce, also fell from the pinnacle, was targeted by forgetful critics, and faded from memory, as many Ohio State football coaches seem to do. After winning those Western Conference titles with Harley in 1916 and 1917 and another one in 1920 without him, a few non-championship seasons turned him into a coaching idiot. The fans began to question his methods and his strategy, and by the mid 1920s, there were calls for him to resign. People who had never played football, people who had never coached a down of football knew more about it than he did, knew that he wasn't bringing in the right kind of players and running the right kind of offense, knew that the game had already passed him by.

Wilce was as stubborn as he was smart. He hung around for a few years and stressed that he, not disgruntled alumni, would decide if and when he would

LOUISE HAVENS

BAKER ART GALLERY.

When Chic returned in 1948, he spent an hour with Louise Havens, a poignant moment. Above is her page from the Ohio State yearbook from when they were in school.

quit, and then in June, 1928, he announced his retirement from coaching. It was a decision that local reporters interpreted as fulfillment of a vow he had made numerous times that his enemies would never force him out.

Even so, the case can be made that Wilce was the first true corpse in a place that became famous as the graveyard of the coaches. Though others were buried before him, they had neither his success nor his durability. They were mostly part-time coaches who worked for a year or two and either weren't rehired or surveyed the situation, heard the criticisms, and chose to move on. Wilce helped create the all-encompassing monster that was Ohio State football and was ultimately consumed by it. He said that he had decided to practice medicine and teach, and he did both, working out of an office in a building at 206 East State Street, occupied today by Planned Parenthood of Central Ohio. He studied data, wrote numerous papers, and gave speeches on the effect of athleticism on the health of the human heart. But even during the twenty-four years (1934-1958) he also served as director of the University Health Center, there were signs that his fall from grace as a coach stung him deeply.

In an article in the *Columbus Citizen* on November 9, 1952, writer Chester Smith retold an old Wilce story that had apparently been around town for years:

"When the doctor finally resigned, he was quoted as saying that if he ever coached again, it would only be on the team at the Ohio Penitentiary because that was the one place that the alumni never wanted to go back."

TWELVE YEARS AFTER HE COACHED HIS LAST GAME, it's clear in a note from OSU journalism professor James E. Pollard to Wilce at his OSU office at 101 Hayes Hall that the old coach had expressed some regret over his lost legacy. Pollard sent Wilce a clipping from an article by Frank Graham in the *New York Sun* that mentioned Wilce's name and wrote, "So you see, you're far from forgotten and perhaps it wasn't in vain after all!"

Harley's work certainly wasn't forgotten, although a once-resplendent picture seemed to devolve into a faded black and white photo that many didn't recognize. After he died of pneumonia on April 21, 1974, in the Danville V.A. hospital where he had spent a large chunk of his life, Ohio State's five football captains—Archie Griffin, Arnie Jones, Steve Myers, Neal Colzie, Pete Cuzick—and tackle Kurt Schumacher served as his pallbearers, and there was a brief flurry of articles in the

Columbus newspapers about his exploits. If his name wasn't on Ohio Stadium, old-timers at least referred to it as the "House That Harley Built," a takeoff on the more-famous "House That Ruth Built" nickname given to Yankee Stadium. But the name never stuck the way it did in the Bronx.

Harley and Babe Ruth were born in the same year—1895—they both helped usher in what became known as The Golden Age of Sports, and they are probably the only athletes almost personally responsible for the construction of massive stadiums that were still in use in the 21st century. But in later years, Ruth's legacy continued to grow while Harley's seemed to fade until only the most devoted college football fans knew his name.

Unfair as it seems, it is just as understandable. Baseball was king in those days and Ruth was the king of baseball, a man who, by popularizing the home run, changed the way the game was played. He was a larger-than-life figure who made news on and off the field, a man who seemed to grow larger during the 1920s, a man who was more famous when he retired in 1935 than he was the day Yankee Stadium opened in 1923.

Harley never played an official game in the stadium that might have been named for him. He played one inglorious season of pro football before it became popular, experienced mental problems, and all but dropped out of sight.

He lived on in old black and white photos that graced the walls of many Columbus restaurants and bars, in frayed albums of yellowed newspaper clippings in the basements and attics around the state, and in the memories of people whose lives were nearly over.

In August, 2000, the wall sculpture of Harley that Leo Yassenoff had carved into the façade of his new University Theater in 1947 was stationed a few feet above a neon sign advertising "Burritos as big as your head." The sculpture was partially obscured by the restaurant's La Bamba awning, and the guy at the counter looked perplexed when a reporter asked him if he knew who that football player on the building was.

"I have no idea," he said. "You might want to ask somebody at our management company."

In the fall of 2002, the *Dispatch* and WBNS-TV conducted a "Best of the Bucks" survey designed to pick the five greatest players in Ohio State football history. Only one player before 1970 made the list—Howard "Hop" Cassady.

Chic

On October 30, 2004, one of the numbers Harley wore—47—was retired during a halftime ceremony of the Ohio State football game with Penn State, his name and number joining those of the school's then-six Heisman Trophy winners on the north façade between B and C decks. It was long overdue—he would have been the school's first Heisman winner if the trophy had existed when he played—and a bit understated. His name might have been on the stadium; now it was on a small sign on one of the stadium's concrete walls, sharing the space with a half-dozen others. Any tribute is better than none, but coming as late as it did, seemed almost as if his name had been removed from some dusty, dog-eared scrapbook that had never been opened.

So here it is, the plain, unvarnished truth: If Chic Harley had never been born, the passion for Ohio State might well have become a passion for something else. Instead of building a colossal concrete horseshoe-shaped stadium on the banks of the Olentangy River, Ohio State officials might have elected to add a few more bleachers to Ohio Field. The Buckeyes might still be stuck there in a patched-together 50,000- or 60,000-seat stadium, playing for a program that makes a bowl appearance once every eight or ten years, playing for a program that's not a lot different than those at Indiana or Kentucky.

Most Ohio State fans today don't know it, but Chic Harley changed their lives. He gave them an avocation, a devotion, and a fanaticism that borders on religion, gave them a game to both savor and fret over 24/7, 365 days a year. Without Harley, some of them, many of them, might be spending their fall Saturdays napping, puttering around the garden, playing euchre, or washing the family car.

Isn't it possible that another Ohio State athlete might have come along and set the chain in motion the way Harley did?

Sure, it is.

But we'll never know.

Chic

the years after

Chic Harley

By the time Harley died of bronchial pneumonia at the age of 78 on April 21, 1974, in the Veterans Administration Hospital in Danville, Illinois, he was little more than a familiar name and a fading photographic image to many Ohio State fans. But school officials knew he was football royalty. Then OSU football coach Woody Hayes said, "He was the man who really got Ohio State off to a great start in football." The funeral procession from Schoedinger Northwest Chapel on Zollinger Road in Columbus made a detour through campus en route to Chic's final resting place in Union Cemetery, about two miles north of the campus. It briefly stopped as it passed the mammoth horseshoe-shaped stadium that served as Harley's real monument.

Six Buckeye football stars, including a team co-captain named Archie Griffin, served as his pallbearers. Like Harley, Griffin was an undersized Columbus high school star who exceeded expectations when he arrived at OSU. The Eastmoor product—the modern-day Harley—eventually became history's first two-time Heisman Trophy winner. If the Heisman had been around in Harley's time, Griffin would very likely have been the second.

Bill Harley

After Chic's older brother lost his quest to wrestle control of the Chicago Bears away from George Halas at the 1922 NFL meeting in Canton, Ohio, it wasn't the end of his NFL ambitions. The league owners granted him the Toledo Maroons franchise, as well as the rights to the three players he had taken to Halas in 1912—brother Chic and OSU teammates Pete Stinchcomb and Tarzan Taylor—but none of them ever played for him. The Maroons were a success on the field but a failure at the turnstiles, and the team folded after two seasons. An excellent athlete who played years of semipro baseball around Chicago, Harley ran other franchises and became a longtime sports promoter in the Chicago area. He reconciled with Halas near the end of his life, was elected to the Chicago Sports Hall of Fame, and retired to Daytona Beach, where he died in 1964 at the age of 75.

Frank Gullum

Chic's first football coach at East High School, Gullum was an Athens native who played baseball and football at Ohio University. After coaching Harley at East in 1912 and 1913, he returned to OU to teach chemistry, coached the baseball, basketball, and football teams, and served as OU's athletic director. He retired in 1955 after 37 years as a faculty member, and died in Athens in 1965 at the age of 79.

Palmer Cordray

Chic's coach at East in 1914, Cordray was also a math teacher before serving in World War I as a first lieutenant in the Medical Corps. He entered OSU's medical school after the war and became a general practitioner in Columbus, dying suddenly in his office in 1955 at the age of 65.

John Vorys

A year ahead of Chic at East and captain of the 1913 football team, he played football at Yale, served in the U.S. Naval Air Service as an overseas pilot during World War I, and taught in the College of Yale in Changsha,

China in 1919 and 1920 before entering law school at Ohio State. He served ten terms in Congress as a Republican and was a delegate to the United Nations before retiring from politics and resuming his law practice. He died in Columbus in 1968 at the age of 72.

John D. Harlor

After six years as East High School principal, Harlor became a teacher at North High, then the superintendent of the Franklin County Children's Home. At 50, he was too old for service in WWI but he became a member of the Spaulding Educational Unit that served overseas. After the war, he returned to East High as a teacher and retired from the Columbus school system in 1934. He died in March of 1954, at the age of 86.

Louise Havens

The Ohio State student and East High graduate whom some family members say was pinned to Harley during her Ohio State days was part of OSU's 1918 yearbook dedicated to the nine women on campus known not only for their beauty, but academic achievement and service to the school. She graduated from OSU and eventually married Russell E. Paul, another East/Ohio State grad and a friend of Harley's. The Pauls had three children, and Louise died in January of 1969 at the age of 72.

Gaylord "Pete" Stinchcomb

Harley's backfield co-star helped the Buckeyes to another Big Ten championship in 1920 and their first post-season appearance in the Rose Bowl. He played for the Decatur Staleys, (which became the Chicago Bears), the NFL's Columbus Tigers and the Cleveland Indians, as well as the league's Louisville team. After his playing days, Stinchcomb moved back near his boyhood home of Fostoria, Ohio, and entered the construction business in Findlay, where he died in 1978 at the age of 78. He was elected to the College Football Hall of Fame in 1973.

Thomas Ewing French

French, who worked his way through OSU as a draftsman, went on to head the school's mechanical engineering department, write a best-selling textbook on engineering drawing, and become the spiritual father of Ohio Stadium. He was, from 1912 until his death in 1944 at the age of 73, the university's first and only faculty representative in the Big Ten. He never missed a Buckeye football game,

and French Field House, still in use by Ohio State track teams, was dedicated in his honor in 1957.

Ferdinand "Fritz" Holtkamp

A 1916 honorable mention All-American from Lakewood, Ohio, Holtkamp coached football at Mississippi State and Western Reserve before entering the construction business. He was working on a construction project for the government during World War II when he was killed in the South Pacific late in 1944. He was 55 years old.

Lynn St. John

St. John, a one-time OSU halfback, coached basketball and baseball at OSU and in 1912 began overseeing the growth of the university's athletic program, which he directed until his retirement in 1947. During that time, he became a leading figure in college athletics, serving (with James Naismith) on the NCAA Basketball Rules Committee from 1912 to 1937, the last eighteen years as chairman, and was a member of the 1936 Olympic Basketball Committee, playing an active role during the inaugural Olympic competition. He died in 1950 at the age of 73 while getting ready to see a football game at his stadium. St. John

Arena, basketball home of the Buckeyes from 1956 to 1998, was named in his honor.

Johnny Jones

The former East High grad, Ohio State cheerleader, and unabashed Harley fan became a theater manager, theatrical press agent, and promoter for the Columbus Zoo and Chamber of Commerce. He was hired by the Columbus *Dispatch* in 1940, and his popular "Now Let Me Tell You" feature became the most widely-read newspaper column in central Ohio. His last column appeared on St. Patrick's Day, March 17, 1971, the day he died.

Leo Yassenoff

Yassenoff's final year as an Ohio State football player (1915) came when Harley was a freshman, but he became Chic's good friend and promoter in later years. After OSU, he went into the construction business, building a string of suburban movie theatres called Academy Theaters. In 1917, he placed a relief of a punting Chic on the facade of his Varsity theatre, across High Street from campus. Yassenoff also built the Orthodox synagogue in Columbus, the original Jewish Community Center, and the Hillel House at Ohio State. Whenever Harley attended a game in his later years, Yassenoff was usually by his side. A noted philanthropist, he left a considerable portion of his assets to a charitable foundation when he died in 1971, and the local Jewish Community Center is named for him.

Harold Joseph "Hap" Courtney

Harley's East High/Ohio State teammate enlisted in the Navy in the early spring of 1918. He trained at Chicago's Municipal Pier, transferred to Philadelphia, and sailed for France in early September. On the transport *Louisville*, where he was quartermaster, he became ill and died of pneumonia on September 11. The war ended a month later.

Howard G. Courtney

Harold's older brother was a cadet in the Aviation Corps, stationed at Fort Sill, Oklahoma, following graduation from OSU in 1918. After the war, he became an engineer with the Bell Telephone Company for twenty-five years, living mostly in Los Angeles. He left a widow, son, and daughter when he died following a long illness in August of 1946.

John C. Harlor

Chic's roommate at the Harlor household during the second part of

235

his junior year at East High School, graduated with an OSU law degree in 1922 and became a senior partner in the law firm of Wright, Harlor, Morris & Arnold, which merged with the law firm of Porter-Stanley in the late 1960s. Harlor specialized in banking and insurance law and argued one case before the United States Supreme Court. He gave the eulogy at Chic's funeral in 1974, and died in 1985 before his 87th birthday.

Harvey A. Miller

The former captain of the Wittenberg College football team and one-time teacher was sports editor of the *Columbus Dispatch* from 1903-1924, when he left to enter the insurance business. His writing didn't end, however; he kept a diary every day of his adult life. He was also an original member of the Upper Arlington Board of Education and died in September of 1952 at the age of 78.

Homer Bostwick

The controversial probate judge who ruled against Harley in 1924 when Chic tried to negate a court lunacy ruling sat on the bench from 1917 to 1931. A huge man of about 380 pounds, he was the first presiding judge of the Columbus municipal court, and after a brief affair with a woman while his wife was ill and not expected to recover (she did), he was relieved of his judgeship. He finished his career as a Columbus lawyer and died in 1952 at the age of 74.

Fred Norton

The multi-sport OSU star enlisted in the Aviation Corps shortly after graduating in 1917, training in Toronto and Texas, where he also became a stunt flyer. In 1918, he was wounded in an air battle near Toul in the St. Mihiel Sector of France and died two days later, on July 23. He was the first of OSU's athletes to fall in action, recommended several times for the Distinguished Service Cross. The first airport in Central Ohio, dedicated in Whitehall in 1923, was named for him.

Walter Chamblin Jr.

After covering OSU sports for the *Ohio State Journal* during his last three years as a student at Ohio State, Chamblin subsequently worked on newspapers in Dayton and Cleveland and as a reporter for the Associated Press. He eventually became the director of the National Association of Manufacturers. He was attending a board meeting in Washington, D.C., when he fell down an elevator shaft and died in September of 1955. He was 56.

Joe Mulbarger

Harley's friend and former East High teammate began his professional football career with the local Mendel Pirates in 1916 and joined the Columbus Panhandles the following year. The 5-9, 200-pound Mulbarger played with the Panhandles until they folded in 1922, then played with the Columbus Tigers, the Portsmouth Spartans, and the Ironton Tanks before retiring as a pro football player at the age of 34. He lived on the South Side of Columbus and worked at Walker's Clothing Store from 1916 until his death of a heart attack on October 31, 1951. He was 56.

Bob Hooey

As a boy, he had moved to Columbus from Wisconsin, watched Chic play football, and became a sportswriter. He wrote for the *Ohio State Journal* from 1924 to 1949, specializing in baseball, and on November 29, 1949, died in a car crash on his way home from picking up his tickets to fly to the 1950 Rose Bowl. He was 52 years old. He was inducted into the Columbus baseball Hall of Fame in 1980.

Ray Pennell

The former North High star played, but didn't letter at Ohio State, and also

attended the Massachusetts Institute of Technology. He became a building contractor, a Columbus city building inspector, and eventually assistant chief building inspector for the city. One of Chic's closest friends, he managed the Harley Fund for several years and was secretary of the Ohio Public Links Golf Association when he died July 26, 1953, at the age of 59.

George Halas

In 1924, Halas won the lawsuit filed against him by Bill Harley that would have given the Harleys a share of ownership in the Chicago Bears—*né* the old Decatur Staleys. (The court essentially ruled that the Bears were a new franchise and not simply an extension of the old Staley franchise.) Halas, a religious man who routinely swore at referees and liked to make them pick their game pay off the ground a dollar a time, was the only man associated with the NFL throughout its first fifty years. He was the Bears' coach for forty years, and his 318 regular season wins remained NFL records until the mid-1990s. He was still owner when he died in 1983 at the age of 88.

Charley Seddon

Harley's former North High rival and teammate on the 1916-1917

Ohio State teams spent World War I at Fort McHenry in Baltimore as campus recreation director. When he returned to Columbus, he parlayed summer jobs with the Columbus recreation department—one summer he managed the first public swimming pool in the city—into a job as assistant recreation director. Each fall, he took ten weeks leave and coached football at Tennessee, Texas, and finally under Jack Wilce at OSU until he quit after the 1928 season. Seddon became city recreation director in 1940 and in 1964 was appointed first chairman of the Franklin County Park and Recreation Commission. He died in August of 1977 at the age of 83.

Edmond "Whit" Dillon

Harley's former East High/Ohio State teammate graduated from Ohio State with a law degree. He was a partner in the Pretzman and Dillon law firm and the supreme attorney for the United Commerical Travelers of America. Before he died in October of 1985 at the age of 88, he was the last surviving member of Chic's high school football team.

James Thurber

Having been rejected for enlistment in the service during the war because of blindness in his left eye due to a childhood accident, the East High grad applied for a job as a code clerk for the State Department in Washington, D.C., and got it in June, 1918. He accepted a transfer to Paris later that year, and was in France in 1919 and missed Harley's last season at Ohio State. Returning to Columbus in 1920, he worked as a reporter at the *Columbus Dispatch* from 1921 to 1924. He was hired by former East/OSU schoolmate Johnny Jones as press agent for the Majestic Theater but soon returned to Paris. He joined *The New Yorker* as an editor in 1927, the springboard of his career both as a writer and as a cartoonist. His first book, *Is Sex Necessary?*, appeared in 1929, and he went on to a career as one of America's legendary literary humorists. He occasionally wrote about Harley and often wrote of his Columbus days, dying in New York in 1961 at the age of 66.

John W. "Jack" Wilce

The coach who once painted OSU's locker room bright red so as to inspire the team's meat eaters, went from genius (when his Ohio State teams won Western Conference championships in 1916, 1917, and 1920) to pariah (when they stopped winning them), although when he announced his retirement from coaching in June of 1928 he had a winning percentage of .695 and, said *Time* magazine, "did more than any coach to give Columbus a permanent football mania." Having earned a medical degree from OSU in 1919, he began his own medical practice and studied the effects of athletics on the human heart (no permanent damage, he reported). He also served as OSU's director of student health services from 1934 to 1958, and died in 1963 at the age of 75. He is a member of the College Football Hall of Fame, and OSU's John W. Wilce Student Health Center is named after him.

Chic

Bibliography

Arter, Bill, Homes of a Hero, Columbus Vignette. *Columbus Dispatch Sunday Magazine*, March 2, 1969.

Barrett, Richard E., *Images of America, Columbus 1860-1910*. Charleston, S.C., Chicago, Portsmouth, N.H., San Francisco: Arcadia Publishing, 2005.

Barrett, Richard E., *Images of America: Columbus 1910-1970*. Charleston, S.C., Chicago, Portsmouth, N.H., San Francisco: Arcadia Publishing, 2006.

Baxter, Oliver J., affidavit, State of Ohio, Franklin County, Nov. 16, 1924.

Berry, Carlton C., *Memory Sketches of Over Fifty Years in Newspaper Composing Rooms*. Columbus: The Dispatch Printing Company, 1954.

Brondfield, Jerry, Rockne, *The Coach, The Man, The Legend*. New York: Random House, 1976.

Cannon, Ralph, Harley to Horvath. *Esquire*, September, 1945, Pages 92-94.

Claassen, Harold and Boda, Steve, Jr., *Ronald Encyclopedia of Football*. New York: The Ronald Press Company, 1960.

Cohen, Richard M., Deutsch, Jordan A., and Neft, David S., *The Ohio State Football Scrapbook*. Indianapolis/New York: Bobbs-Merrill, 1977.

Condon, George E., *Yesterday's Columbus, A Pictorial History of Ohio's Capital*. Miami: E.A. Seeman Publishing, Inc., 1977.

Creamer, Robert W., *Babe, The Legend Comes to Life*. New York: Simon and Schuster, 1974.

Cromartie, Bill, *The Big One*. Atlanta: Gridiron Publishers, 1994.

Danzig, Allison, *The History of American Football, Its Great Teams, Players and Coaches*. Englewood Cliffs, New Jersey: Prentice-Hall, Inc., 1956.

Danzig, Allison, *Oh, How They Played the Game, The Early Days of Football and the Heroes Who Made It Great*. New York: Macmillan and Company, 1971.

Davis, Jeff, *Papa Bear, The Life and Legacy of George Halas*. Blacklick, Ohio: McGraw-Hill, 2004.

East High School, *100 Years of Excellence, East High School 1898-1998*, Columbus, Ohio. Columbus: Central Ohio Graphics, 1998.

Evans, Leland S., affidavit, State of Ohio, Clark County, Nov. 24, 1924.

Garrett, Betty, with Lentz, Ed, *Columbus, America's Crossroads*. Tulsa, Oklahoma: Continental Heritage Press, Inc., 1980.

Grange, Harold E., *Zuppke of Illinois*. Chicago: A.L. Glaser, Inc., 1937.

Halas, George, with Morgan, Gwen and Veysey, Arthur, *Halas by Halas*. New York: McGraw-Hill Book Company, 1979.

Harley, Charles W., affidavit, State of Ohio, Franklin County, No. 43420, November 17, 1924.

Harlor, John. D., Memorial Statement Made at the Funeral of Chic Harley, April 26, 1974.

Henderson, Andrew, *Images of America: Forgotten Columbus*. Chicago: Arcadia Publishing, 2002.

Homan, Marv and Hornung, Paul, *Ohio State 100 Years of Football*. Columbus: 1989.

Howe, Henry, *Historical Collections of Ohio, Vol. 1*. Columbus: Henry Howe and Son, 1889.

Howells, William Dean, *Years of My Youth*. New York and London: Harper and Brothers, 1916.

Huffman, Iolas M, affidavit, State of Ohio, Clark County, November 24, 1924.

Hunter, Bob, *Buckeye Basketball, Ohio State University*. Huntsville, Alabama: The Strode Publishers, 1981.

Hunter, Bob, "Forgotten Family." *Columbus Dispatch*, January 27, 2002, Page D-1.

Hunter, Bob, "Harley's Absence Calls Top Five List Into Question." *Columbus Dispatch*, November 22, 2002, Page H-1.

Hunter, Bob, "Harley Should Be Honored With Statue at Horseshoe." *Columbus Dispatch*, March 5, 2003, Page B-1.

Hunter, Bob, "Legend Loses Step to Time, Years Have Clouded Memories of Chic Harley, OSU's First Superstar." *Columbus Dispatch*, August 27, 2000, Page E-1.

Hyman, Mervin D. and White, Gordon S. Jr., *Big Ten Football, Its Life and Times, Great Coaches, Players and Games*. New York: Macmillan Publishing Co., Inc., 1977.

Jones, Johnny, *Now Let Me Tell You*. Columbus: The Dispatch Printing Company, 1950.

Kinney, Harrison, *James Thurber, His Life and Times*. New York: Henry Holt and Company, Inc., 1995.

Lentz, Ed, *As it Were, Stories of Old Columbus*. Dublin, Ohio: Red Mountain Press, 1998.

Lentz, Ed, *Columbus, The Story of a City*. Charleston, South Carolina: Arcadia Publishing, 2003.

Madej, Bruce, *Michigan, Champions of the West*. Champaign, Illinois: Sports Publishing, 1997.

Martin, William T., *History of Franklin County: A Collection of Reminiscences of the Early Settlement of the County; with Biographical Sketches and a Complete History of the County to the Present Time*. Columbus: Follett, Foster and Company, 1858.

McCabe, Lida Rose, *Don't You Remember?* Columbus: A.H. Smythe, 1884.

McCallum, John and Pearson, Charles H., *College Football U.S.A., 1869-1971*. Hall of Fame Publishing, Inc.

McClellan, Keith, *The Sunday Game, At the Dawn of Professional Football*. Akron, Ohio: The University of Akron Press, 1998.

Michelson, Herb and Newhouse, Dave, *Rose Bowl Football Since 1902*.
New York: Stein and Day, Publishers, 1977.

Montville, Leigh, *The Big Bam, The Life and Times of Babe Ruth*. New York:
Broadway Books, 2006.

Ohio State University Archives, Biographical Files, Wilce, John W.

Ohio State University Archives, Director of Athletics (Record Group 9/e–1/8),
"Harley, Charles W. Correspondence: 1919, 1922, 1924, undated."

Ohio State University Archives, Director of Athletics (Record Group 9/e–1/8),
"Harley Fund, 1922-1948."

Ohio State University Archives, *The Makio*, yearbooks for 1915-1930.
Columbus: Ohio State University.

Ohio State University Archives, Wilce, Dr. John W, Box 1, 141-222-1,
Series I: Correspondence; 2. Athletics: 1937-1956; 14. Football, Fun, Facts and
Friends, 1946-1956; 26. Personal: 1940-1949.

Ohio State University Archives, Wilce, Dr. John W., Box 6, 141-222-6,
Reference File; 8. Talks, by Dr. Wilce, 1925-1938.

Ohio State University-University of Illinois football program, Oct. 10, 1953, Tributes to Chic Harley. Pages 22-23.

O'Neal, Bill, *The American Association, A Baseball History*, 1902-1991.
Austin, Texas: Eakin Press, 1991.

Park, Jack, *The Official Ohio State Football Encyclopedia*. Champaign,
Illinois: Sports Publishing , L.L.C., 2001.

Perry, Will, *The Wolverines, A Story of Michigan Football*. Huntsville,
Alabama: The Strode Publishers, 1974.

Peterson, Robert W., Pigskin, *The Early Years of Pro Football*. New York, Oxford:
Oxford University Press, 1997.

Pollard, James. E., *Ohio State Athletics, 1879-1959*. Columbus: Ohio State University Athletic Department, 1959.

Pollard, James E., *History of the Ohio State University, The Story of its First Sev-
enty-Five Years, 1873-1948*. Columbus: The Ohio State University Press, 1952.

Porter, David L., *Biographical Dictionary of American Sports–Football*.
Westport, Connecticut: Greenwood Press, 1987.

Probate Court, Franklin County, Ohio, Inquest of Lunacy in the matter
of Charles W. Harley, No. 43420, December 2, 1922.

Probate Court, Franklin County, Ohio, Decision by Judge Homer Z. Bostwick in
the matter of Charles W. Harley, No. 43420, December 12, 1924.

Probate Court, Franklin County, Ohio, Medical Certificate in the Matter of
Charles W. Harley, Inquest of Lunacy, Epilepsy and Feeble-Mindedness, No.
43420, December 2, 1922.

Probate Court, Franklin County, Ohio, Memorandum in the Matter of Charles W.
Harley, No. 43,420, filed by James J. Trainor, Joseph J. Nagle and Timothy S.
Hogan, attorneys for Harley, November, 1924.

Rea, Mark, A Talent Never to be Forgotten. *Buckeye Sports Bulletin*, Vol. 24, No.
7, October, 23, 2004, Pages 24-25.

Rea, Mark, Legendary Scribe Called Harley a Cyclone. *Buckeye Sports
Bulletin*, Vol. 24, No. 8, October, 30, 2004, Pages 34-35.

Rea, Mark, Harley Leaves Legacy, But Meets Sad Ending. *Buckeye Sports
Bulletin*, Vol. 24, No. 9, November 6, 2004, Pages 30-31.

Roberts, Howard, *The Big Nine, The Story of Football in the Western Conference*. New York: G.P. Putnam's Sons, 1948.

Roberts, Howard, *The Chicago Bears*. New York: G.P. Putnam's Sons, 1947.

Roseboom, Eugene H. and Weisenburger, Francis P., *A History of Ohio*. Columbus: The Ohio State Archaeological and Historical Society, 1953.

Scheibeck, Irven, Chic Harley, the one and only. *Columbus Dispatch Sunday Magazine*, Sept. 18, 1966.

Smith, Robert, *Illustrated History of Pro Football*. New York: Madison Square Press, Grosset & Dunlap, Publishers, 1970.

Snypp, Wilbur and Hunter, Bob, *The Buckeyes, A Story of Ohio State Football*. Huntsville, Alabama: The Strode Publishers, 1982.

Superior Court of Cook County, State of Illinois, General No. 384,732, William G. Harley et al. vs. George S. Halas et al., filed October, 1924.

Superior Court of Cook County, State of Illinois, Bill of Complaint, William G. Harley and Charles W. Harley vs. George S. Halas and Edward C. Sternaman, filed December, 1922.

Superior Court of Cook County, State of Illinois, No. 384,732, Complainants' Objections to Master's Report, filed October, 1924.

Taylor, William Alexander, *Centennial History of Columbus and Franklin County, Ohio, Vol. 1*. Chicago-Columbus: The S.J. Clarke Publishing Co., 1909.

Time, The Weekly News Magazine, Chick Harley, Vol. IV, No. 22, Dec. 1, 1924.

Tootle, James, *Baseball in Columbus*. Chicago: Arcadia Publishing, 2003.

Thomas, Robert D., *Columbus Unforgettables, A Collection of Columbus Yesterdays and Todays*. Columbus: Robert D. Thomas, publisher, 1983.

Thomas, Robert D., *More Columbus Unforgettables, A Further Collection of Columbus Yesterdays and Todays, Vol. 2*. Columbus: Robert D. Thomas, ublisher, 1986.

Thurber, James, *My Life and Hard Times*. University Days. New York and London: Harper and Brothers, 1933. (Passage reprinted with the permission of Rosemary Thurber.)

Thurber, James, If You Ask Me. *P.M.*, Oct. 22, 1940, Pg. 11.

Veterans Administration Facility, Danville, Illinois, Psychiatric Social History, Charles W. Harley, investigation upon admittance, Oct. 15, 1938.

Veterans Administration Facility, Danville, Illinois, Clinical Record, Charles W. Harley, brief and laboratory examination, Oct. 15, 1938,

Watterson, John Sayle, *College Football, History, Spectacle, Controversy*. Baltimore: The John Hopkins University Press, 2000.

Wilce, J.W., Football, *How to Play It and Understand It*. New York: Charles Scribner's Sons, 1923.

Wilce, Dr. John W., as told to Dohn, Norman H., My 16 Years at Ohio State. *Columbus Dispatch Sunday Magazine*, November 14, 1954.

Willis, Chris, *The Columbus Panhandles, A Complete History of Pro Football's Toughest Team, 1900-1922*. Lanham, Maryland: The Scarecrow Press, Inc., 2007.

Wilson, Kenneth L. (Tug) and Brondfield, Jerry, *The Big Ten*. Englewood Cliffs, New Jersey: Prentice-Hall, 1967.

WOSU, Greene, Brent (producer), *The Birth of Ohio Stadium*. Columbus: television documentary, 1999.

X-Rays, The, East High School, Columbus, Ohio, student newspaper, 1914.
Micofilms and hard copies of the following newspapers and magazines were also
    consulted extensively:

The Columbus Dispatch.
The Columbus Citizen.
The Dayton Daily News.
The Ohio State Journal.
The Ohio State Lantern.
The Chicago Sun-Times.
The Chicago Tribune.
The New York Times.
The Ohio State Quarterly.
The Ohio State Monthly.

The city directories for Columbus published by R.L. Polk & Co., were also fre-
    quently consulted for the years 1880 through 1978.

Chic